Let's Talk Turkey

The Stories
behind America's
Favorite
Expressions

Let's Talk Turkey

The Stories behind America's Favorite Expressions

by Rosemarie Ostler

Prometheus Books

59 John Glenn Drive
Amherst, New York 14228-2119

Published 2008 by Prometheus Books

Inquiries should be addressed to
Prometheus Books
59 John Glenn Drive
Amherst, New York 14228–2119
VOICE: 716–691–0133, ext. 210
FAX: 716–691–0137
WWW.PROMETHEUSBOOKS.COM

12 11 10 09 08   5 4 3 2 1

Library of Congress Cataloging-in-Publication Data

Ostler, Rosemarie
    Let's talk turkey : the stories behind America's favorite expressions / by Rosemarie Ostler
        p. cm.
    Includes bibliographical references and index.
    ISBN 978–1–59102–625–9 (pbk. : acid-free paper)
    1. English language—United States—Terms and phrases. 2. Americanisms—History. 3. English language—United States—Slang—History. 4. Figures of speech. I. Title.

PE2839.O88 2008
427'.973—dc22

2008017659

Printed in the United States on acid-free paper

TABLE OF CONTENTS

INTRODUCTION

Let's Talk Turkey

Let's Talk Turkey gets to the roots—or as close to the roots as possible—of more than one hundred and fifty familiar figures of speech. All are distinctly American. Either they originated in the United States or colonial America, or their meanings changed drastically when they crossed the Atlantic. These metaphors grew out of the places, people, and events that captured the American imagination. They add zest to the language and contribute greatly toward giving American English its own unmistakable character.

The figures of speech in this book are grouped into four sections and thirteen chapters, organized by topic area. When an expression could reasonably have been classified under more than one category, it went into the category most strongly associated with it. Most people think of gangsters when they hear *sing like a canary*, so that phrase went into the "Cops and Robbers" chapter rather than "Behaving Like an Animal." *Go whole hog*, on the other hand, works in a variety of situations. It is therefore listed with the animal expressions, although its first widespread use was political.

Certain aspects of American life seem to trigger linguistic invention more than others. A large number of the expressions in this book—at least one or two in every chapter—can ultimately be traced to the American frontier. Beginning in the eighteenth century, when "the West" meant West Tennessee, Kentucky, and the Ohio Valley, frontier residents created a distinctly American way of talking. Their colorful jargon was a combination of hyperbole and down-home pithiness. Dr. Thomas L. Nichols, an American who moved to England, explained American speech habits to British readers in his 1864 memoir, *Forty Years of American Life*: "A Western man 'sleeps so sound, it would take an earthquake to wake him.' . . . He tells of a person 'as cross as a b'ar with two cubs and a sore tail.' . . . He 'goes the whole hog.'" Dr. Nichols's examples have the genuine ring of homespun Westernisms. Among the frontier figures of speech discussed in this book are *play possum, eat crow, go west, pass the buck, be loaded for bear, die with your boots on, throw a necktie party,* and *paint the town red.* Davy Crockett, the most famous frontiersman of them all, introduced a number of picturesque expressions to a broader public. Two included here are *have more than you can shake a stick at* and *bark up the wrong tree.*

The necessity of grappling with the land also colors American speech patterns. The challenge of the North American terrain overwhelmed the first English settlers. Common figures of speech reflect their awareness of the country's vastness, as well as the settlers' desire to transform the wilderness into farms and ranches—*be up a tree* or *out on a limb, be stumped, make a stump speech, go haywire, pull up stakes, mend your fences, let the chips fall where they may, ride herd.*

The way of life of the people already living in North America also had a strong impact on the colonists. British settlers observed the natives closely and wove their impressions—accurate or not—into the English language. Two figures of speech discussed here, *bury the hatchet* and *hold a powwow*, started as literal descriptions of activities the colonists witnessed. Later they evolved into metaphors. Other expressions relating to Native Americans found in this book are *bite the dust, put an ear to the ground, send smoke signals*, and *walk Indian file.* These and many other references—*the warpath, the happy hunting grounds, the Great Spirit*—have become so central to the American language that we use them without even considering their origins.

Travel also holds a fascination for Americans. The coming of the transcontinental railroad and, later, the invention of the automobile, marked major events in the life of the country. The vast, borderless continent encouraged restless movement and relocation. Chapter 6, "Ways to Travel," includes the iconic *go south* and *go west*, as well as several expressions that allude to traveling by horse, train, or car—*ride herd, ride the gravy train, be taken for a ride*. A number of entries in other chapters also touch directly or indirectly on the travel impulse. These include *come from the wrong side of the tracks, go like a bat out of hell, push the envelope, make a whistle-stop tour, go to town*, and *take a powder*.

Another facet of American life that powerfully influenced the way Americans express themselves is the world of sports. Sports-related metaphors permeate the culture. Recently, *USA Today* printed a piece titled "Do Foreign Executives Balk at Sports Jargon?" The article described the puzzlement that descends on CEOs from Brussels or Buenos Aires when their American business partners start tossing around terms like *step up to the plate* and *hit one out of the park*. The metaphorical implications of expressions like these are obvious to Americans, even those who don't follow baseball. In Japan, even avid baseball fans are left scratching their heads over such terms. Although the Japanese are enthusiastic about the game, they don't normally apply its jargon to their business dealings. Americans, on the other hand, just naturally interpret life in terms of sports.

Chapter 8, "Playing the Game," is the longest in the book. Various figures of speech listed in other chapters also allude to games and sports. These include *take a rain check, keep the ball rolling, throw your hat in the ring, win one for the Gipper, jump the gun, keep your shirt on*, and *be ready at the drop of a hat*. Dozens of sports metaphors are not discussed here because their origins are obvious—for instance, *slam dunk, par for the course, no holds barred, batting a thousand, the ball's in your court, hit a grand slam, cover the bases*, and *play your cards close to your vest*.

Politics also generates colorful speech. The American political scene has been boisterous since 1776, when John Hancock signed his name in extra-large writing to make sure King George III would be able to read it. Since then, a host of terms has been invented to describe the workings of American politics. (John Hancock's story is told in chapter 5, "People and Places.") The nineteenth century, a time of fiery oratory and untrammeled backroom deals, is an especially rich source of political jargon. *Spoils system, split ticket, lame duck, dark horse, filibuster, fence sitter, lobby, pork barrel, junket,* and *favorite son* all date from this era. Imaginative names also abounded for political parties—*Barnburners, Loco-Focos, Know-Nothings, Plug Uglies, Old Hunkers, Popocrats.*

Besides the figurative expressions listed in chapter 4, "Politics as Usual," several others scattered throughout the book are connected to the political world. These include *let the chips fall where they may, change horses in midstream, beat the Dutch, jump on the bandwagon,* and *whistle Dixie.*

Besides their American roots, the expressions featured here share another characteristic. Although their figurative meanings are clear, their origins are not. Many commemorate now-forgotten trends or events. *Keep the ball rolling* comes from the ancient game of shinny, once as popular on college campuses as football but now virtually unknown. The exploits of Steve Brodie (*take a brodie*), Mickey Finn (*slip someone a Mickey Finn*), and the Joneses (*keep up with the Joneses*) have long since disappeared from the public consciousness, although their names live on in the language. The Civil War incident that led to *hold the fort* was headline news nearly one hundred and fifty years ago. Now the phrase is far more famous than the battle that inspired it. A handful of phrases arose within the last few decades—*go ballistic, twist in the wind, drink the Kool-Aid.* Even in these cases, the incidents that inspired them are fading from American memories.

Other figures of speech have become obscure because of convoluted linguistic histories. For example, *take it on the lam* started out life as a verb—*to lam*—meaning to beat someone up. The meandering path leading to its present meaning is a perfect illustration of ingenious wordplay. The phrase *sell someone a bill of goods* is based on a now-obsolete usage for *bill,* and *play hookey* probably originated from the Dutch name for hide-and-seek. The *cop* in *cop a plea* is the product of centuries of meaning change. The literal meaning of *blaze a trail*—peel chunks of bark off trees to mark a path—relies on *blaze*'s ancient connotation of whiteness.

The exact moment of an expression's birth is seldom discoverable. *Slang*—a term that fits most of these entries—often exists in the culture for years or decades before being captured in writing. Then it pops up in several places at once. Sometimes early uses of a phrase provide a clue to its origin—for example, the first recorded use of *play both ends against the middle* includes the information that it's a gambling term. Other terms, like *fight fire with fire*, are used literally for a while before taking on figurative meanings. Many expressions, however, seem to arise full-blown as figures of speech. The mysterious phrase *go the whole nine yards* is a prime example of this. Its origin remains a puzzle, although one with tantalizing possibilities.

Expressions like *go the whole nine yards* provide hours of entertainment for language enthusiasts. Faced with the intriguing mystery of its derivation and ultimate meaning, they let their creative juices flow. Popular explanations for this phrase and a number of others included in this book show impressive ingenuity. However, solutions based on imaginative speculation usually don't stand up to much scrutiny.

Etymologists base their reconstructions of word histories on the appearance of those words in print. A proposed explanation that doesn't match the earliest recorded uses of a phrase is less likely to be right. For instance, *hit the ground running* cannot have originated as World War II slang, contrary to what some have claimed, for the simple reason that the expression was being used figuratively at least twenty years earlier. Likewise, explanations that claim an expression derives from a far-distant historical time and place are unrealistic. *Spill the beans* and *cry uncle* first became popular in the early twentieth-century United States. Speculations that these expressions come from classical Roman and Greek traditions fail to account for how they bridged the enormous gulf separating the ancient world from modern America. An origin closer to home is more likely.

Fortunately for American word historians, Americanisms have been collected from early days. John Russell Bartlett published the first dictionary of the American language in 1848. Bartlett adopted the modern etymologists' method of illustrating his definitions with quotes from American books and newspapers. He provides valuable context for such nineteenth-century idioms as *make a stump speech*, *bark up the wrong tree*, and *go whole hog*. Another important nineteenth-century work is Maximilian Schele de Vere's *Americanisms: The English of the New World*, published in 1872. Schele de Vere discusses the possible derivations of many words and expressions, including two listed in this book—*pull up stakes* and *face the music*.

Historical dictionaries are another valuable source of citations. Two important records of Americanisms are Sir William Craigie's *Dictionary of American English on Historical Principles* and Richard Thornton's *American Glossary*, both published in the early decades of the twentieth century. The *Random House Historical Dictionary of American Slang* and the *Dictionary of American Regional English* are more recent works that provide thorough and up-to-date citation records. For Americanisms that are now part of mainstream English, which includes most of those listed here, the *Oxford English Dictionary* online is an incomparable resource. It contains the first known use of a host of expressions and is updated frequently. These dictionaries are the first line of research for anyone tracking the life story of an American expression.

Newly coined figures of speech often make their first appearance in a newspaper. Newspaper writers love a colorful colloquialism and can be relied on to popularize handy new expressions such as *drink the Kool-Aid*. A newspaper article's context sometimes offers a clue about an expression's original milieu—gambling houses, criminal circles, or the western prairie.

The writings of certain authors also provide rich material for etymologists. Davy Crockett, Mark Twain, and James Fenimore Cooper all had a sharp ear for Americanisms. The works of the now-obscure J. K. Paulding, who wrote some of the first American plays, and Canadian Thomas Haliburton, creator of the stereotypical Yankee Sam Slick, contain a treasury of American linguistic inventions. Early twentieth-century authors whose stories preserve many slang words and expressions from their era include P. G. Wodehouse, O. Henry, George Ade, and the cartoonist Thomas A. Dorgan. *Let's Talk Turkey* frequently cites these writers for early examples of an expression.

Since the 1990s, much vintage material that was once inaccessible is now on the Internet. Books put online through Google, newspapers accessed through Lexis-Nexis, and other texts that are searchable on the Internet have made it easier to discover very early examples of new coinages. Word historians are finding examples that predate, sometimes by a decade or more, what were once thought to be the first uses of a figure of speech. In some cases, this new evidence has substantially changed etymological history. One instance where antedating put a new spin on a word's history is *hot dog*, discussed in the *hot dog it* entry found in chapter 12, "Eating Well." Online sources like Google's news database are also helpful for pinpointing current shifts in an expression's usage. For example, evidence that *other shoe* in the phrase *waiting for the other shoe to drop* is changing to *other shoes* comes mainly from news sources.

Along with the citation record, word historians consider the relevant historical context when deciding how a familiar expression arose. *Let's Talk Turkey* sets each listed expression in a historical frame. Figures of speech that seem odd or nonsensical are often illuminated this way. It's helpful to know, for example, that when O. Henry first used *cut the mustard* in 1907, bottled mustard was a brand-new product. It piqued the interest of Americans at that time and might easily have inspired a metaphorical turn of speech. *Bite the dust*, a surprising instance of a classical idea that really did inspire an Americanism, makes more sense when we understand late nineteenth-century literary fads. If nothing else, taking an expression's cultural context into account helps eliminate questionable explanations of origins. *Let's Talk Turkey* presents a capsule history of each listed expression, tracing a trajectory from the phrase's first known appearance in print to its modern usage. The back stories thus revealed offer fascinating slices of Americana—United States history viewed from a different angle.

ACKNOWLEDGMENTS

I would like to express my thanks to Linda Greenspan Regan, my editor at Prometheus Books, whose incisive comments and suggestions helped make this a much stronger book. I also appreciate copyeditor Julia DeGraf's careful work.

Thanks also go to my agent, Janet Rosen of Sheree Bykofsky Associates, for her commitment to the project and her professional expertise; to Deanna Larson, Mary-Kate Mackey, and Sally Sheklow for their valuable comments on the manuscript, as well as their support and encouragement over the years; and to John Reed for much helpful advice. I am grateful to Scott Landfield and David Rhodes of Tsunami Books in Eugene, Oregon, for making their bookstore a welcoming gathering place for writers.

I am especially thankful to my husband, Jeffrey Ostler, not only for his unswerving support while I was writing this book, but also for acting as a kind of walking reference resource for my questions about American history.

PART 1:
THE NATURAL
WORLD

Chapter 1

THE GREAT AMERICAN OUTDOORS

Until well into the twentieth century, most Americans lived rural, outdoor lives. No wonder some of their earliest colloquialisms incorporate basic outdoor materials. Several expressions are based on dirt, that most fundamental of outdoor substances: *do someone dirt*, *eat dirt*—meaning to make a humiliating admission—and the now old-fashioned *cut dirt*, meaning to leave. Americans were also the first to speak of *dirt farmers* and being *dirt poor*. And of course, *dishing the dirt*, listed below, has always been a popular national pastime. *Pay dirt*, also described in this chapter, was one of the few kinds of desirable dirt.

Other noticeable features of the landscape are captured in such classic American expressions as *clear out the underbrush*, *be swamped with work*, *make tracks*, *head for the high hills*, *visit the old stamping/stomping grounds*, *be up the creek without a paddle*, and perform a task that's *easy as falling off a log*. Americans also allude to rivers, wind, woods, and plains in their figurative speech, as the following entries show.

CARRY A CHIP ON YOUR SHOULDER.
Be resentful or quick to take offense.

Carrying a chip on your shoulder, or knocking it off someone else's, was apparently a popular nineteenth-century activity. The *Long Island*

Telegraph for May 20, 1830, describes it as a way of conducting a childish quarrel: "When two churlish boys were determined to fight, a chip would be placed on the shoulder of one, and the other demanded to knock it off at his peril." A *Harper's Magazine* article from the 1850s confirms that chip knocking was a genuine activity. The article's author talks about "a provocation to a fight, after the fashion of some 'shoulder-hitters' in placing a chip upon a man's shoulder and daring another to knock it off." Since wood chips are light and flimsy, knocking one off someone's shoulder would be fairly easy to do—about as easy as offending someone who's already spoiling for a fight.

By the middle of the nineteenth century, the chip on someone's shoulder could be figurative. Carrying a chip on your shoulder meant harboring a sense of grievance, being quick to take offense. Somerset Maugham's 1930 *The Gentleman in the Parlour* offers a good illustration of the expression's new meaning: "He was a man with a chip on his shoulder. Everyone seemed in a conspiracy to slight or injure him."

Actual wood chips are scarce since the advent of electricity and gas, but *a chip on the shoulder* has remained a metaphor for belligerent behavior. These days, however, the verb *carry* has been dropped. Instead people say *has*, as in, *That guy has a real chip on his shoulder*.

LET THE CHIPS FALL WHERE THEY MAY.

Do the right thing without regard to consequences.

Roscoe Conkling, New York senator from 1867 to 1881, is credited with popularizing this expression. He used a version of it during a speech nominating Ulysses S. Grant for president at the 1880 Republican convention. Speaking of Grant, Conkling said, "[P]opular or unpopular, he would  hew to the line of right, let the chips fly where they may." In spite of Conkling's stirring oration, Grant, who had already served as president from 1869 to 1877, was not asked to run. Instead, James Garfield received the nomination and was later elected.

The chips alluded to in this phrase are the small bits of wood that fly all around when woodcutters split logs or cut down trees. Although the image conjured up is one of colonial settlers clearing the forest, the idea is actually much older. It comes from a proverb first written down in the fourteenth century and usually rendered into modern English as "Hew not too high, lest the chips fall in thine eye." The lesson seems to be that people should not take on too ambitious a task. If so, "let the chips fall where they may" could be interpreted as a response—"I will do the appropriate thing, no matter how awkward and messy it turns out to be."

This saying appeared in print in the United States at least once before Senator Conkling used it. The spiritualist publication *Brittan's Journal* for 1874 contains the sentence "Hew to the line, let the chips fall where they may." It is mentioned as the motto of a Methodist preacher of that time. During the nineteenth and early twentieth centuries, the expression is virtually always as it appeared in *Brittan's Journal*: *Hew to the line, let the chips fall where they may.* Conkling's use of *fly* instead of *fall* was his own innovation.

The expression lost its status as a motto by the mid-twentieth century, and the first part of the sentence—*hew to the line*—was dropped. These days, letting the chips fall where they may simply means accepting the consequences of your actions. For example, you could say *I intend to see this through, let the chips fall where they may.*

HAVE MORE THAN YOU CAN SHAKE A STICK AT.
To be faced with some overwhelming number of objects, too many to be counted.

This colloquial phrase was frowned on as backwoods slang when it first appeared in the early nineteenth century. John Russell Bartlett, author of the 1848 *Dictionary of Americanisms*, calls it "a ridiculous phrase very often heard in low language." Backwoodsman Davy

Crockett's use of the expression in his 1835 *Account of Col. Crockett's Tour to the North and Down East* seems to confirm Bartlett's view. Crockett writes, "We got a little dry or so, and wanted a horn; but this was a temperance house, and there was nothing to treat a friend to that was worth shaking a stick at."

Davy Crockett, who was born in 1786 in the rugged Tennessee wilderness, introduced citified nineteenth-century Americans to a number of pithy idioms. To Americans on the East Coast, he was the epitome of the linguistically flamboyant, tall-talking frontiersman. He described himself as a two-fisted mountain man who could whip his weight in wildcats and hug a bear too close for comfort. When Crockett was elected to Congress in 1827, he captivated easterners with his colorful backwoods slang. People traveled to Washington, DC, from many miles away just to stare at him. Crockett also popularized *bark up the wrong tree*, found in chapter 2, "Behaving Like an Animal."

Although *more than you can shake a stick at* was associated with Crockett, it appeared in print as early as 1818, nearly twenty years before *An Account of Col. Crockett's Tour to the North and Down East* was published. People tended to use it in colloquial and joking contexts, as in this quote from a book titled *May-day in New York*: "New York is an everlastin' great concern, and . . . there's about as many people in it as you could shake a stick at."

The exact significance of shaking a stick at something is unclear, but it implies a threat of violence. One possible interpretation is that no one would want to challenge more people than he could successfully fight off. Shaking a stick at a large, hostile crowd would be a tactical error. Given this interpretation, the folksiness of the phrase also makes sense—it implies that your only weapon is a stick picked up on the spur of the moment.

The expression *more than you can shake a stick at* is now common in both the United States and England and is more mainstream than it was in the nineteenth century. It is used often in serious contexts, such as *We've gotten more complaints about those defective cell phones than you could shake a stick at.* The expression is occasionally rephrased for effect, as in "more . . . than a prudent man would shake a bundle of twigs at," found in the spring 1982 issue of *Folio.*

GO HAYWIRE.
Become excited or distracted; go out of control.

Haywire has meant "substandard" or "out of whack" since the beginning of the twentieth century. Some of the earliest recorded uses come from the logging industry. A 1905 *Forestry Bureau Bulletin* defines *haywire outfit* as "a contemptuous term for loggers with poor logging equipment." A 1925 article in the journal *American Speech* explains that loggers use *haywire* to describe "everything from Calvin Coolidge to the calks in their boots." Although *haywire* was first applied to defective equipment or poorly functioning systems, it began to mean "going crazy" around the 1920s. A typical example comes from the 1936 mystery novel *Flowers for the Judge* by British writer Margery Allingham: "I suppose some wives would have gone haywire by this time."

Haywire, true to its name, is wire used for bundling bales of hay. The most common explanation of the origin of *go haywire* is that the wire has a tendency to twist up, making it difficult to work with. Another option is that pieces of old haywire were often used for makeshift repairs in earlier times. This explanation would account for why the expression is first recorded to have been in use among loggers rather than farmers. The term *haywire outfit* also makes more sense given this theory.

These days, computers as well as the stock market are often described as going haywire. Human beings can also go haywire. In fact, *go haywire* can be plugged into just about any sentence where you can say *go crazy.*

BITE THE DUST.

Be wounded or die in action; fail or be defeated.

For most modern Americans, the phrase *bite the dust* conjures up scenes from old-time Westerns. In these films, both the black-hatted bad guys and the marauding Indians routinely bite the dust. Men are shot off their horses while doing battle on the dusty plains, or plugged during a gunfight in the middle of Dodge City's dusty main street.

The imagery of warriors hitting the dust goes back much further than the American West. It first appears in Homer's *Iliad*. Translators interpret the phrase in various ways, for example, "bite the bloody sand." Versions of the phrase also appear in the King James Bible. For example, a line from Psalms reads, "They that dwell in the wilderness shall bow before him and his enemies shall lick the dust." These passages would have been familiar to many nineteenth-century Americans. Educated people read the *Iliad*, and nearly everyone read or listened to the King James Bible.

The exact phrase *bite the dust* first appears in print in *Our Army on the Rio Grande*, a report on the Mexican War of 1846. The sentence occurs in a vignette describing ferry passengers crossing the river from Mexico to the United States. The author, a newspaperman, colorfully describes a "ranchero" who makes his living by selling a broken-down nag, stealing it back from the customer, and reselling it. The author predicts that this con man will continue his dishonest ways until he sells the horse to the wrong person. Then, the author concludes ominously, "when he is found out, his days will be numbered, and his father's son will bite the dust for his rascality." The American poet William Cullen Bryant also used *bite the dust* in his 1870 translation of the *Iliad*, writing, "May his fellow warriors . . . Fall round him to earth and bite the dust."

Bryant may have been influenced by American popular culture of the time. Throughout the 1860s, dust-biting villains appeared frequently in a form of sensational fiction known as the dime novel. The first dime novel, published in 1860, was titled *Maleaska, the Indian*

Wife of the White Hunter. Dime novels provided something for everyone—romances, detective stories, war stories, schoolboy adventures. However, novels of the western frontier, with series titles like *Wild West Stories* and *Buffalo Bill Stories*, were among the most popular. These cheap, flimsy little books were the mass entertainment of their day. They were affordable to nearly everyone—although called dime novels, they sold for anywhere from a nickel to a quarter—and many series characters had devoted fans. Americans back then followed their exploits the way they follow the antics of popular sitcom characters today. Dime novels sold by the millions. Some series remained in wide circulation until the 1920s.

Stereotypical Native Americans were stock characters in dime Westerns. Many stories featured titles like *Out against the Redskins*, with cover illustrations depicting the white hero successfully challenging a crowd of warlike Indians. Rustlers, gunslingers, and other assorted troublemakers also figured as villains in these books. Even before the earliest Western movies hit the screen at the turn of the twentieth century, dime Westerns had firmly established the image of the bad guys biting the dust.

By 1887 the expression *bite the dust* was being used metaphorically to imply failure. The following line appears in a story in an 1887 New Orleans newspaper: "If he ain't careful, he'll bite the dust [get broke and go begging]." The fact that the writer thought he had to provide a definition for this use of *bite the dust* suggests that the phrase's new meaning was not yet widespread. In modern times, *bite the dust* is still sometimes used to describe literally falling dead. More often it means being vanquished or defeated in some lesser way. According to newspaper headlines over the past few years, estate taxes, favorite ball teams, certain hapless CEOs, and a growing number of unpopular blogs have all bitten the dust.

PUT AN EAR TO THE GROUND.

Proceed cautiously, especially by collecting relevant information before taking action.

Like *bite the dust*, this expression draws on folklore of the Old West. In *Western Words*, published in 1994, Ramon Adams describes the plainsman's practice of placing a silk neckerchief on hard ground, pressing an ear to it, and listening for the sound of horses' hooves. Supposedly, sounds coming through the ground carried much farther than sounds in the air. Adams calls this technique *to long-ear*. Plainsmen claimed to have learned the skill from Native American trackers (although presumably the silk neckerchief was an added refinement).

Native Americans may have put an ear to the ground, but it could not have been a common tracking technique. Nineteenth-century army observers such as W. P. Clark and Richard Irving Dodge don't mention it in their accounts of trackers on the Great Plains. Listening for the sound of hooves would have had limited usefulness. Its only purpose would be to locate horses or bison that were not yet close enough to be visible. Most tracking involved following people or animals that had already passed through a territory.

For instance, Clark describes the activities of a Cheyenne army scout trying to identify an unknown band of Native Americans by studying their abandoned camp. The tracker brushed away the ashes from the dead fires and felt the ground underneath, scrutinized scraps of fabric and moccasins that had been left behind, studied traces left by tepee pegs, observed the number of animal droppings, and noted the remains of a sweat lodge (a saunalike structure used for ritually sweating out impurities). Eventually, he determined that the unknown band was Lakota Sioux and that they had camped in that spot for only a single night.

Even if Native American trackers did not put an ear to the ground, white plainsmen might have been inspired to invent the technique from their observations of how trackers worked. Another possibility is that the phrase *an ear to the ground* was always meant to be an exaggeration. Trackers often held their faces very close to the ground to get a better view of footprints or other telltale clues at that level. *He put an ear to the ground* could simply have been a colorful way of describing this action, similar to saying that someone sleeping hard is pounding his ear. Over time, as the days of the plainsmen grew further away, American English speakers might have invented a literal explanation to account for a now-puzzling phrase.

The earliest figurative use of *put an ear to the ground* occurs in a 1900 *Congressional Record*, where it is defined as "to use caution, to go slowly and listen frequently." Putting, keeping, or having an ear to the ground is now most closely associated with business and politics. It suggests that someone has insider connections, as well as some skill at interpreting subtle clues. For example, you might prefer to deal with a realtor or investment manager who keeps an ear to the ground for the latest business developments.

BLAZE A TRAIL.
Mark out a path for others to follow; be an innovator.

The verb *to blaze* dates from at least 1750, when Thomas Walker wrote in his journal of frontier explorations, "I blazed a way from our house to the river." Blazing meant peeling a piece of bark off the side of a tree. The resulting white patch was the blaze. Thus blazes were usually cut for the purpose of marking a trail. A biographer of Daniel Boone writes in 1833, "The brothers left such traces—or blazes as they are technically called—of their course as they thought would enable them to find it again."

The original meaning of *blaze* is a white mark on the face of an animal. The white marks on trees became blazes by extension. British settlers from the earliest days marked out property with blazes. A record from 1662 notes that a meeting house will be built by a small oak "marked at the sou[th]west side with two notches and a blaze." Sometimes blazes were combined to indicate different paths. For example, in one locality, trees were marked with a single blaze to indicate the route of a future neighborhood road and with three blazes to mark out a state road.

By 1850 *blaze a trail* had gained its figurative meaning of leading the way. An early example comes from the 1902 book *How Words Grow*, which includes the sentence "Professor Bréal has blazed the way for future explorers in the wilderness of philology." Blazing a trail today usually means being an innovator—an intellectual rather than a physical pioneer.

Blaze may be regaining some of its physical aspects in recent teen slang. Since the 1980s, *blaze* has meant to leave, especially by car. *Newsweek* for September 25, 1989, reports that *I'm blazin'* means that a teen is on his or her way out the door.

SEND SMOKE SIGNALS.

Give an indication of your intentions; send an indirect message.

Native Americans may never have placed a literal ear on the ground, but they did send smoke signals. Many books about the nineteenth-century West mention the long columns of smoke, visible at great distances. In 1891, Samuel Cozzens wrote in *The Marvellous Country*, "After leaving the Organos Mountains we had noticed Indian smoke signals."

Army scout Richard Irving Dodge describes the method for sending smoke signals: "A small fire is built on which is placed damp grass, creating a large volume of smoke. As it begins to ascend a blanket is held horizontally above, and when the space beneath is quite full, the blanket is slipped off sideways and then quickly brought back to its place." Moving the blanket in this way caused the smoke to ascend in short, rounded puffs. Single puffs—"a single smoke," as Dodge calls it—were typically a warning to all tribal members within sight that strangers were in the area. Puffs were also grouped in different ways to send a variety of simple or instant messages.

It's unclear when sending smoke signals first became a metaphorical activity. The earliest examples appear in print around the mid-twentieth century. Usually, the phrase implies a subtle, nonverbal form of communication. This typical example is from the January 20, 1978, *Times* of London: "Mr. Enoch Powell['s] . . . delphic remarks certainly got Mrs. Thatcher asking herself what smoke signals he intended."

FIGHT FIRE WITH FIRE.
Respond in kind to an attack or threat.

Settlers on the frontier fought prairie fires by deliberately starting a fire in the wildfire's path. The backfire, as this purposeful burn was called, cleared the ground of flammable material like wood spars, grass, and other plants. When the advancing wildfire reached the edge of the burned patch, it would die out for lack of fuel. At least, that was the plan. Fighting fire with fire is a dangerous business. Backfires occasionally flamed out of control, enlarging the original wildfire rather than causing it to burn out. Modern wildfire fighters still set backfires, although they also employ other tactics such as digging fire-breaks—deep trenches that the fire will, it is hoped, not cross.

Backfire in the sense of a plan that goes awry is unrelated to prairie backfires. In this case, the term comes from the word for a premature explosion in the cylinder or exhaust of a car's engine. People have been using this *backfire* figuratively since the early twentieth century to describe an action whose result is the opposite of the one intended.

Nineteenth-century examples of *fight fire with fire* come mostly from settlers' narratives. They use the phrase literally while describing prairie fires. One of the earliest figurative uses in print comes from the 1943 novel *Down among the Dead Men*: "The only way I know how to fight fire is with fire." However, the expression was almost certainly being used as a metaphor much earlier. Today, fighting fire with fire implies not only employing the same techniques as your opponent—say, meeting charges with countercharges—but also throwing yourself into the fray with equal fervor and commitment. As with prairie wildfires, fighting fire with fire sometimes causes a volatile situation to flare up rather than to die down.

HIT PAY DIRT.

Find wealth or success; find what you are looking for.

The earliest uses in print of *pay dirt* refer to real dirt. For example, an 1856 newspaper reports, "On the Merced the miners are doing well, many getting out pay dirt." To the miners working along California's Merced River, hitting pay dirt most likely meant retrieving chunks of gold ore from the gravel of the riverbed, an activity known as placer mining, or panning for gold. In 1856, these miners would have been latecomers to the California gold rush.

The gold rush started on January 24, 1848, when the foreman at John August Sutter's newly built Coloma, California, sawmill fished several pieces of shiny rock out of the millrace. Tests showed that the shine came from gold. The banks of the American River, where the mill was located, were soon overrun with gold-bedazzled forty-niners, as they were called, desperately digging for pay dirt. By the end of 1849, the forty-niners had swelled California's population from around fourteen thousand to one hundred thousand. The gold boom continued through the mid-1850s. Gradually, as pickings got scarcer, mining companies replaced individual speculators on the gold fields.

At least one enterprising word historian has suggested that *pay dirt* derives from the Chinese *pei*, which means "to give." This argument was evidently inspired by the presence of Chinese immigrants in the California gold fields. However, the Chinese did not arrive in any numbers until 1852, several years after the gold rush was in full swing. *Pay dirt* was almost certainly an established term by that time. This etymology seems to be an example of another metaphor—*going around your elbow to get to your thumb*. The transparent derivation of *pay dirt*—dirt that pays—is much more likely to be right. By the 1880s, *pay dirt* was being used as slang for money or general wealth. An article in the November 1884 issue of *Century Magazine* includes the line "He lives . . . in a style that proves that he has lots of pay dirt somewhere." Since the mid-twentieth century, hitting or striking pay dirt can describe any kind of desired result, as in *The Yankees have been hitting pay dirt since acquiring a new relief pitcher* or *After searching through every closet in the house, Megan at last hit pay dirt. Pay dirt* can also be used to refer to the scoring area of a playing field, such as a football field's end zone.

DISH (THE) DIRT.

Gossip; make spiteful remarks about someone.

Dishing dirt has been a popular way of sharing information since at least the 1920s. An early example of its use comes from Meyer Levin's 1936 novel *The Old Bunch*: "The seven wise virgins got together in Ev Goldberg's ritzy house and proceeded to dish the dirt." *Dirt* has been slang for scandal or an embarrassing fact since the middle of the nineteenth century. In a typical use, Hemingway's narrator in the 1926 *The Sun Also Rises* asks, "Do you know any dirt? . . . None of your exalted connections getting divorces?"

The *dish* part of the phrase probably comes from *dish up* or *dish out*, meaning to put food on dishes and serve it. Someone who dishes dirt is offering partakers a tempting helping of scandalous news or gossip. The word may also be connected with the sense of *dish out* that means to hand out physical or verbal punishment. "You can dish it out, but you can't take it" is a common way of accusing someone of being unable to accept criticism, particularly someone who often gives it.

In earlier times, the verb *dish* could mean to ruin or defeat someone. Francis Grose's 1788 *Dictionary of the Vulgar Tongue* gives this example: "'He is completely dished up': 'He is totally ruined.'" George Ade uses the expression in the 1901 *Forty Modern Fables* to indicate that a girl's parents have spoiled her chances of finding a suitor: "Jeanette was a dutiful Child and respected her parents, but after they had dished many a Bright Prospect she had to rise up and have her Say." According to the *Oxford English Dictionary*, this meaning of *dish* also derives ultimately from *dish out*. The idea in this case is that the ruined person is "done," like cooked food, and served up on a dish. (*Dish* does not appear to be related to the verb *dash*, meaning to smash an object or, figuratively, to spoil someone's hopes.)

In recent decades, the noun *dish* has become a synonym for "scandal," with the dirt implied. *New Yorker* magazine for February 2, 1998, quotes literary agent Lucianne Goldberg explaining why she encouraged her friend Linda Tripp to tape-record Tripp's conversations with former White House intern Monica Lewinsky: "I love dish! I live for dish!" *Dish* can also be used as a verb on its own, as in this line from a *New York Times* article for February 21, 2005: "In the dynamic that exists between gossip magazines and celebrities, each party has a particular role: the magazines dish and the celebrities try to dodge." Another way to dish up gossip that may be more palatable to some is to *spill the beans*. (See chapter 12, "Eating Well.")

TAKE A RAIN CHECK.

Postpone an event until a more convenient time.

The first rain checks were literally checks—tickets—that allowed their holders to attend a future baseball game in place of one that had to be postponed because of rain. Abner Powell, owner of the early baseball team the Atlanta Crackers, is widely credited with inventing rain checks in 1889. He claimed to have introduced them in Sportsman's Park in New Orleans. The tickets were dated so they could be used for only the next game.

Although Powell may have introduced dated rain checks, he did not invent the concept. An article in an 1884 *St. Louis Post-Dispatch* notes that several games in the city had to be canceled because of heavy rain and "the audience had to be content with three innings and rain checks." It's obvious from this context that *rain checks* is meant literally. A ticket preserved from an 1888 Detroit game reads, "In case rain interrupts the game before three innings are played, this check will admit the bearer to grounds for the next league game only."

Tickets to early ball games at most parks were made out of reusable cardboard strips. Eventually, because of the need for rain checks, tickets were cut with perforations across the middle so the stub could be kept in case of a postponement due to the weather.

By the 1930s, *rain check* had taken on the general meaning of a postponement or a future possibility. An early figurative example occurs in Raymond Chandler's 1939 novel, *The Big Sleep*. One character uses the phrase to describe her family's penchant for making losing bets: "The Sternwoods have money. All it has bought them is a rain check."

FEEL A DRAFT.
Detect hostility.

This piece of slang was coined by jazz saxophonist Lester Young in 1945. Young, who began playing in jazz bands in the 1930s, was known for his obscure private vocabulary, which was understood by his friends but not by outsiders. For example, he called women *hats*, with different headgear, such as skull caps, referring to specific women. He had *bulging eyes* for things he approved of. When encouraging fellow players to take another chorus, he said, "Have another helping." The "draft" that Young referred to came from the chilly, uncomfortable atmosphere that hostile people create.

By the 1950s, the expression *feel a draft* was widespread among jazz musicians, although less so among the general public. Jazz players typically used it to describe hostility from an audience or from strangers at large. It often applied specifically to the racism that African American musicians encountered while on tour. A 1960 *Esquire* magazine article on jazz defines *feel a draft* as "evidence of Jim Crow in a restaurant or elsewhere." Musicians, baseball players, and others who traveled through the South in the early twentieth century were harassed by the "Jim Crow" laws, named for an early nineteenth-century plantation song. These remained in effect in some places until the 1960s. Among other things, the laws mandated separate eating, bathroom, and sleeping facilities for blacks and whites.

Although *feel a draft* mainly refers to the hostility of racism, it can apply to other negative feelings as well. The draft will sometimes waft over from fellow musicians. An example of this usage is found in an August 1960 *Playboy* article referring to celebrated jazz trumpeter Miles Davis: "'If somebody like J. J. or Gil Evans or John Lewis is not impressed by what he's doing,' says a friend, 'Miles feels a draft.'" Musicians can also feel a draft related to the music itself. For instance, *I'm playing and all of a sudden I feel a draft* means that something doesn't sound quite right. Nonmusicians occasionally use the term to describe the feeling that they are failing to make a good impression on their chosen audience.

BE SENT UP THE RIVER.
Be sent to prison.

The prison up the river is Sing Sing, about thirty miles north of New York City on the banks of the Hudson. Sing Sing Prison was built in 1825 and soon became notorious for the harshness of its conditions. During its early years, these included the imposition of complete silence on the prisoners. The prison was named for the nearby town of Ossining, which was originally called Sing Sing. It currently houses about seventeen hundred inmates.

The expression *up the river* to refer to Sing Sing Prison has been in use since at least 1891. It appears in *Darkness and Daylight*, a social worker's narrative of rescue work in New York City. A former inmate, describing his postprison experiences, says, "Lager beer had come up since I went up the river." Early gangster movies like the 1932 film *20,000 Years in Sing Sing* also helped popularize the phrase, besides making Sing Sing the most famous prison in the country.

Up the river began to be used for prisons generally by the 1940s. The phrase frequently appears in hard-boiled novels, usually modified with the phrase *a long stretch*. Mickey Spillane writes in his 1947 thriller, *I, the Jury*, "He had been a pickpocket until a long stretch up the river gave him a turn of mind." The expression is still used this way. Joseph Hallinan's 2001 book about the private prison system in the United States is titled *Going Up the River: Travels in a Prison Nation*.

COME FROM THE WRONG SIDE OF THE TRACKS.

Socially or economically inferior.

This expression has been current since at least the 1920s. It refers to the railroad tracks that once ran through nearly every town in the United States. In a 1929 novel titled *The Stray Lamb* by Thorne Smith, the author explains, "In most commuting towns . . . there are always two sides of which the tracks serve as a line of demarcation. There is the right side and the wrong side."

Railroad tracks were a central feature of American towns until the 1950s. The first railway lines were built in the 1820s, and, by the early twentieth century, a network of more than two hundred thousand miles of track crisscrossed the country. In fact, many towns owed their existence to the proximity of the railroad. Train stations bustled from morning till night with travelers boarding passenger trains and businesses loading goods to be shipped.

How did the tracks get a right and a wrong side? One possible explanation is that property on the upwind side of the tracks was more desirable than downwind property. The first locomotives ran on steam created by burning coal or wood. The resulting smoke and other residue blew mainly into the downwind side of town. The property in this area was consequently less valuable, and factories and warehouses were often built there. Cheap housing was also sometimes located on the wrong side of the tracks. Townspeople with plenty of money built their houses on the cleaner, more attractive upwind side.

Although railroad tracks no longer have significance in most Americans' lives, the expression has survived. However, *wrong side of the tracks* no longer refers literally to a geographic location. It simply means being from a low socioeconomic class. This change of perspective may be due to the fact that the interstate highway system, built after World War II, now plays a more crucial part in the survival of towns along its routes.

✻✻✻

As spectacular as the landscape appeared to the first colonists, they would hardly have considered it complete without the presence of free-roaming wildlife. The wild turkeys, oppossums, and other native North American animals impressed the English as much as the rivers and forests—especially the edible ones. As we will see, they, too, contributed to the American vocabulary.

Chapter 2

BEHAVING LIKE AN ANIMAL

Animals are always a rich source for metaphors. American colloquialisms pay special attention to animals that were significant for the English colonists and later, for settlers on the frontier. One that looms large (literally as well as figuratively) is the hog. Pigs were among the first domestic animals to arrive in America and the most important meat source until recent times, so expressions referring to hog parts and hog behavior are no surprise. It's also no surprise to find turkeys on the list. That mistakenly named North American animal played a big part in saving the Pilgrims from starvation. This collection also includes the opossum, another native American animal. The millions of pigeons that darkened the eighteenth-century sky are commemorated in the chapter 7 entry *sing like a canary*, which also discusses the origin of *stool pigeon*.

Besides their interest in the local fauna, the colonists evidently retained the well-known English attachment to all things dog. To the many doggish expressions already in the language—*to be an old*, *lucky*, *impudent*, or *sly dog, lead a dog's life, die like a dog, not have a dog's chance, go to the dogs*, and many more—Americans added the now-obsolescent *put on the dog*, meaning to dress extra well, *stay until the last dog is hung*, a western expression meaning to stay until the bitter end, and *see a man about a dog*, explained next.

SEE A MAN ABOUT A DOG.

Leave, with the implication that you would rather not reveal your destination.

Over the years, people on their way to see a man about a dog have been headed for a variety of places. The phrase was coined during the Victorian era of verbal delicacy as a euphemism for engaging in any crude activity or behavior that a person would rather not mention. For example, it could suggest a visit to a prostitute. Eventually the phrase evolved into an all-purpose excuse for leaving. A popular nineteenth-century American play includes the line "Excuse me Mr. Quail, I can't stop; I've got to see a man about a dog." The audience of the time would have understood that the speaker wanted to get away from Mr. Quail in a hurry.

During the Prohibition era of the 1920s, seeing a man about a dog (or more jocularly, seeing a dog about a man) meant going out to buy illegal liquor. Places for buying and consuming liquor were known in the Old West as *doggeries*, or *dog-holes*, possibly a combination of *dog* with *groggery*, a low-class drinking place. (A few decades earlier, men stepping out for a tipple used the even shorter excuse that they wanted to *see a man*, with or without a dog.)

Why would anyone genuinely want to see a man about a dog? Possibly to get a tip for the dog races or to place a bet. Coursing meets—events where two greyhounds competed at chasing a rabbit—were popular during the last quarter of the nineteenth century. County fairs also sponsored greyhound races. The heavy betting that usually accompanied dog races would have attracted all sorts of unsavory characters, so it wouldn't be surprising if seeing a man about a dog race became a metaphor for any low-class activity. The occasional use of the alternative euphemism *see a man about a horse* supports the idea that racing was involved.

The meaning of the phrase *see a man about a dog* began to change again around the 1960s. For the past few decades, people who announce an urge to inquire about dogs are assumed to be headed for the bathroom. *The Third Deadly Sin*, a 1981 novel by Lawrence Sanders, features these lines: "'Make yourself at home,' Fred said. 'I gotta see a man about a dog.' He went into the bathroom, closed the door."

BARK UP THE WRONG TREE.

Misdirect one's efforts as a result of misunderstanding a situation.

This colloquialism comes from the colonial frontier, where nocturnal raccoon hunts were common events. Hunters cornered their game using dogs that chased the raccoons up trees. The dogs then kept the raccoons pinned down by standing at the base of the tree and barking until the hunters arrived. Unfortunately for the hunters, raccoons are wilier than dogs. They were often able to slip through the branches of neighboring trees and make their escape while the gullible dogs remained barking in their original spot, unaware that the tree was now empty.

Bark up the wrong tree is yet another of the down-home expressions attributed to Davy Crockett. Crockett very likely popularized it, but the phrase first appeared in print in 1832 in *Legends of the West* by James Hall: "You are barking up the wrong tree, Johnson." Davy Crockett is quoted as using the expression in *Sketches and Eccentricities of Col. David Crockett of West Tennessee* ("the meanest thing on earth, an old coon dog barking up a tree"), which was published in 1833. A version of it also appears in *An Account of Colonel Crockett's Tour to the North and Down East*: "some people are going to try to hunt for themselves, . . . and seem to be barking up the wrong sapling."

Bark up the wrong tree passed into the general vocabulary by the twentieth century. It's no longer considered a colorful regional colloquialism but rather a part of standard English. It appears in newspaper stories without explanation or quotation marks, not only in the United States but in other parts of the English-speaking world.

TALK TURKEY.

Talk frankly about serious matters; get down to business.

In the early nineteenth century, *talking turkey* meant affably chatting or making pleasant remarks—in other words, having a conversation. This meaning is probably behind the related old-fashioned expression *not say turkey* or *not say pea-turkey*, meaning not to speak at all, as in *She didn't say pea-turkey to me about it.*

By the turn of the twentieth century, the meaning of *talk turkey* had shifted from making general conversation to discussing cold, hard facts. The journal *Dialect Notes* for 1903 defines the expression as "talk plainly" and gives the example "I'm going to talk turkey with him and see if I can't get him to mend his ways."

Native to North America, turkeys have been a feature of American life since colonial days. Wild turkeys were an abundant food source for the early settlers and were essential to their survival during the first years of settlement. The domesticated variety of the bird was already familiar to British colonists. They were introduced into Europe in the sixteenth century by Spanish explorers returning from North America. Tradition has it that turkeys were part of the first Thanksgiving feast in 1621. William Bradford, writing about that year's harvest in *Of Plymouth Plantation*, notes, "[T]here was great store of wild turkeys, of which they [the Pilgrims] took many." Benjamin Franklin approved of these creatures so much that he argued for their claim to "national bird" status over that of eagles. As for modern Thanksgiving dinners, nothing is more of a cold, hard fact of life than leftover turkey.

Etymologists are unsure of how turkeys came to be associated with talking. Various, more or less farfetched guesses can be concocted. Perhaps the colonists noticed that wild turkeys are sociable birds. Turkeys gather in large flocks, and the males often go courting in pairs. Possibly the gobbling noises that turkeys make reminded people of certain conversations they'd heard. All we know for sure is that *talk turkey* was being used as a metaphor for conversing from at least the late eighteenth century.

A widely repeated but highly doubtful explanation for the origin of *talk turkey* began appearing early in the nineteenth century. One version goes like this: An Indian and a colonist went hunting together and bagged several birds, including a turkey and a crow. When it came time to divide the day's takings, the colonist tried to tilt the odds for good eating in his favor. He offered the Indian a choice: "You can take the crow and I'll take the turkey, or I'll take the turkey, and the crow can be yours." The Indian was unfazed by this blatant attempt to gain an unfair advantage. "You don't talk turkey to me," he said, "but I'll talk turkey to you." (For more about dining on crows, see *eat crow* in chapter 4, "Politics as Usual.")

This unlikely story has persisted through the years. It was apparently already well established in 1824 when it was recounted in a book of humor called *A Little Bit of Tid-Re-I*. Author Roderick Roundelay writes that he hopes no one will accuse him of "not talking turkey" in his essays. Although the quote implies that talking turkey meant being businesslike and factual, other instances of the phrase from as late as the 1880s show that *talk turkey* was still widely used as slang for chatting.

The expression is most often used today in business contexts. It suggests detailed negotiations, as in *Let my lawyer know when you're ready to talk turkey.*

GO COLD TURKEY.

Stop an activity suddenly and completely; suddenly withdraw from drug use.

This expression is almost certainly connected with *talk turkey*. In the early decades of the twentieth century, people spoke of *talking cold turkey*, meaning to get down to the unvarnished basics. Carl Sandburg wrote in a 1922 letter, "I'm going to talk cold turkey with booksellers." As the English newspaper *Daily Express* explained to its readers in a 1928 article, "She talked cold turkey about sex. 'Cold turkey' means plain truth in America."

Cold turkey could also mean an event that happened without warning, as in *I lost five hundred dollars cold turkey* or *They performed the number cold turkey, without rehearsal.* This use seems to have died out. Also during the 1920s, the meaning of a sudden, unaided withdrawal from drugs was gaining ground. *Cold turkey* is given this definition in a 1936 *American Speech* article listing narcotics addicts' slang.

An alternative explanation for the "drug withdrawal" meaning is that going cold turkey leaves the addict's skin looking pale and goose pimpled, like a plucked turkey. However, it's more likely that the phrase draws on the original *talk turkey* or *talk cold turkey* idea of facing up to the hard facts. These days, *cold turkey* can refer to any sudden and complete abandonment of some substance and is often used less than seriously, as in *I recently went off chocolate cold turkey.*

LIVE HIGH ON THE HOG.
Live in a luxurious style.

All the best parts of the hog—for example, expensive chops and roasts—are located high up on its body, so those who can afford to live high on the hog must be doing very well financially. Most Americans from colonial days through the nineteenth century couldn't afford to live that high. They ate every part of the hog, high and low, from the ears to the feet. Pigs were by far the most common meat-providing domestic animal. They were relatively easy to raise and transport, compared with herd animals like cattle. Colonial Virginian William Byrd writes in his diary that his compatriots ate so much pork that they became "extremely hoggish in their temper . . . and prone to grunt rather than speak."

Nineteenth-century Americans ate a heavy diet of salt pork. It kept well and was a convenient staple for travelers and those living in isolated areas. Hog and hominy, a dish of salt pork with grits or cornbread, was a frequent meal in the South. In fact, the plentiful availability of pork was probably the main reason for Americans' reputation as prodigious meat eaters. European visitors of the time often note in their writings that Americans live mainly on meat. In most European countries, only the upper classes could afford to eat animal protein every day.

The expression *live high on the hog* and its variants, *live high off the hog* and *eat high off the hog*, began appearing in print around the 1940s. Possibly the first use appears in H. L. Mencken's 1941 autobiography, *Newspaper Days*. Writing about two colleagues on the Baltimore *Herald* who claimed to be descendants of French aristocracy, he says: "Both were content to let it be known that they . . . would be eating very high on the hog if they could only get their rights." Another early quote, which refers literally to eating well, comes from the editorial page of the May 27, 1946, San Francisco *Call-Bulletin*: "I have to do my shopping in the black market because we can't eat as high off the hog as Roosevelt . . . and all those millionaire friends of the common man."

The expression is now common in England as well as in the United States. It usually refers to prosperity, generally—for example, *Since she received her raise, she's been living high on the hog.*

GO (THE) WHOLE HOG.

Commit oneself to some activity or idea unrestrainedly; be enthusiastically in favor of a thing.

The first widespread use of *go the whole hog* was political, from the time of the 1828 presidential election, when Democrat Andrew Jackson challenged Federalist incumbent John Quincy Adams. Ardent Jackson supporters were known as *whole hoggers*. The Democratic Party during this time stood for government by the common people, as opposed to the Federalist preference for strong central government by a political elite. Jacksonian Democrats introduced high-intensity campaigning, rousing the populace with raucous speeches and pithy slogans. They were noisy, enthusiastic, and committed. A newspaper quoted in John Russell Bartlett's *Dictionary of Americanisms* comments, "[T]he Democrats . . . generally go the whole hog—they never scratch or split differences." The slogan for Jackson's 1832 reelection campaign was "Jackson forever: Go the whole hog!"

A whole hog is a lot—two hundred pounds or more. The 1852 edition of *Household Words* offers this possibility for the origin of the phrase: "When a Virginian butcher kills a pig, he is said to ask his customers whether they will 'go the whole hog,' as, in such case, he sells at a lower price than if they pick out the prime joints only." Obviously, going the whole hog would have meant a serious undertaking for his customers, especially before the days of refrigeration. (*Go* in this case is evidently being used in the sense of accepting some item, as in *Could you go another beer?* This phrasing was common in the nineteenth-century United States.)

Another possible explanation connects *whole hog* to the slang meaning of *hog* in the nineteenth century—a British shilling or an American ten-cent piece. In those days, many people would have considered it extravagant to spend a whole ten-cent piece at once.

In his book *Presidential Campaigns*, Paul Boller relates an anecdote about a Kentucky farmer who arrived at the Lexington market late one night with two halves of a dressed pig to sell. He hung the meat up on hooks, then settled down to sleep on some old sacks nearby until the market opened in the morning. On awakening, he discovered that one pig half had been stolen during the night. Furious, he began pacing and shouting in front of his stall. "I know the sort of man that stole that pork," he yelled to the gathering crowd, "He was a Clay man!" (referring to Jackson's opponent in the 1832 presidential race, Henry Clay). Clay was a Kentucky native, so the people of Lexington were his solid supporters. They angrily demanded an explanation for the farmer's outrageous remark. Quickly backtracking to avoid trouble, the farmer explained, "Why, if he had been a Jackson man he would have gone the whole hog!"

Joking paraphrases of this expression were popular during the nineteenth century—*proceed the whole pork, go the entire swine, go the entire animal,* or the shortened form *go the whole* all appeared in newspapers and books of the era. In modern times, the phrase has lost its political meaning and simply refers to any extreme amount of activity or a very thorough approach. Usually it is said without *the*, as in *Dana has really gone whole hog for skiboarding*.

GET SOMEONE'S GOAT.
Annoy or anger someone.

Various origins have been proposed for this colloquial phrase, popular since the beginning of the twentieth century. One story is found in H. L. Mencken's *The American Language*. Mencken writes that he has been told the phrase originated with the old-time horse trainer's habit of calming a nervous horse by stabling it with a goat. If some unscrupulous competitor managed to steal away the goat before a big race, the horse would become unnerved and could then be easily defeated at the track.

Mencken's explanation is ingenious but unlikely. No connection has been discovered between the horse racing world and the first uses of the phrase. One of the earliest examples comes from a letter Jack London wrote in 1910: "Honestly, I believe I've got Samuels' goat! He's afraid to come back." London is obviously using *get someone's goat* in the same way it would be used today—to describe exasperating or disturbing someone.

A few people have suggested that the expression comes from the French *prendre la chevre*, "take someone's goat," meaning to deprive someone of his last resource. This explanation is not entirely satisfactory either, as the French and American meanings aren't that similar. Although annoyance would certainly be one result of having your goat stolen, the main point of the French phrase is deprivation, or taking advantage, rather than irritation.

Yet another possibility is that the expression is somehow connected with *goatee*, the word for a small pointed beard, first heard in the mid-1800s. Goatees were sometimes called *goats*, presumably because of their resemblance to a billy goat's beard; for example: *His admirers were greatly impressed by his long silky goat.* Yanking someone's goat would certainly cause annoyance. A 1930 quote from *The Last Rustler* actually uses the phrase "That country around there would get a man's goatee," but this may well be a play on words based on a saying that was widespread by 1930.

If goatees were once connected to getting someone's goat, they are no longer. Both men and women commonly say *That really gets my goat* to let others know what annoys and infuriates them.

PLAY POSSUM.
Pretend to be sick, dead, or asleep; lie low when attacked.

This expression has been in use since at least the beginning of the nineteenth century and probably before. An early example comes from William Ioor's 1807 *The Battle of Eutaw Springs and Evacuation of Charleston*: "They little thought I was playing 'Possum all the while! . . . Now, if I could only stumble upon proof positive that I was the first clever fellow who saved his life by dying." Other ways to *play possum* in the nineteenth century were to *act possum* and *to come possum over someone*. Occasionally *possum* is also heard as a verb—*I closed my eyes and possumed sleep*. Possums (or more formally, opossums) have a habit of lying still when attacked and pretending to be dead. This very sensible behavior causes their predators to grow impatient and abandon the chase.

William Simmons describes an encounter with a possum in his 1822 travelogue, *Notices of East Florida*. While walking through the pine barrens with a guide, Simmons observed a possum running up a tree. At his instructions, the guide fired a shotgun at the creature four or five times. He was unable to dislodge it from the tree, although he believed he had hit it. However, the possum still had enough wherewithal to retain its perch. Although Simmons and his guide waited patiently for quite some time, the possum gave no sign of intending to move. Eventually they abandoned the effort and walked on.

Simmons concludes by remarking that possums have been known

to lie as if dead for several hours after being wounded, only to escape when their attackers tire of waiting and leave the coast clear. "Hence," he concludes, "the expression of 'playing possum' is common among the inhabitants, being applied to those who act with cunning and duplicity." Today, playing possum usually means pretending to be asleep. It doesn't necessarily imply serious duplicity.

GO LIKE A BAT OUT OF HELL.
Move very fast.

This expression may have originated in the southeastern United States. *Dialect Notes* for 1909 lists it as an Arkansas regionalism meaning "very quickly." However, it was clearly in use in other parts of the country by the early twentieth century. A 1903 Western by Harry Leon Wilson titled *Lions of the Lord* contains the line "if I knew anyplace where the pinches was at, you'd see me comin' the other way like a bat out of hell!" The expression most often refers to physical movement, either on foot, horseback, or in modern times, in a car or plane. However, it can be used more abstractly, as in this 1912 quote from George Patullo's *The Sheriff of Badger*: "whenever I have any [money] and get to town, it goes like a bat out of hell."

Bats have long been associated with the underworld. The Greek play *The Birds* by Aristophanes refers to a bat from hell. The fact that they sleep in dark caves during the day and come streaming out at dusk may have contributed to the connection between bats and the nether regions. There's something uncanny about their frightening appearance and the suddenness of their swooping just as night falls.

Even if bats don't really fly out of hell, they do move quickly. Using the sonar system called echolocation, bats can move without hesitation through total darkness. The Web site *Bat House* reports that Bat Conservation International has clocked one species flying as fast as sixty miles per hour.

Like a bat out of hell has remained a common description for someone moving with speed and confidence, even recklessly. Some have speculated that the 1977 album *Bat out of Hell* by the musician Meat Loaf may have helped maintain the expression's popularity.

GO BELLY-UP.

Go bankrupt; die; become defunct.

Many people share the sad childhood memory of goldfish floating belly-up in the aquarium. Fish turn belly-up when they die because, as they decay, their abdomens fill with gas. Their bodies then flip over, with the heavier, backboned part underneath and the lighter, gas-filled belly above. There is no more obvious symbol of death than a belly-up fish—its condition is unambiguous.

Belly-up as a metaphor for being in a defunct state has been around at least since 1920. One of the first uses of the phrase in print comes from a letter by writer John Dos Passos, dated September 12 of that year: "Labor's belly up completely—the only hope is the I.W.W. [Industrial Workers of the World]." Belly-upness is usually a financial condition. Bankrupt businesses are frequently said to be belly-up. Mechanical devices like computers can also go belly-up. The phrase is used occasionally to describe a sudden failure in other areas, for example, *My golf game has gone belly-up. Belly-up* is also possible as a verb. The 1980 book *Wait Until Dark* by R. L. Morris includes the sentence "Payoffs and bribes . . . caused the majority [of speakeasies] to belly-up."

JUMP THE SHARK.

To have reached a peak of performance and to start declining in quality or appeal.

Jump the shark is a highly unusual colloquial phrase in that its origin can be pinpointed exactly. Its figurative meaning evolved from the Web site *www.jumptheshark.com*, which went online on December 24, 1997. Dedicated to critically analyzing popular television shows, the site defines jumping the shark as that moment "when you know that

your favorite television program has reached its peak . . . from now on
. . . it's all downhill." Ways that a series can jump the shark include
two characters marrying or having a child, the death of a character, a
child actor in the series growing to adulthood, the frequent appearance
of special guest stars, or substituting one actor for another to play the
same character.

The site's founder, Jon Hein, credits his college roommate with
coining the phrase. It refers to the television series *Happy Days*, which
aired from January 1974 through July 1984. Set in 1950s Milwaukee,
the show featured a leather-jacketed high school dropout named
Arthur Fonzarelli—Fonzie for short—played by actor Henry Winkler.
In the opinion of Hein's roommate, *Happy Days* started its downhill
slide with the episode of September 20, 1977. During this show,
Fonzie, dressed in a leather jacket and a pair of swimming trunks, goes
waterskiing and literally jumps over a shark. Although the show ran
for another seven seasons, some purists believe it was never the same.

Musicians, filmmakers, politicians, and anyone else in public life
can jump the shark. The jump often takes the form of an over-the-top
stunt, staged in a desperate effort to regain a lost audience or a for-
merly high approval level. People in the public eye can also jump the
shark simply by declining in popularity, without a defining "jump-the-
shark" moment.

※ ※ ※

An even better-known shark than the one that appeared on *Happy
Days* is that American predator known as the *loan shark*, a term used
since the beginning of the twentieth century. Along with the bears and
bulls of the stock market, the loan shark was a force to be reckoned
with. Like many business titans, he would do whatever it took to make
a profit.

PART 2: BUSINESS, POLITICS, AND SOCIETY AT LARGE

Chapter 3

BUSINESS DEALINGS

"The chief business of the American people is business," said President Calvin Coolidge in 1925. Coolidge was speaking at the height of the boom times known as the Roaring Twenties. However, Americans have always put plenty of energy into buying and selling at the right time. Metaphors like *get down to business*, *bank on it*, *deliver the goods*, and *look at the bottom line* reflect the cultural centrality of business dealings.

Different kinds of money-making ventures have captured Americans' interest during different eras. In the nineteenth century, thousands rushed to California and Alaska to search for gold, adding *gold digger* and *mother lode* to the figurative vocabulary (as well as *pay dirt*, discussed in chapter 1, "The Great American Outdoors"). *Peter out*, which once applied only to veins of ore, can now refer to any enterprise that gradually dwindles to a stop. Likewise, *pan out*, originally a reference to gold being left in the miner's pan after he sifted through the rocks and debris, is now something that can happen with any successful business gamble.

In the 1920s, and again in the 1980s, the country went wild for stocks and bonds. American English showed a net gain from this obsession, with metaphors that include *buy into an idea*, *be a sellout*, *sell someone short*, *trade up*, *trade down*, and *trade off*.

Now that businesses—and the rest of us—have embraced computer technology, terms from the online world are slowly seeping into the vocabulary. Americans have learned how to "multitask" like computers, and consumers now demand that cookbooks, films, and other unlikely items be "user friendly." Whereas once only computer software was beta-tested—tried out during development—today, plans and ideas of all kinds have their beta versions.

SELL SOMEONE DOWN THE RIVER.
Betray someone.

The origins of this phrase apparently come from the antebellum practice of sending troublesome slaves to plantations along the lower Mississippi River. Among the first to use the expression was Harriet Beecher Stowe, author of *Uncle Tom's Cabin*. References to selling slaves down the river occur in several places in her narrative, first published as a serial in 1851. For example, a slave owner explains to his companions how he handles male slaves who threaten to cause trouble: "I've had one or two of these fellers and I just sold 'em down river." Another character, trying to persuade a slave against running away, says, "If you're taken, it will be worse with you than ever; they'll only abuse you and half kill you and sell you down river." These examples don't specifically mention Mississippi plantations. However, *down river* clearly represents a literal threat of being sold into greater hardship.

Another example of the phrase used literally appears in Mark Twain's 1894 novel, *Pudd'nhead Wilson*. The slave owner Driscoll terrifies his slaves into admitting their petty pilfering by shouting, "Name the thief. . . . I will give you one minute. If at the end of that time you have not confessed, I will not only sell all four of you *but*— I will SELL YOU DOWN THE RIVER!" The narrator describes this threat as "equivalent to condemning them to hell."

It's unclear why Mississippi plantations were considered more wretched than plantations elsewhere. Like most Southern plantations, those along the Mississippi grew cotton. The workload would presumably have been similar to that of other cotton-growing estates. It is possible plantations in Mississippi simply did more slave buying during the nineteenth century than older, better-established places on the East Coast. The Mississippi slave population tripled in the decades before the Civil War, as the demand for cotton exploded. During this time, it may have been most convenient for plantation owners in other parts of the South to sell unwanted people down the Mississippi River.

By the twentieth century, *sell someone down the river* was a metaphor for betrayal. P. G. Wodehouse includes an early example in his 1927 novel, *The Small Bachelor*: "When Sigsbee Waddington married for the second time, he to all intents and purposes sold himself down the river." The phrase implies not only self-betrayal but a kind of oppression. As the speaker goes on to explain, "He [Waddington] does what his wife tells him—that, and nothing more." In recent decades, someone who is sold down the river could also be the victim of a con game or other dishonest dealings.

SELL SOMEONE A BILL OF GOODS.
Make false promises; trick or swindle someone.

The Americanism *bill of goods* originally meant a list of merchandise on consignment. In the late nineteenth century, *bill* often stood for an order to a sawmill for wood cut to a specific size, as in this quote from the April 16, 1881, *Chicago Times*: "Last fall our mills shut down with contracts for bill stuff still on their order books." However, a bill of goods could list any kind of merchandise. Bookkeepers' ledgers often noted items like *bill of crockery* or *bill of linen*. This meaning of *bill* no doubt led to another Americanism, *fill the bill*, which has been slang for "meet all the necessary requirements" since the middle of the nineteenth century, as in *The doctor thinks this new medicine will fill the bill for curing my insomnia*.

The first recorded slang use of *bill of goods* is from Eugene O'Neill's 1927 play, *Marco Millions*. The character Maffeo Polo jokes with two business competitors by saying, "Selling a big bill of goods hereabouts, I'll wager, you old rascals?" The remark is obviously meant to suggest sharp dealings as well as genuine selling. By the 1940s, *sold a bill of goods* had become a common synonym for being cheated or fooled. Consumers in most cultures tend to mistrust the motives of people trying to sell them something, especially an item the seller doesn't actually have on hand. Paying for a bill of goods in the hope that the goods themselves will arrive in the near future might well strike cautious buyers as a mug's game.

Another way in which bills of goods might have gotten a bad reputation stems from a traditional use for bills of lading. In the days when merchandise was sent to buyers on ships, the ship's master presented the seller with a bill of lading before he sailed. This detailed receipt committed the master to delivering the shipped items safely to the buyer. Depending on the merchant ship's destination, delivery and payment could take up to a year. To ease cash flow problems in the meantime, holders of bills of lading often used them as security for bank loans. If, for some reason, payment was not forthcoming after all, the lender was left holding a worthless bill of goods. Between accidents at sea and dishonest merchant sailors, this situation must have arisen fairly often.

Today, people who claim to have been sold a bill of goods usually mean that someone has persuaded them to believe a false story. Politicians are often accused—and accuse each other—of trying to sell the American people a bill of goods.

BUY THE FARM.
Crash; be killed.

Buying the farm originated in military circles, although it's unclear whether Americans or the British were the first to employ the phrase. Most sources attribute it to the United States military. However, the shorter term *buy it* was current in England as early as 1825. W. N. Glascock's *Naval Sketchbook* includes the phrase, "we didn't buy it with his raking broadsides." Another British example, recorded in 1920 but dating from World War I, is from a book on the Bristol Fighter Squadron: "The wings and fuselage, with fifty-three bullet

holes, caused us to realize . . . how near we had been to 'buying it.'"
A soldiers' and sailors' slang dictionary from the same era further
defines *buy it* as being forced to accept something you don't want,
such as an unpleasant task, or being made to look foolish. This
meaning of *buy* comes close to the modern meaning of "naively
believe," as in *Thank goodness—the boss bought my lame excuse!*

Buying a piece of property—usually the farm, but occasionally a
ranch, plot, or shop—does not appear as a metaphor until World War
II. Originally it referred specifically to a pilot's fatal crash. Two explanations of the phrase are common. The first, current during the war,
claimed that it came from the fighter pilots' tendency to talk about
how they would leave the military after the war, buy a farm, and settle
down. By the 1950s, the more usual explanation was that farmers on
whose land a plane had crashed would sue the government for dam-
ages, typically demanding a sum large enough to pay off the mortgage.
Since the pilot almost always died in the crash, he essentially paid for
the farm with his life. It seems more likely that *buy the farm* originally
alluded to the sense of *buy* that implies a person has lost out, as in the
earlier meanings of *buy it*. The *farm* part of the expression might have
been tacked on as a reference to the fields that fighter planes often
crashed into. A 1938 volume of *American Speech* records the variants
buy a car and *buy a telephone pole* as long-distance bus drivers' slang
for causing an accident.

Since the 1960s, any sort of death can buy someone the farm. It
does not necessarily have to be an airplane crash or other accident. In
his 1989 novel, *Midnight*, Dean Koontz's narrator says, "I was in sur-
gery, having a bullet taken out of my chest, and I almost bought the
farm." People can even buy the farm without dying, simply by getting
into very serious trouble, as in *You boys have really bought the farm
this time!*

BUILD A BETTER MOUSETRAP.
Make a significant improvement to a popular product.

The lecturer and essayist Ralph Waldo Emerson may have been the first to mention better mousetraps. Sarah Yule, in her 1889 anthology, *Borrowings*, attributes the following quote to Emerson: "If a man can write a better book, preach a better sermon, or make a better mouse-trap, than his neighbor, though he build his house in the woods, the world will make a beaten path to his door." The writer Elbert Hubbard, famous in the early twentieth century for his pithy sayings, also claimed authorship of the quote.

Yule responded to Hubbard's claim by explaining that she had noted down the quote while listening to Emerson lecture in 1871. A similar passage is recorded in Emerson's journal, a frequent source of ideas for his talks. Emerson was a leader of the American Transcendentalist movement, devoted to the individual discovery of an ideal, "transcendent" spiritual state. A powerful orator, he drew large, enthusiastic crowds to his lectures.

Build a better mousetrap was a familiar allusion by the 1930s. One of the earliest examples in print appears in a 1934 *New York Times* article that asks how Babe Ruth gained world-class fame: "By building better mousetraps?" Modern business writers often refer to this adage, usually in the shortened form *Build a better mousetrap and the world will beat a path to your door.*

PUSH THE ENVELOPE.
Go beyond the established or permissible boundaries.

During World War II, pilots operated according to flight envelopes—the combination of speed, altitude, engine thrust, and other factors that defined the performance limits for various makes of airplane. The urge to go beyond the established limits compelled daring pilots to push the flight envelope. Variations on the phrase are *push the edge of the envelope* and *push the outside of the envelope.*

The expression gained popularity with the general public when author Tom Wolfe used it in his 1979 book about the early space program, *The Right Stuff*. Besides defining the phrase, Wolfe makes clear that it meant not merely ascertaining limits but going beyond what was safe. Pushing the envelope was part of the excitement and fascination of flying. Writing about the program's pilots, he says, "One of the phrases that kept running through the conversation was 'pushing the outside of the envelope.' The 'envelope' was a flight-test term referring to the limits of a particular aircraft's performance, how tight a turn it could make at such-and-such a speed, and so on. 'Pushing the outside' . . . seemed to be the great challenge and satisfaction of flight test."

Since the 1980s, any sort of innovative or edgy move is known as pushing the envelope. For example, in a 1989 profile of Apple founder Steve Jobs in the *New York Times Magazine*, he is quoted as telling an audience, "What we want is to create the next computing revolution. We want to push the envelope." Recent news stories describe modern novelists, computer scientists, advertising firms, comedians, stationery designers, and architects pushing their respective envelopes. The term is also still used in aeronautics.

THINK OUTSIDE THE BOX.
Be creative.

Thinking outside the box was first mentioned in print around 1975. It almost always appears in a business context, as in this 1984 quote from *Fortune* magazine: "He tells his managers . . . to 'think outside the box' of their own specialty." The box is a grid of nine dots—

three rows of three—known as the nine dots puzzler. To solve the puzzler, players must connect the dots in one continuous line without lifting the pencil from the paper. This task is doable only if part of the line veers outside the perimeter of the "box" created by the rows of dots.

Although business consultants discovered the box in the 1970s as a way to challenge their clients' creative capacities, the game first appeared in 1914 in a children's book called *Cyclopedia of Puzzles*. The puzzle may have been invented by the book's author, Sam Loyd, or he may have borrowed it from some unknown source. In the *Cyclopedia*, the puzzle is called "Christopher Columbus's Egg Puzzle." The illustration shows King Ferdinand and Queen Isabella of Spain sitting at a table, studying a grid arrangement of nine eggs. This puzzle is apparently meant to be a companion to Columbus's better-known challenge of how to make an egg stand on end. (Hard-boil it and crack the larger end so it's flat.)

While outside-the-box thinking is still a desirable trait for businesspeople, it is also possible to think inside the box. *New York Magazine* reports in an article about architecture from April 25, 2000, "Skidmore stayed safely inside the box."

HIT THE PANIC BUTTON.

Overreact; act too hastily out of panic.

The original panic button was probably connected to the bell system installed in World War II bombers. When a plane was extensively damaged, the pilot signaled "prepare to abandon" with a series of rings, then "jump" with another set of rings. Bomber crews developed their own ring codes for different emergency situations. Occasionally, a pilot would hit the button prematurely, causing the crew to bail out of a plane that had sustained only minor damage.

In an *American Speech* article from October 1956 titled "Which Panic Button Do *You* Hit?" Lt. Col. James L. Jackson interviews several Air Force Academy pilots to determine how they identify the panic button. The most common candidate is the feathering button, hit during flight to turn off a malfunctioning engine. Another potential panic button triggers a burst of extinguisher materials designed to put out engine fires. Yet a third button can be punched to tip out part of a dangerously heavy fuel load, making it easier to gain altitude. Finally, pilots can hit a button triggering the ejection seat. This final panic button seems especially well named. If any situation calls for rational people to panic, it's almost certainly when they have to jettison themselves out of a plane in midflight.

However, Lieutenant Colonel Jackson points out that none of these four devices had been introduced when pilots first started using the phrase. He concludes that the bell-system button of World War II bombers inspired *panic button*, and the term then spread to various other emergency gadgets.

Hit, *push*, *press*, or *punch the panic button* was in figurative use by the 1950s. Anyone who appears to be overreacting to a tense political situation or sounding a premature alarm is said to be hitting the panic button. Several emergency buttons are also sometimes labeled panic buttons. These include under-the-counter buttons that convenience store clerks, bank tellers, and other workers in danger of being robbed can press to call for help. Devices that the elderly use to summon emergency services are also called panic buttons.

BLOW YOUR BUFFER.
Lose your train of thought.

A buffer is a device for temporarily storing information on computers. Different computer systems process information at different speeds. The buffer holds, or "remembers," data input from a faster system until it can be processed by the slower system. For example, material to be printed is fed from the word processor into a buffer, where it remains until the printer can reproduce it on paper. Buffers may have been so named because they mediate between different parts of the computer and allow them to function compatibly, serving a similar purpose to buffer states or buffer zones. When the computer's buffer receives too much data all at once, the computer blows its buffer and the memory quits functioning.

Blow your buffer as a metaphor first appeared, appropriately enough, online—as a posting on the American Dialect Society's e-mail discussion list. In a forwarded message titled "Cyberslang," the term is defined as what happens when the person you're speaking to won't let you "get a word in edgewise," or makes a statement so astonishing that you forget what you were about to say. Either way, you lose what you were holding in your memory.

Although the computer savvy typically define the phrase as losing your train of thought, recent Internet uses of *blow your buffer* indicate a broadening in the meaning. For example, a new movie described as "guaranteed to blow your buffer" suggests an analogy with the 1960s expression *blow your mind*, meaning to cause amazement. Other uses indicate a meaning closer to losing control, such as, "Ever blow your buffer at work?" This expression, which is still very new, might appear in many versions (1.0, 2.0, and so on) before it settles down to a standard meaning.

GO POSTAL.

Lose your temper; behave with irrational violence, especially as a result of workplace stress.

Before 1986, few Americans would have equated post offices with violence. On August 20 of that year, Patrick Sherrill, an Edmond, Oklahoma, postal worker, killed fourteen of his fellow employees and wounded six before fatally shooting himself. According to news reports, Sherrill entered the post office at 7:00 a.m., dressed in his postal uniform and carrying three handguns. He locked the door behind him. Sherrill then walked through the building shooting people. Although Sherrill had a history of disciplinary problems, the immediate cause of his outbreak is still unknown.

Sherrill's killing spree is generally attributed with inspiring the term *go postal*. However, several copycat incidents involving postal workers who were fired or forced to retire might have contributed to the expression's spread. By the early nineties, *go postal* was well entrenched in the vocabulary. Its earliest known appearance in print is in a *St. Petersburg Times* article for December 17, 1993. The *Times* reports that the US Postal Service is sponsoring a symposium on workplace violence. The article notes that the post office has seen so many recent outbursts "that in some circles excessive stress is known as going postal." *Go postal* is used twice in the 1994 movie *Clueless*, indicating that the phrase was mainstream slang by this time. An alternative is *going postal worker*. A 1994 *Chicago Tribune* article on "Chicago speak" offers this definition: "going postal worker: . . . overwhelmed with work and about to go crazy with frustration."

The US Postal Service, understandably disturbed by this negative publicity, hastens to point out that relatively few incidents of workplace violence happen in post offices. After making a broad-based survey of occupations, the service concluded that working at the post office is one of the safer jobs—far safer than driving taxis, for instance. The report concludes, "If 'going postal' is meant to suggest that postal employees are more violent than the national workforce, it is simply untrue."

The post office's high profile might have encouraged the expression's spread. The phrase might also have been memorable because Americans have a positive image of mail carriers as responsible people who deliver their letters in spite of "snow, rain, heat, or gloom of night."

Since at least the late nineties, *go postal* has lost its connection to workplace-related violence and can now refer to any kind of rage. It is increasingly used to mean an ordinary, nonlethal loss of temper, as in *If my boss catches me surfing the Web on office hours, she'll go postal.*

WHEEL AND DEAL.

Scheme, bargain, or negotiate, with the implication of unscrupulousness.

Wheeling and dealing is the province of big wheels, characters who appeared on the American scene around the 1930s. Big wheels, sometimes just called wheels, were originally gang leaders or prominent members of the underworld.

Wheeler-dealer and the verb form *wheel and deal* did not become part of the vocabulary until around the 1950s. By this time, the criminal connotations of being a wheel had disappeared, or at least faded, and wheeler-dealers could be important people from any walk of life. The 1961 edition of *Webster's Dictionary* defines *wheel and deal* as "to take the part of a leader . . . and to take charge of affairs or arrangements."

Wheel and deal has inspired several theories of origin. *Picturesque Expressions* suggests that the phrase originated as World War II military slang. Among mechanics of that era, *roll a big wheel* meant to hold an elevated position. World War II mechanics could not have invented the figurative meaning of *big wheel*, as it was already a familiar term in the 1930s underworld. However, they may have popularized it after the war.

Several sources suggest that *wheel and deal* could be connected with *wheels within wheels*. This phrase derives from the biblical verse found in Ezekiel, chapter 1, verse 16: "their appearance and their work was as it were a wheel in the middle of a wheel." However, this expression refers to complex forces at work—not exactly the same meaning as *wheel and deal*. Also, *wheels within wheels* has been in use as a figure of speech since at least the seventeenth century, whereas big wheels are a twentieth-century phenomenon. Such a long gap argues against the later phrase directly evolving from the earlier one.

Yet another common explanation derives the phrase from gamblers' slang, with the wheel in question being a roulette wheel. Heavy gamblers spun a big wheel frequently. As with the Ezekiel theory, the weakness of this derivation is the time gap involved. Roulette wheels were at their most popular during the nineteenth century, when Americans living in the West were mad for gambling in all its forms. (See chapter 8, "Playing the Game.") However, *wheel and deal* does not appear in print until the 1950s.

Wherever the figurative *wheel* came from, it seems fairly certain that *deal* is the result of repeating a sound for emphasis—this form of wordplay is popular in English, creating combinations like *bow-wow*, *nitty gritty*, *razzle dazzle*, *walkie-talkie*, and dozens of others. (See also *flip-flop* in chapter 4, "Politics as Usual.") Connecting the two words also makes sense—big wheels cut big deals. *Deal* to mean a business arrangement or other type of negotiation has been current since the fourteenth century.

Wheel and deal is most often used in modern times to describe business and politics, but anyone can potentially be a wheeler-dealer. The phrase usually connotes getting some benefit not available to everyone.

HOLD A POWWOW.

Hold a meeting or confer together, especially with more noise and bluster than necessary.

The word *powwow* comes from the Algonquian language of Narragansett. It refers to a shaman or spiritual leader—literally, "he who dreams." Powwows, spelled in various ways, are mentioned in the earliest colonial records. Edward Winslow's 1648 description of colonial settlement, *Good News from New England*, explains, "The office and duty of the Powah is to be exercised principally in calling upon the Devil; and curing diseases of the sick or wounded." *An Account of Two Voyages to New England*, published in 1674, also mentions tribal members known as powwows, describing them as "Indian priests."

The colonial British extended the term to cover native ceremonies, councils, and other public gatherings that they witnessed. The shaman would normally have been an integral participant in these events. For example, one observer records, "the Indians at the Wigwams, near the Fort, had a Powwow, or sort of Conjuring." Another source describes the powwow as "an ancient religious rite."

Using *powwow* to mean a meeting, especially a political gathering, dates from the early nineteenth century. Early examples of the term are almost always jocular. The *Salem Gazette* of June 5, 1812, reports,

"The Warriors of the Democratic Tribe will hold a powwow at Agawam on Tuesday next." *Powwow* implied an exaggerated bustle and show. Mark Twain uses the word this way in his 1897 book, *Following the Equator*. He describes the Mumbai (Bombay) tradition of driving around the seashore to Malabar Point every evening, a showy event featuring clusters of footmen clinging to the backs of the carriages. The footmen's job was to look flashy and to harry pedestrians out of the way. Twain remarks, "It all helps to keep up the liveliness and augment the general sense of swiftness and energy and confusion and powwow."

In most modern uses, holding a powwow means holding a meeting to discuss some issue or to plan strategy. Native Americans have also reclaimed the word *powwow* in the twentieth century as a cross-tribal term for a Native American gathering. Modern Native American powwows typically include traditional singing and dancing, as well as socializing.

DON'T TAKE ANY WOODEN NICKELS.
Don't let anyone trick you or take advantage of you.

The first occurrence of this expression in print doesn't actually name the type of coin. It appears in Christy Mathewson's 1915 novel, *Catcher Craig*: "He was instructed . . . not to take any wooden money." Nickels usually are specified in this phrase, which was popular as a casual farewell in the early decades of the twentieth century. *Don't take any wooden nickels* warned innocents going abroad to steer clear of con artists. In the 1920s, the phrase was briefly college slang, an injunction to fellow students to stay alert during classes.

Wooden nickels were never part of the American monetary system. The expression probably grew out of an earlier version of the phrase *Don't take any wooden nutmegs*. As the story goes, a favorite trick of the spice peddlers who traveled from town to town in the early United States was to substitute nutmegs carved from wood for the costlier genuine article. Nutmegs, imported from the exotic Spice

Islands of Indonesia, were a scarce luxury item. Inexperienced house-wives might easily have been fooled by a carved version. Con-necticut's nickname, "the Nutmeg State," is an allusion to its large colonial population of Yankee peddlers. Whether peddlers really did sell wooden nutmegs is open to question. J. R. Dolan, author of *The Yankee Peddlers of Early America*, believes the story of the wooden nutmegs was an early form of urban legend—always happening to the friend of a friend, never to the storytellers themselves.

Peddlers were ubiquitous in pre–Civil War America. The scat-tered, mostly rural population of the time relied on door-to-door salesmen for a wide assortment of essential goods, from small notions like needles and buttons to big-ticket items like spinning wheels and firearms. It wouldn't be surprising if, among these thou-sands of merchants, a few maximized their profits with an imagina-tive swindle or two.

More frauds may have been attributed to them than they actually committed. Yankee peddlers were the national stereotypes of dis-honest rogues. The Englishman Thomas Hamilton, who wrote *Men and Manners in America* in 1833, claims that Yankee peddlers "are proverbial for dishonesty. They go forth annually in the thousands to lie, cog [deceive], cheat, swindle. . . . They warrant broken watches to be the best timekeepers in the world; sell pinchbeck trinkets for gold; and always have a large assortment of wooden nutmegs." Wooden nut-megs were evidently already a metaphor for worthless goods.

As peddlers disappeared from the American scene at the close of the nineteenth century, the term *wooden nutmegs* would have been increasingly puzzling. Valueless nickels made more sense. Nickels often stand in for money generally—for example, in the expressions *nickel and dime someone, not worth a plug* (or *plugged*) *nickel, nickel nurser* (a miser), *It's your nickel,* and *If I had a nickel for every time.* Around the turn of the twentieth century, when the expression *Don't take any wooden nickels* first came into use, many everyday items cost a nickel, including candy bars, cheap paperback novels, bus rides, cigars, and the moving picture theaters known as *nickelodeons.* The term *wooden nickel* would have conjured up a double-dealing disaster that anyone could understand.

Don't take any wooden nickels is not as common a send-off as it once was. However, it is still heard occasionally in joking situations.

DO NOT FOLD, SPINDLE, OR MUTILATE.

Do not treat individuals in an impersonal, mechanical way; do not damage people or things by rough treatment.

This expression was popular during the 1960s as a protest against what many people saw as the increasing impersonalization of daily life. The phrase originated as an instruction on punch cards—a nearly obsolete format for recording information digitally. Punch cards are stiff paper cards marked with predefined columns, usually twelve rows of eighty columns. They are coded by punching holes in the appropriate columns. The punched cards are then fed into a reader for interpretation. One of the few remaining uses of punch cards is to record and tabulate votes.

Punch cards were invented in late eighteenth-century France as a way to program textile looms. In 1890, an American statistician named Herman Hollerith adapted punch cards so they could be used to tabulate the data collected during that year's census. His system was a success—the Census Bureau completed the 1890 census tabulations in less than half the time of the 1880 census. Within a few decades, businesses were using punch cards to keep track of sales numbers, client records, and similar information. The army and other branches of government also stored data on punch cards.

In the 1950s, IBM (an outgrowth of Hollerith's original company) developed a computer that read and tabulated data off punch cards. After that, the cards were everywhere. Utilities companies and department stores began sending out their bills on punch cards. Social Security checks were issued as punch cards. Most important for the future of punch cards as a metaphor, college students were handed stacks of them when they arrived to register for classes. Since computers couldn't process the cards properly if they were bent or otherwise damaged, warnings were usually printed across one side—"Do not fold or bend this card"; "Do not fold, tear, or mutilate this card"; "Do not fold, tear, or destroy." For unknown reasons, "Do not fold, spindle, or mutilate" became the archetype of these warnings, although that exact phrase may never have appeared on an actual card.

The expression has outlived some of its terms, as well as nearly outliving the cards themselves. Everyone knows what folding and mutilating are, but hardly anyone spindles papers anymore. When businesses started printing their warnings on the cards sometime in the 1930s, most offices still organized receipts, notices, and other loose pieces of paper by impaling them on sharp, upright spikes called spindles. Spindling punch cards—poking a random, unreadable hole in them—would have caused computer havoc.

Do not fold, spindle, or mutilate was reborn as a metaphor on the campus of the University of California at Berkeley during the 1960s. To the rebellious youth of that era, punch cards were symbols of enforced regimentation. Students saw them as a bureaucratic attempt to reduce individuals to numbers—standardized bits of data. As the campus newspaper *Daily Californian* explained in a September 15, 1968, editorial, "The incoming freshman has much to learn . . . perhaps lesson number one is not to fold, spindle, or mutilate his IBM card." The students' response to this instruction was to flip it around and apply it to themselves. *Do not fold, spindle, or mutilate* became a slogan that told the adult establishment, "We are individuals. Treat us with at least as much respect as you would treat a punch card." Posters and T-shirts began to appear with the legend "Human being: do not fold, spindle, or mutilate."

Although *do not fold, spindle, or mutilate* is still occasionally used as a plea for gentle treatment, more often it's a shorthand reference to the world of computing. It forms the title for several books and articles about the early days of computer technology. *Do Not Fold, Spindle, or Mutilate* was also the title of a 1971 movie about the perils of computer dating.

NEVER GIVE A SUCKER AN EVEN BREAK.

Don't be too scrupulous about taking advantage of another's inexperience.

This trenchant piece of advice was the signature phrase of the great American comic actor W. C. Fields. It is the title of a 1941 film that Fields wrote, reportedly jotting down the plot on the back of an envelope and subsequently selling it to Universal Studios for $25,000. In the movie, Fields plays himself—"The Great Man"—in his final starring role. The slapstick plot follows Fields's attempts to sell a film script to Universal.

According to the *Oxford Dictionary of Catchphrases*, Fields first ad-libbed the slogan *Never give a sucker an even break* in the 1923 stage musical *Poppy*. He speaks the phrase again in the 1936 film version of *Poppy*, in which he plays Professor McGargle, a carnival snake oil salesman. In one scene the professor tells his daughter, "If we should ever separate, my little plum, I want to give you just one bit of fatherly advice: Never give a sucker an even break!" The line pops up yet again in the 1939 film *You Can't Cheat an Honest Man*: "As my dear old grandfather Litvak said (just before they swung the trap), he said 'You can't cheat an honest man. Never give a sucker an even break or smarten up a chump.'"

Several quotation books attribute the original phrase to a remark by vaudeville theater owner Edward F. Albee. Grandfather of the playwright Edward Albee, the elder Albee began his career touring with P. T. Barnum. Barnum is associated with a similar phrase, *There's a sucker born every minute*, although no record exists of his ever having said it. (Barnum is also supposed to have said, "You can't cheat an honest man.")

Alternatively, volume 2 of William and Mary Morris's *Dictionary of Word and Phrase Origins* credits Wilson Mizner with the original remark. Mizner, a playwright and entrepreneur during the early decades of the twentieth century, was known for his clever repartee.

W. C. Fields might have heard some version of *Never give a sucker an even break* from either of these sources. Taking advantage of suckers was no doubt a basic principle in the world of vaudeville and circus entertainment. However, his movies are the reason why the general American public adopted the expression as a familiar cliché.

※※※

Speaking of suckers—if the chief business of the American people is business, the second most important activity is politics. Too many of us, after voting, unfortunately feel that we've been sold a bill of goods.

Chapter 4

POLITICS AS USUAL

Election banners reading "Vote early and vote often" flew openly in New York City streets during the nineteenth century. This slogan neatly represents traditional American political jargon, which tends to reflect a freewheeling approach to the democratic process. Among the colorful terms inspired by nineteenth-century politics are *spoils system, lobby, filibuster, gerrymander, pork barrel*, and *bunkum*, not to mention *snollygoster*, now sadly obsolete. The *Columbus Dispatch* for October 28, 1895, offers this lively definition of the word: "A snollygoster is a fellow who wants office, regardless of party, platform or principles, and who, whenever he wins, gets there by the sheer force of monumental talknophical asumnancy."

The expressions listed in this section show an energetic approach to politicking. Eager candidates mend fences, roll campaign balls through the streets, and leap onto tree stumps to make speeches. Such expressions as *twist in the wind* and *eat crow* hint at the down side of politics.

TAKE A STRAW POLL.
Take a nonbinding vote; conduct an unofficial survey.

Straw polls are also known as *straw votes*. The term originally signified a casual opinion survey, often conducted by a newspaper reporter looking for a story. The first use of the phrase appears in an 1866 *Cleveland Leader* article concerning President Andrew Johnson. Johnson had been elected Abraham Lincoln's vice president in 1864 and was sworn in as president after Lincoln's assassination. He clashed with Congress when he opposed recently passed civil rights laws and tried to reverse post–Civil War Reconstruction policies. The American public evidently sided with Congress. The *Cleveland Leader* reported to its readers, "A straw vote taken on a Toledo train yesterday resulted as follows: A. Johnson 12; Congress 47." The *Leader*'s opinion poll was right on the mark. Two years later, the House of Representatives passed a resolution of impeachment against this deeply unpopular president. However, he was acquitted in the Senate by one vote.

Most etymologists believe that the term *straw poll* alludes to the practice of holding up a straw to test which way the wind is blowing. Seventeenth-century British scholar John Selden used the idea metaphorically when he wrote, "Though some make slight of libels, you may see by them how the wind sits: as take a straw and throw it up into the air, you shall see by that which way the wind is, which you shall not do by casting up a stone." Straw polls are like straws in the wind. Although casual and nonbinding, they can indicate emerging trends.

An alternative phrase for a *straw vote* in the nineteenth century was *steamboat vote*. Steamboats were a popular means of travel for most of the nineteenth century. By polling steamboat passengers, reporters and political operatives could collect a representative cross-section of opinions. Newspapers often tracked trends with steamboat votes during this era.

Straw polls are now much more scientifically organized, large-scale affairs. They are conducted by professional pollers and are almost always aimed at discovering which candidate would win an election if a real vote were taken on the day of the poll. Political caucuses also take straw polls to get a sense of how opinions are running without having to be bound by the results. Participants at meetings also take straw votes to decide whether they all agree on a particular issue. If they do, they can conduct a real vote immediately. If not, they can discuss the issue further. The mock elections often held in grade schools around the time of a national election are also known as straw votes.

MAKE A STUMP SPEECH.
Make a political speech; advocate a cause.

Stumps were plentiful in colonial America. They made a convenient platform for a speaker who wanted to raise himself a foot or so above the crowd. According to a Tory jingle that was current during the Revolution, George Washington was a stump speaker. The song goes, "Upon a stump he placed himself, / Great Washington did he." Early uses of the phrase indicate that it often referred to a real stump. This example from the 1844 *Knickerbocker* magazine even names the type of tree: "A western orator recently delivered himself of it [an opinion] from the summit of a sugar maple stump."

Making a stump speech, or stumping, as it was also called, was considered a showy political trick—not quite dignified. One essayist of the time complains about "the devices of the stage and the stump." Candidates for public office who were suspected of being out for personal gain were called *stumps*. Congressmen who engaged in overheated oratory were accused of behavior more appropriate to the stump than the serious business of government. By the late nineteenth century, stump speeches could be made from any kind of platform, not just tree stumps.

In American English, the verb *to stump* has the additional meaning of puzzling or obstructing someone. People who are at a loss for an answer admit *You've got me stumped*. This use also relates to tree stumps. The *Oxford English Dictionary* suggests that the meaning refers to the difficulty of plowing a piece of land from which the stumps have not been cleared. In early settlement days, potential farmland was nearly always covered with trees. Before planting could begin, these had to be cut down and the stumps removed, a piece of backbreaking but necessary labor. Otherwise, the plow would have to swerve around them. *Stump* to mean baffle was in use by the first decade of the nineteenth century.

All political campaigning is now known as stumping, especially if it involves travel. Campaign speeches are stump speeches, no matter where they take place. *Stump speech* is sometimes used to describe a candidate's standard statement of his or her positions on the issues. Supporters of a candidate can also make stump speeches. Headlines during the 2004 presidential election included "Bush Twins Stump for Dad" and "Gore to Stump for Kerry in Florida." Supporters can stump for a piece of legislation as well as for a person.

MEND YOUR FENCES.
Attend to neglected business; make peace with someone.

This phrase is attributed to Senator John Sherman of Ohio, author of the Sherman Antitrust Act and brother of the Civil War general William T. Sherman. Sherman served as the state's Republican senator from 1861 to 1897, with a break from 1877 to 1881 to serve as secretary of the treasury. In 1879, when Sherman was contemplating a run for the presidency, he retired to Ohio to think the matter through. The standard version of the story tells of an enterprising reporter who tracked Sherman down one day when he was repairing a broken fence on his farm. When the reporter asked him what he was doing in Ohio, he replied that he was mending his fences. This literal answer failed to impress the newsman, who put his own political spin on the phrase.

Sherman's memory of the event is slightly different. According to the account published in his recollections, he had returned to Ohio to take care of various pieces of business. He stayed at a local hotel, as his farm was occupied by tenants. Visiting the farm one afternoon, he noticed that several of the fences were broken down and he decided to repair them. That evening a group of reporters accosted Sherman at the hotel, wanting to know if he was thinking of running for governor (another possibility besides president). Sherman replied that he had come home on private business—"to repair my fences and look after neglected property."

Either way, the expression *mend fences* almost immediately became a synonym for taking care of political business. A slang dictionary published in 1889 defines *mend fences* as "for a man . . . to attend to his interests." The phrase was most often associated with politicians who traveled home to reconnect with their constituents. The *Congressional Record* for August 16, 1888, includes a dry comment on absent members: "I presume they are at home seeking renomination or looking after their fences." An April 1906 article in the *Forum* explains that "an early adjournment of the [legislative] session is deemed essential in order that the members may go home to mend their fences, as the saying is."

Today, the expression is often used as a general term for repairing a broken relationship, either personal or political. That includes making up after a disagreement, as in *Jennifer tried to mend fences after the argument by inviting her friend to dinner*. Although *mend fences* appears frequently in political contexts, it usually does not refer to a representative's relationship with constituents anymore. More typically, it is used in a sentence like *China and Japan recently took steps to mend some fences*.

SIT ON THE FENCE.
Be neutral or undecided.

This expression was familiar to Americans by the 1820s. The August 1, 1828, *Richmond Whig* editorializes about the fence-sitting editors of other newspapers: "There are certain Administration Editors, Editors for a long time on the fence, who occasionally undertake . . . to sit as censors upon their fatigued and dusty brethren." In the nineteenth century, newspaper editors were not expected to sit on the fence. They were frankly partisan when it came to politics. Many newspapers were known as "Democratic" or "Whig" papers. The above quote refers to "Administration Editors." These would have been supporters of President John Quincy Adams, the incumbent in 1828, rather than his opponent, Andrew Jackson. The 1828 presidential campaign was heated, and fence sitters would hardly have been appreciated by either side. (For more on the Andrew Jackson campaign, see *go (the) whole hog* in chapter 2, "Behaving Like an Animal.")

By the middle of the nineteenth century, *on the fence* was a typical way to describe a politician who remained neutral on an issue or waited to see how events turned out before throwing his weight to whoever was victorious. As John Russell Bartlett points out in his 1848 *Dictionary of Americanisms*, "A man sitting on top of a fence can jump down on either side with equal facility." Bartlett goes on to say disapprovingly, "Selfish motives govern him, and he is prepared at any moment to declare for either party."

As the above quote indicates, fence sitting was generally viewed with contempt. However, author James G. Blaine seems to be using the term admiringly when he writes about Carl Schurz in the 1886 *Twenty Years of Congress: From Lincoln to Garfield*. Schurz was a senator from Missouri during the first half of the 1870s. Later he was appointed secretary of the interior. Blaine says of Schurz, "He aspires to the title of 'Independent,' and has described his own position as that of a man sitting on a fence, with clean boots, watching carefully which way he may leap to keep out of the mud."

Although anyone waffling over a decision can be described as being *on the fence*, the term is still used most often to describe politicians who have not yet taken a firm stand on a particular issue. Other ways to refer to someone's position with respect to the fence include *come down on the right side of the fence*, *stand on the other side of the fence*, and *keep on the same side of the fence*.

BURY THE HATCHET.
Make peace after a dispute; lay down arms.

This phrase is one of the earliest that British settlers adopted from Native Americans. It refers to the tradition among some tribes of cementing a peace pact by burying their weapons—not only hatchets but also long knives and war clubs. The first Englishman to describe this practice is Samuel Sewall, a Puritan who immigrated to the Massachusetts colony in 1661. Sewall writes in his diary for 1680 about "the mischief of the Mohawks." The colonists' problems with the natives had led to a Major Pynchon traveling to Albany, where he met with the Mohawks' chief and "they came to an agreement and buried two axes in the ground." Sewall adds that this ceremony is more significant and binding to Native Americans than any other form of treaty, "the hatchet being a principal weapon."

Later, the British initiated hatchet burying themselves. A New York colonist records in 1754, "We have ordered our Governor . . . to hold an interview with them [the Iroquois] for delivering those presents, [and] for burying the hatchet." The expression *bury the hatchet* was not used figuratively until the late eighteenth century. Even then it most often referred to settlers' relations with Native Americans. The variants *lay down the hatchet, bury the tomahawk*, and *bury the axe* were also used.

To the colonists, hatchets were synonymous with war. It was possible to pick up—or more colorfully, dig up—the hatchet as well as bury it. Writing about the Seven Years' War against the French and their Native American allies, George Washington notes, "Three Nations of French Indians . . . had taken up the hatchet against the English."

By the early nineteenth century, burying the hatchet simply meant to make peace or repair personal or political relations. A typical example comes from the *Annals of the Congress of the United States*: "I had long been persecuted by the General, but wished to bury the hatchet." The expression is still used this way today. *Dig up the hatchet* and *bury the tomahawk/axe* are now obsolete.

HOLD THE FORT.
Take temporary responsibility; remain at your post.

This expression is attributed to the Civil War general William T. Sherman. When the Confederate army threatened to disrupt Sherman's supply line near Allatoona, Georgia, in early October 1864, Sherman sent General John M. Corse to secure the fort at Allatoona Pass. Corse arrived with around two thousand men on the morning of October 5.

A few hours later, Confederate general John T. French arrived with over three thousand troops. French sent a message to Corse, suggesting that he surrender "to avoid a needless effusion of blood." Corse refused. According to stories of the battle, he had received a signal from Sherman saying, "Hold the fort, for I am coming." He did hold the fort, and eventually French's troops were forced to withdraw.

Sherman denied having sent Corse a message in those words. He claimed to have signaled the more mundane "Hold out, relief is coming." Considering that Sherman was signaling by flag—the telegraph lines having been cut—it's likely that his message was as basic as possible. Turning it into *Hold the fort, for I am coming* is an example of a common phenomenon—polishing up a quote so it sounds more quotable. In 1870 Philip Paul Bliss, a writer of spiritual music, published the gospel song "Hold the Fort!" The song includes the lines "'Hold the fort, for I am coming,' Jesus signals still; Wave the answer back to heaven, 'By Thy grace we will.'" The popularity of this song ensured that Sherman's message would be preserved in these words.

By the early twentieth century, *hold the fort* was used figuratively as a request to keep a situation under control when the person who would normally be in charge couldn't be there. An early example comes from Erle Stanley Gardner's 1936 mystery, *The Case of the Sleepwalker's Niece*: "I want to put in a telephone call. You hold the fort." In modern times, *hold the fort* usually carries the implication that someone will be arriving or returning soon to relieve you.

KEEP THE BALL ROLLING.

Keep a conversation or an activity moving smoothly forward.

Other versions of this expression are *get the ball rolling* and *start the ball rolling*. The saying has been around since at least the early nineteenth century, but it rose in popularity during William Henry Harrison's 1840 presidential campaign. The 1840 campaign was among the first to approach elections as a form of public entertainment. Harrison's Whig Party held barbeques and bonfire rallies and composed campaign ditties ridiculing the Democratic opponent, Martin Van Buren. As an ongoing campaign stunt, Whig Party stalwarts rolled parade balls for hundreds of miles, traveling from rally to rally. These ten-foot paper and tin balls were covered with campaign slogans. As campaigners rolled the balls through town, they encouraged the gathering crowds to "Keep the ball rolling for Harrison."

Although Harrison's people popularized *keep the ball rolling* with the general public, they clearly did not invent it. The phrase wouldn't have had much impact as a slogan unless people already understood its potential double meaning. A more likely possibility is that the term originated earlier with a game called shinny. Shinny is the American version of a very old European game called bandy, a cross between soccer and ice hockey. Bandy players push a tiny, three-inch ball around an icy surface using bent sticks. In the old days, the surface was a frozen pond or an icy field. Today, it's an ice rink. The ball must keep moving throughout the game. Originally *to bandy* meant simply to toss a ball back and forth—giving us the expression *to bandy words with someone*—but a game with bandy-like rules has been played since the Middle Ages.

Shinny, the American version of bandy, was wildly popular all along the East Coast during the latter half of the eighteenth century. College students played ferocious games of shinny, accompanied by the kind of mayhem now associated with European professional soccer. In 1787 Princeton banned the game. Other schools also restricted its play, and shinny disappeared as a popular cultural phenomenon. A mild form of the game is still played in the modern United States, but bandy is much better known in Scandinavia and Russia.

By the 1850s, setting or keeping the ball rolling was a common metaphor for keeping up your end of a conversation. It was also used to suggest spreading an idea, opinion, or political movement. Walter Colton, an early California settler, writes in his 1850 book, *Deck and Port*, of "that courageous organisation which set the ball of Anglo-

Saxon supremacy rolling in California." These days, *Let's get the ball rolling* can refer to starting any kind of activity.

CHANGE HORSES IN MIDSTREAM.

Change leaders or switch loyalties in the middle of a project or crisis.

Abraham Lincoln is often credited with inventing this metaphor. He used a version of it during a speech to the National Union League acknowledging his nomination for a second term as president. Aware that many people felt he had mishandled the war, Lincoln said that the circumstances reminded him of "an old Dutch farmer, who remarked to a companion once that 'it was not best to swap horses when crossing streams.'" Lincoln then said, "I do not allow myself to suppose that either the Convention or the League have concluded to decide that I am either the greatest or best man in America, but rather they have concluded that it is not best to swap horses while crossing the river, and have further concluded that I am not so poor a horse that they might not make a botch of it in trying to swap."

Lincoln's tale of the Dutch farmer was probably already familiar to his audience. However, even if Lincoln did not coin the expression, his speech is certainly responsible for popularizing it. Horses were the most common means of transport in mid-nineteenth-century America, so the imagery would have struck a chord with Lincoln's listeners. Many of them would have ridden horses across streams themselves and understood the difficulties of changing from one horse to another while in the water.

It's interesting to note that Lincoln lent his speech a folksy touch by choosing the word *swap*. *Swap* or *swop* has meant "exchange" or "barter" since the sixteenth century, but by the 1800s it was seldom used in England. It was considered an Americanism and routinely condemned as vulgar by British language critics. Lincoln's use of it would no doubt have pleased his patriotic audience.

The current version of this expression is *change horses in mid-*

stream, but the meaning has remained the same as when Lincoln used it. It still conveys the idea that changing tactics in the middle of a project could lead to disaster. The phrase is almost always used with a negative—*Let's not change horses in midstream.*

FLIP-FLOP.
Change sides on an issue; habitually change your opinion.

Flip-flop became a buzzword during the 2004 presidential race. In the spring of that year, supporters of incumbent president George W. Bush began running campaign ads that labeled Democratic candidate John Kerry as a "flip-flopper" on the issues. They particularly targeted his alleged change of position on the 2003 US invasion of Iraq from support to opposition. The Democrats returned the favor, charging that President Bush had also "flip-flopped," or changed position, a number of times over the years on his reasons for invading Iraq.

Although most Americans now associate the term with the 2004 campaign, accusing politicians of flip-flopping is not a new tactic. The word was used as early as 1894 when the *Chicago Tribune* for March 27 made this comment about a local politician: "That incomparable political flip-flopper . . . was rewarded for his last flop with a fat diplomatic position." Around this time, someone who deserted his party for the opposite side was often called a *flopper*.

The American noun *flip-flop* originally meant a somersault. For example, the November 30, 1929, issue of *Liberty* magazine describes a performer as "turning hand-springs and flip-flops all over the sawdust covered floor." The meaning soon broadened to cover any change of direction, whether physical or philosophical. The verb *to flip-flop*, meaning to change your position on an issue, has been in use since at least the mid-twentieth century. The word derives ultimately from the "flop" sound that accompanies turning over, such as a fish that flops around after it lands on the pier. The *flip* part of the term was probably added for emphasis. *Flip-flop* is one of the many words in English that uses sound repetition for greater intensity—for instance, *ding-dong*, *fiddle-faddle*, *wishy-washy*, *shilly-shally*, and *pitter-patter*, to name a few. (See *wheel and deal* in "Business Dealings" for more examples.)

Long-haul truckers have assigned a special meaning to *flip-flop*. Building on the idea of changing directions, they use the term to refer to a return trip. One example is found in E. W. Rukuza's 1990 novel, *West Coast Turnaround*, which includes the CB radio signoff, "See ya on th' flip-flop."

EAT CROW.

Be forced to admit you were wrong, usually in public.

Eating crow, or eating boiled crow, was originally a mid-nineteenth-century form of political humiliation. Politicians who made missteps were regularly forced to eat figurative crow. The expression implied public groveling—or simply public embarrassment—usually through the newspapers. An 1877 quote from the periodical *Notes and Queries* indicates that newspapers themselves sometimes had to choke down a little crow: "A newspaper editor, who is obliged . . . to advocate 'principles' different from those which he supported a short time before, is said to 'eat boiled crow.'" This definition probably refers to the fact that many nineteenth-century newspapers served as mouthpieces for a particular party or faction. If the politicians the paper supported shifted position on an issue, the newspaper would have been forced to shift also. Thus they would have been humiliated—made to eat crow—in front of their readers.

An excellent example of the distastefulness of crow comes from a comment in the *Nation* on *New York Tribune* editor Horace Greeley's 1872 presidential campaign. Greeley's nomination was the result of an unlikely coalition between the Democrats and a group calling themselves Liberal Republicans. He was not a popular candidate. Eventually he lost by a landslide to Ulysses S. Grant. From the *Nation*'s perspective, "Mr. Greeley appears to be 'boiled crow' to more of his fellow citizens than any other candidate . . . boiled crow he is to his

former Republican associates; and now the Democrats are saying . . .
that to them also he is boiled crow."

In 1888 the *Atlanta Constitution* published a story claiming to
explain the origin of this expression. It tells of an incident that supposedly occurred toward the end of the War of 1812. An American soldier
stationed near the Niagara River took advantage of an armistice to go
hunting one day. In his enthusiasm he crossed the river into British territory, where he soon bagged a crow. Before he could escape back to
American territory, he was discovered by a British soldier.

As the story goes, the British soldier tricked the American into
handing over his gun, then forced him to take a humiliating bite out of
the crow. After issuing a stern warning, the Englishman then foolishly
returned the weapon, whereupon the American forced him to eat crow
also. The story ends with the British soldier complaining to the American's commanding officer that the American had broken the
armistice. The American reluctantly admits that he recognizes the
Englishman, saying that, in fact, they had dined together only the day
before.

Like other stories of the sort, this one is almost certain to be false.
Besides the unlikelihood of such an obscure incident giving birth to a
piece of popular slang, the expression did not appear in print until the
1870s. Such an elaborate explanation is unnecessary anyway. It's
more reasonable to suppose that nineteenth-century Americans simply
considered crows bad eating, especially when served plainly boiled.
At a time when many people lived in rural areas and hunted their own
meat, crows may well have been a food of last resort when nothing
better was available.

Is crow really such a terrible thing to eat? Opinions vary. Crows
are scavengers, which automatically disqualifies them as a food choice
for many people. They've acquired a bad reputation through being
portrayed in several movies as voracious carrion eaters that attack
humans. On the other hand, some hunters claim that crows are as tasty
as any game bird. The hunters' Web site *Crow Busters* features a
number of recipes, including Crow Kabobs and Crow Casserole.

By the 1880s, *eat crow* meant to admit you were wrong on any topic, without necessarily implying a political context. It can also mean to apologize. A typical modern use would be the sentence *I had to eat crow and admit that I'd been careless.* The *boiled* part of the phrase disappeared by the end of the nineteenth century.

TWIST IN THE WIND.

Be kept in suspense; be abandoned by former allies.

This phrase entered American folklore in 1973 during the Watergate scandal. Shortly before the 1972 presidential election, five men were arrested for breaking into the Democratic National Committee headquarters, located in Washington, DC's Watergate Hotel. Their bungled mission had been to plant listening devices. The subsequent investigation uncovered links between the burglars and the inner circle of the recently reelected president, Richard Nixon.

Among those who rushed for the barricades when the scandal broke was White House counsel John Ehrlichman, coiner of *twist in the wind*. He used the line during a strategy session in the Oval Office, in reference to Nixon's nominee for director of the FBI, L. Patrick Gray. Gray, acting head of the FBI since J. Edgar Hoover's death in 1972, was responsible for investigating the Watergate break-in. Many felt that he handled the matter poorly. When the Senate confirmation committee posed some sharp questions about it, Gray made damaging admissions that implicated the White House in a cover-up attempt. A furious Ehrlichman suggested that Gray be abandoned to his fate. "I think we ought to let him hang there," he said, "Let him twist slowly, slowly in the wind." Ehrlichman's advice was recorded on tape and became public during the Senate's later Watergate hearings. Ehrlichman himself was eventually convicted of conspiracy and obstruction of justice, among other charges. He served one and a half years in prison.

Twisting in the wind conjures up an image of hanging, and *twist* was in fact underworld slang for being hanged during the eighteenth and early nineteenth centuries. A dictionary of early nineteenth-century criminal's cant translates *He was twisted for a crack* as *He was hanged for burglary*. When Ehrlichman uttered his verdict on Gray, he may have been thinking of the tradition of allowing the corpse of a condemned man to remain hanging in a public place as a warning to others.

Today, *twist in the wind* is often used to suggest that someone is being made a scapegoat or abandoned by his or her superiors. It is most commonly used in political contexts. Examples from recent editorials include the opinion that a judge who postponed his veto of a legislative pay raise let "lawmakers twist in the wind of constituent anger," and the view that former aide to Vice President Dick Cheney, Lewis "Scooter" Libby, "was left to twist slowly in the wind by his comrades." In modern uses, *wind* often features a qualifying adjective, such as *political wind*. The phrase is not only for politics—it can be used in nearly any situation where people are left in doubt. Two possible examples are *Late arrivals were left to twist in the wind* and *The Olympics Committee let her twist in the wind while deliberating on their decision.*

GO BALLISTIC.
Fly into a rage; become wildly enthusiastic.

Ballistics is the science of projectiles. A ballistic missile is guided while taking off but falls freely when in its downward trajectory. Americans were introduced to the term *ballistic* in the 1950s, when the United States began developing the intercontinental ballistic missile (ICBM) system for delivering nuclear warheads over a long range. However, it didn't really become a household word until the early 1980s, the era of President Reagan's proposed Strategic Defense Initiative. The Strategic Defense Initiative, informally known as "Star Wars," was designed to protect the country from ICBM attacks. Partly because of the $1 trillion price tag and partly because its effectiveness was in question, the program was never implemented. Meanwhile, the missiles inspired the figurative expression *go ballistic*. Presumably the meaning derives from the missiles' free-falling phase.

The figurative use of *go ballistic* dates from the early 1980s. The *Washington Post* for July 11, 1985, quotes a Pentagon official as saying, "Wickham went ballistic when he heard about the recommendation." *Go ballistic* entered the pop culture when President George H. W. Bush used it to describe himself in a November 7, 1988, *New York Times* article: "I get furious. I go ballistic. I really do and I bawl people out."

Since the 1990s, going ballistic can be a good thing. It can mean going wild with enthusiasm, as in this example from a 1998 issue of the *Lapidary Journal*: "I went ballistic over the amazing patterns . . . found *inside* the rocks!" Going ballistic can also mean explosively reaching a whole new level of achievement, as in a musician whose career goes ballistic when his album hits the top of the charts.

MAKE A WHISTLE-STOP TOUR.
Take a trip that includes a number of brief stops.

In the nineteenth-century United States, people relied on trains for trips of any distance. However, small towns didn't provide the railroads with enough passengers to justify a regularly scheduled stop. Instead, whenever a resident of a small town wanted to catch the train, he or she informed the station master, who then flagged down the train as it passed. Likewise, train passengers who wanted to alight at a small town told the conductor, who pulled the train's signal cord. The engineer responded with two toots of the whistle to let the conductor know that he'd gotten the message. Because of that system, small towns without regular train service were called whistle stops.

Whistle-stop tours (sometimes spelled *whistlestop*) entered the public consciousness during Harry Truman's 1948 presidential campaign. Truman crisscrossed the Midwest and the West on his campaign train, pausing at up to eight whistle stops a day. At each small town, he stood on the platform at the back of the train and delivered a short campaign speech. A *New York Times* article for September 7, 1948, quotes Truman as telling a crowd gathered at one railroad station, "Before this campaign is over I expect to visit every whistle stop in the

United States." The news media referred to Truman's strategy as a whistle-stop campaign. The term *whistle-stop tour* appeared in print by 1952. The verb *to whistle-stop* was also a possibility, as in this sentence from the July 26, 1952, *News* of Birmingham, Alabama: "In a sort of swan song to the Democratic Party . . . he offered to whistle-stop for his successor."

Most of the early appearances of *whistle-stop* in print involved Truman. However, by the late 1950s, other politicians were described as whistle-stopping or taking whistle-stop tours. Gradually the expression broadened to cover any kind of trip that involves stopping at a large number of places over a short time, usually for business. It can also mean a brief tour of a single place, such as a school or a movie studio. The term has been adopted in other English-speaking countries as well. A typical modern example of its use comes from the *Business Daily Africa* for June 25, 2007: "A high-powered delegation consisting of top government and private sector executives visited the United States on a whistle-stop tour." Interestingly, whistle-stop tours are almost never taken by train these days.

THROW YOUR HAT IN THE RING.
Announce your intention to run for office.

Theodore Roosevelt used this expression in a 1912 interview to announce that he intended to run for president against William Taft: "My hat's in the ring. The fight is on and I'm stripped to the buff." Roosevelt was making figurative use of a boxing term that had been around since at least the early nineteenth century. The phrase commonly appeared in sports magazines that followed boxing matches, as in this quote from an 1818 issue of *Sporting Magazine*: "Johnson . . . threw his hat in the ring." Professional boxers at this time made money by traveling to fairs, men's clubs, and other venues and challenging all comers. A man who wanted to take up the challenge signaled his interest by throwing his hat into the boxing ring. No doubt this method was adopted because boxing matches, then as now, were crowded, noisy events. Just shouting or waving wouldn't have been enough to attract attention.

Nowadays nearly all candidates for political office are described in the newspapers as having thrown their hats into the ring. Any office qualifies, from president to city councilor. When Shirley Temple Black ran for Congress in 1967, the *New York Times* dismissively declared that she had thrown her curls in the ring. Other kinds of job seekers can also toss their headgear into the ring, especially those competing for a high-profile position such as coach of a professional ball team.

WAVE THE BLOODY SHIRT.

Foment trouble, especially political strife.

After the Civil War, Northern politicians who used incendiary rhetoric to stir up bitter feelings against the South were accused of waving the bloody shirt. Usually the shirt wavers were congressional Republicans trying to gain ascendancy over their Southern Democratic colleagues. The expression was in use by the 1870s, as this example from an 1879 *Nation* shows: "Senator Sherman has gone up to Maine . . . and delivered a long speech. . . . He opened by a wave of the bloody shirt, showing that to repeal the legislation of the war directed against the South was 'state rights' and 'nullification' and 'revolution and anarchy' . . ."

Fiery Massachusetts congressman Benjamin F. Butler once waved a literal bloody shirt during an 1868 speech in the House. Butler was a fervent supporter of postwar Reconstruction policies. Supposedly, the bloodstained nightshirt that he brandished before his fellow congressmen belonged to an Ohio carpetbagger who had been horsewhipped by night riders of the Ku Klux Klan. Butler's actions may have been the source of the post–Civil War adoption of *wave the bloody shirt*. However, the phrase, as well as the idea behind it, has a long history.

One common explanation traces *the bloody shirt* to traditions of the Corsican blood feud. When such feuds led to killing, the murdered man was laid out on a bier with his weapons around him and his bloodstained shirt hanging from a pole near his head. As emotions heated up during the funeral ceremony, the victim's widow or other female relative would seize the pole. In an upsurge of grief, she would wave the shirt in front of the other mourners and galvanize them into taking revenge.

A similar story claims that the expression originated after the Scottish battle of Glenfruin in 1603. Members of the MacGregor clan ambushed the Colquhouns, slaughtering more than one hundred of them. Tradition has it that when King James VI held a review of the incident, the grieving Colquhoun widows rode past the king one by one, waving their husbands' bloody shirts and exhorting him to vengeance. Displaying a murder victim's bloody clothes is a predictable rabble-rousing tactic—it probably happened in many times and places. For instance, Mark Antony showed the Roman crowd the murdered Julius Caesar's bloody toga at Caesar's funeral. This scene is dramatized in Shakespeare's play *Julius Caesar*, where Antony tells the Romans, "If you have tears prepare to shed them now."

Wave the bloody shirt in modern times refers to troublemaking generally, although it is mainly heard in politics. Contentiousness on almost any issue tends to be attacked by members of the opposition as an instance of "waving the bloody shirt."

✖ ✖ ✖

Contentiousness has always been part of the American political scene. Long before Representative Butler waved a bloody shirt in the United States Congress, political dramas were unfolding between the colonial British and their rivals, especially the Dutch. As with later political clashes, these encounters also had an impact on the American vocabulary.

Chapter 5

PEOPLE AND PLACES

Dutch settlers, although relatively small in numbers, had a powerful impact on the American language. Four years after the Pilgrims made landfall on Plymouth Rock, the Dutch established the colony of New Netherland. They held onto it for only forty years before their colonial rivals, the British, scooped it up and changed the name to New York. However, the colony's culture didn't change nearly as abruptly as the ownership. Dutch influence remained strong, and the language of the original New Netherlanders could still be heard in certain corners of New York and New Jersey in the early twentieth century.

American English adopted a number of Dutch words, including *boss*, *bedspread*, *sleigh*, *waffle*, *coleslaw*, *cookie*, *cruller*, *spook*, *snoop*, *stoop* (meaning front porch), *poppycock*, *dope*, *dumb*, and *Santa Claus*. The quintessential Americanism *Yankee* is probably also a gift from the Netherlands. This derisive nickname was first recorded in the seventeenth century. Its most likely origin, suggested by linguist Harold Davis in a 1938 *American Speech* article, is the Dutch nickname *Jantje* (pronounced *Yantyuh*). *Jantje* translates as "Johnny" or "little John." (Adding the ending *je* is a common Dutch way to make a word diminutive. Another example is *koekje*, "little cake," the origin of *cookie*.) The term no doubt alluded to John Bull, the stereotypical Englishman. As lesser Englishmen, Americans were designated "little John" Bulls.

American attitudes were no more flattering toward the Dutch.

They applied the adjective *Dutch* to a number of less-than-positive situations: *get in Dutch* (owe money or otherwise be in trouble); *have Dutch courage* (from drinking alcohol); *do a Dutch act* (desert or commit suicide); *make a Dutch book* (bet foolishly); *give a Dutch rub* (rub your knuckles against the nape of someone's neck, a popular small boy's trick); *hold a Dutch auction* (where prices start high and are gradually lowered until someone bids); *offer Dutch comfort* (be glad things aren't worse); *talk double Dutch* (talk gibberish; little girls also jump double Dutch with two jump ropes); as well as the three "Dutch" expressions listed below. The first one, *beat the Dutch*, explains why no love was lost between Anglo-Americans and Netherlanders.

Besides the Dutch, this section features several other individuals and locations whose names have done their part to add color to the American vocabulary.

BEAT THE DUTCH.
Cause amazement.

This expression is usually heard in the negative, as in *If that don't beat the Dutch!* It was first recorded in 1775 in a Revolutionary song lyric: "Our cargoes of meat, drink and clothes beat the Dutch." By 1837, when *Davy Crockett's Almanack* describes him boasting to the Congress, "I can . . . frighten the old folks—astonish the natives—and beat the Dutch all to smash," the phrase was a common colloquialism. Linguist Maximilian Schele de Vere reports in his 1872 collection of Americanisms that *beat the Dutch* is used "whenever a peculiarly astonishing fact is announced."

For Englishmen of the colonial period, beating the Dutch might well have been a cause for astonishment. In the early 1620s, when the Dutch and the English were first making rival claims to North American territory, competition between the two countries was fierce. It appeared that the Dutch were winning. The Netherlands boasted the most powerful navy in Europe. Dutch trading outposts reached around the globe, including into India and China, countries where the British also hoped to gain a foothold. Dutch colonists slipped in ahead of the British to contract a trade agreement with the powerful Iroquois Confederacy. They were also strong-arming their way into England's North Atlantic herring fishing waters.

The English started challenging Dutch naval and commercial supremacy in the 1650s. Although the struggle between the two countries was prolonged, Great Britain eventually triumphed. By the nineteenth century, the English could claim the strongest navy and most far-flung colonies of any European country.

They conspicuously beat the Dutch in America on at least one occasion. In 1664, King Charles II of England decided to consolidate his American holdings. The Dutch colony of New Netherland was situated squarely between New England and the king's southern colonies, breaking up British territory, so Charles sent his brother the duke of York to claim it. When the duke sailed into Manhattan harbor accompanied by an impressive fleet of warships, governor Peter Stuyvesant surrendered the colony without a fight. Overnight New Netherland turned into New York. That really beat the Dutch.

Although *that beats the Dutch* is still heard and read occasionally, it has an old-fashioned ring these days. Less colorful substitutes, such as *that beats everything*, are more common.

GO DUTCH.

Go on an outing where each person pays his or her own way.

Go Dutch has been in use since at least the early twentieth century. *Dutch* in this expression is a shortened form of *Dutch treat*, an occasion when everyone pays his or her own expenses—in other words, no treat at all. The *Oxford English Dictionary* cites an 1887 *Lippincott's Magazine* story for the first instance of this term in print: "'You'll come along too, won't you?' Lancelot demanded of Ormizon. 'Dutch treat.'"

An even older version of a skimpy Dutch social event is a *Dutch feast*, defined in Francis Grose's *Classical Dictionary of the Vulgar*

Tongue as a party at which the host gets drunk before the guests. This term was obsolete by the end of the nineteenth century. Although the message—the Dutch are stingy—is similar (and similarly unfair), *Dutch treat* probably did not derive from *Dutch feast*. It's more likely that both were separately invented slurs.

Both *Dutch treat* and *go Dutch* continue to be used in modern English. Going Dutch is usually associated with dating, but sometimes announcements of organizational events like luncheons or cocktail hours will use terms like *Dutch treat lunch* or *Dutch treat drinks*.

TALK TO SOMEONE LIKE A DUTCH UNCLE.
Talk to someone in a severe or scolding manner.

This expression is first recorded in Joseph Neal's 1837 book of stories, *Charcoal Sketches*: "If you keep a'cutting didoes [fooling around], I must talk to you both like a Dutch uncle." By 1853 the expression was becoming familiar. The periodical *Notes and Queries* published a letter asking about the saying's origin, in which the letter writer offered this definition: "[W]hen a person has determined to give another a lecture, he will often be heard to say, 'I will talk to him like a Dutch uncle.'" The expression has been common in England as well as the United States since the mid-nineteenth century. It implies giving advice to someone in a situation that may not be strictly your business.

The phrase's origins are unclear. One possibility is that it grew out of the American view of the Dutch as stern, no-nonsense people. The original Dutch settlers in New York were known for their orderly ways. Their uprightness and severity may have been thought to extend to the area of child raising. Another possibility is that *Dutch* in this case refers to the German settlers often called Pennsylvania Dutch (the German word for *German* is *Deutsch*). Pennsylvania Germans, whose descendants include the Amish and the Mennonites, began arriving in America around the beginning of the eighteenth century. Because they were known to be religious and held close family ties, they would also have been considered strict child rearers.

Dutch uncles are still around. A 2006 biography of Milton Hershey by Michael D'Antonio quotes someone using the phrase during an interview: "I talked to him like a Dutch uncle."

SAY UNCLE.

Surrender; ask for mercy.

This expression has inspired some intriguing theories of origin. It has been familiar since the late nineteenth century. A typical example appears in the *Chicago Herald-Examiner* for October 11, 1918: "Sic him Jenny Jinx—make him say 'Uncle.'" Michael Quinion of the Web site *World Wide Words* has found the expression's earliest known appearance in print. It comes from the *Iowa Citizen* of October 9, 1891, and is part of a joke. The joke concerns a gentleman who wants to show off his pet parrot to guests. He urges the parrot to repeat the word "uncle," but the parrot stubbornly refuses. Finally losing his temper, the man grabs the unfortunate bird and half twists its neck, shouting, "Say uncle, you beggar!" Then he angrily tosses the creature into the fowl yard. Sometime later, having cooled down a bit, the man returns to the yard to retrieve the parrot. To his astonishment, the bird is not dead. However, nine of his ten fowl are lying with their necks wrung, while the parrot stands on the tenth bird's head, screeching, "Say uncle, you beggar!"

This joke itself is unlikely to be the origin of *say uncle*. The humor of the punch line depends on the phrase being already familiar to the audience as an expression for conceding defeat. The joke's appearance at this time may indicate that *say uncle* was just becoming popular as a figure of speech. It was still enough of a novelty to make a good laugh line.

One theory of the phrase's origin harks back to ancient Roman days. Supposedly, when one Roman boy bested another in a fight or wrestling match, the winner would make the loser cry out, "*Patrue, mi Patrissimo,*" meaning "Uncle, my best uncle." Uncles were important relatives in the Roman Empire. This was especially true of paternal uncles, who had great influence over their nephews' lives. (*Patrue* means "paternal uncle," as distinct from *avunculus*, "maternal uncle.") Crying "uncle" could have been an appeal to a powerful family member for help. Alternatively, it could have been a way for the winner of the fight to force the loser to address him as "uncle," thereby acknowledging him as a superior person. Lacking from this explanation is any reason why the expression disappeared with the fall of the Roman Empire and did not resurface until the twentieth century in the United States.

Celia M. Millward, writing in *American Speech*, has advanced another idea. In a 1976 article titled "Two Irish Loans in English," Millward suggests that *uncle* is a corruption of the Irish word *anacol*, meaning "the act of protecting; deliverance; mercy, quarter, safety." She explains that the expression dates back one thousand years to the tale of an ancient Irish hero who gives his defeated opponent a chance to surrender and save his life, or in other words to ask for *anacol*. (In the legend, the defeated warrior refuses and is killed.) Millward points out that modern Irish contains an idiom *deinim anacol*, meaning to spare or give quarter to. As with the Roman explanation, a problem with this story is that the phrase *say uncle* arose in the United States and is not found in Ireland. Millward attributes its origin to the large numbers of Irish immigrants who arrived in the United States at the end of the nineteenth century.

Alternative versions of this figure of speech are *cry uncle* and *holler uncle*. It is mostly associated with small boys on playgrounds. However, it does occasionally appear in print, usually in the context of forcing someone to admit political or moral, rather than physical, defeat.

SHOW A LOT OF MOXIE.
Show courage, stamina, or aggressiveness.

Moxie started life with a capital letter. It is not the name of an individual, however, but of a soft drink. Moxie was the inspiration of nineteenth-century medical man Dr. Augustin Thompson. In the late 1800s, patented health drinks were all the rage. Typically, these elixirs came in the form of a syrup to be mixed with soda water. They were concocted of sugar, various flavorings, and one or two "secret" ingredients that usually included herbs. According to their inventors, they cured a wide range of ailments from upset stomachs to dementia. They pepped you up, helped build strong muscles, gave you an appetite, and kept you mentally alert.

In 1876 Dr. Thompson added his special formula to the dozens of patent medicines already on the market, registering it under the name Moxie Nerve Food. As well as flavorings, the mixture contained gentian, a flowering plant believed to have medicinal benefits. In spite of its unusual flavor, it sold well as a health beverage, both in bottles and as a soda fountain syrup. Thompson claimed that he named the drink after a classmate at West Point, Lieutenant Moxie, who was responsible for discovering its secret ingredient. However, Thompson did not attend West Point, and Lieutenant Moxie was probably a spur-of-the-moment invention. The *Dictionary of American Regional English* suggests that the word may derive from the Algonquian word *maski*, meaning "medicine." A flowering plant called moxie plant or moxie vine grows in New England. Thompson was a native of Maine, home of Moxie Falls and Moxie Pond.

The first recorded use of *moxie* as a figure of speech appears in Henry C. DeMille's 1890 play, *Men and Women*: "Young man, you've got enough nerve to start a Moxie factory." This quote plays on the different definitions of nerve. Moxie Nerve Food was meant to cure nervousness, but *nerve* can also mean arrogance or effrontery.

The figurative *moxie* has the feel of street slang. It often appears in stories about gangsters or other lowlifes. A typical quote comes from a Damon Runyon story that appeared in *Collier's* magazine in 1930: "I always figure Louie is a petty-larceny kind of guy, with no more moxie than a canary bird." In the 1930s and 1940s, *moxie* was also commonly attributed to skilled baseball players. Depending on how people handle their moxie it can be a positive or negative trait—

gutsy or obnoxious. *I like this kid—he's got moxie* or *You've got a lot of moxie, asking me for a loan.*

Moxie the soft drink is still manufactured. Today, it is mostly found in New England. People in other areas of the United States might be familiar with the metaphorical *moxie* without being aware of its status as a beverage. The expression *show moxie* is still fairly common, especially in the world of sports. One recent example appeared on Fort Wayne's *News-Sentinel* Web site after a win by the New York Yankees: "Yanks Show Moxie."

KEEP UP WITH THE JONESES.

Do as well as the neighbors; keep up appearances.

This phrase was popularized in 1913 as the title of a comic strip by A. R. "Pop" Momand. The strip "Keeping Up With the Joneses" ran for twenty-eight years in newspapers around the country. The Jones family never actually appeared in the strip. They were neighbors of the main characters, named McGinis—Aloysius, Clarice, and daughter Julie, along with their maid Belladonna. Although invisible to the strip's readers, the Joneses were often on the McGinises' minds. The strip is peppered with lines such as "Wait'll the Joneses see that, Julie!" By the 1920s, *keeping up with the Joneses* was a well-understood expression. It implied competitiveness in terms of consumer goods but also the struggle to improve your social status. A 1927 book called *Your Money's Worth* includes the statement "Certain things we buy . . . to keep up with the Joneses, or happily to surpass the Joneses." The urge to keep pace with the Joneses is often attributed to the female members of a family. In her 1953 novel, *Larry Vincent*, Frances Parkinson Keyes writes of a character who is thankful that he does not have a nagging wife, "one who insisted on making a show, on 'keeping up with the Joneses.'"

Some etymologists speculate that Momand chose the name Jones as a reference to George Frederic and Lucretia Stevens Rhinelander Jones, parents of novelist Edith Wharton. When Momand began writing the strip in 1913, the Joneses had long been a prominent and wealthy New York family. However, Jones is a common enough name to have universal associations.

Keeping up with the Joneses is still a familiar phenomenon in the United States. A variation on this theme appeared in a *New York Times* headline for May 3, 1998: "Keeping Up with the Gateses?" a reference to Microsoft founder Bill Gates and his wife, Melinda. *Keeping up with the Joneses* does not appear to be connected with *having a jones* or *jonesing* for something, originally a word for an addict's drug cravings.

PUT DOWN YOUR JOHN HANCOCK.
Sign a contract or other document.

The earliest recorded use of *John Hancock* as a metaphor for a signature appears in a published letter written by Oliver Wendell Holmes. The letter, written in 1846, ends with the words "Avoiding . . . the pretentious boldness of John Hancock . . . I subscribe myself Yours very truly . . ." The expression was almost certainly familiar long before this date.

John Hancock, one of the founders of the United States, was born in Braintree, Massachusetts, on January 12, 1736. He inherited the fortune of a merchant uncle at a young age, making him one of the richest businessmen in Boston. Hancock was an enthusiastic supporter of American independence from Great Britain. He was president of the Second Continental Congress, and on July 4, 1776, he became the first man to sign the Declaration of Independence. Scrawling his name in large letters across the page, he supposedly remarked that King George would have no trouble reading his signature.

John Hancock's signature was in keeping with his personality—bold and showy. According to the *Dictionary of American Biography*, his ostentatious displays of wealth during the Continental Congress alienated many of his fellow signers. He further fell out of favor with members of the Congress when they voted to make George Washington commander-in-chief instead of him. However, he later served as governor of Massachusetts and, in 1788, presided over the convention to ratify the Constitution. Hancock died in 1793.

By the late nineteenth century, *John Hancock* was a common term for a signature. Typical uses are *We just need your John Hancock* or *Put your John Hancock here*. Although the original connotations of the term include large, bold writing, today it simply means any signature. A female can put down her John Hancock as easily as a male. A variation used by westerners is *John Henry*. Possibly, one reason why John Hancock's name became popular as a general term for a signature is that the names *John* and *Johnny* often stand in for everyman. Examples include *John Bull* (the typical Englishman), *John Doe, John Q. Public, Johnny Rebel*, and *John* or *Johnny* with various affiliations, such as *Johnny Lawyer* and *John Harvard*.

Today, the phrase is sometimes shortened to *Hancock*, as in *We need your Hancock on this line*. It's also possible to turn John Hancock into a verb—for instance, *Want me to Hancock it on every page?*

SLIP SOMEONE A MICKEY FINN.
Put knockout drops into someone's drink.

Mickey Finn was a notorious Chicago saloonkeeper at the end of the nineteenth century. Allegedly Finn drugged, robbed, and then somehow disposed of innocent customers who sipped a "Mickey Finn special." The *Chicago Daily News* for December 16, 1903, reports on Finn's trial, describing him as the "proprietor of the Lone Star saloon . . . the scene of blood-curdling crimes through the agency of drugged liquor." The Chicago *Inter-Ocean* for the following day carries the headline "Lone Star Saloon Loses Its License." The paper reports that Finn's alleged use of "knockout drops" led to his business being closed.

At different times, a Mickey Finn could be a drugged drink, the drug itself, or an unusually strong drink meant to put someone under the table. The "queen of crooks," Chicago May Sharpe, seems to use the term both ways in her 1928 autobiography: "I shot a few more Mickey Finns (double drinks) into him. . . . I slipped his little drops into the last drink." P. G. Wodehouse defines the term as the drug itself in this line from the 1951 novel *Old Reliable*: "She had been about to suggest that the butler might slip into Adela's bedtime Ovaltine what is known as a knockout drop or Mickey Finn." The more formal *Michael Finn* was a jocular way to refer to an alcoholic drink in the early decades of the twentieth century.

The *Dictionary of American Slang* suggests an alternative ingredient for Mickey Finns—a strong laxative. The idea behind this suggestion is that bartenders would doctor the drinks of problem customers, causing them to head for home at full speed. Several quotes support this usage. The 1935 book *The Underworld Speaks* defines a Mickey Finn as "a concoction given to offensive drunkards, which rapidly purges or causes vomiting." *Music on My Mind*, the 1964 memoir of jazz pianist Willie Smith, includes the line "A Mickey Finn . . . made it necessary to make frequent trips to the men's room." If the term in fact started with the Chicago saloonkeeper Mickey Finn, it must have meant a knockout drug to begin with. The meaning could later have spread to describe any kind of adulterated drink. In modern times, the expression appears to be used most often to refer to knocking someone unconscious.

WIN ONE FOR THE GIPPER.
Pull an unlikely victory out of difficult circumstances.

The Gipper was George Gipp, a legendary football player for the University of Notre Dame from 1917 to 1920. Originally from the small town of Laurium, Michigan, Gipp entered Notre Dame to play baseball. According to the story, when coach Knute Rockne discovered him casually making drop kicks that traveled sixty to seventy feet, Rockne quickly recruited him for the football team. Gipp played halfback. He became a hero when he led the team to an undefeated season in 1919.

The Gipper led a checkered career off the field. Reputedly he enjoyed gambling and frequenting pool halls almost as much as he liked to play sports. (Already twenty-two when he started at Notre Dame, he was older than most of the students.) These activities caused him to be expelled in 1920, but he was soon readmitted, no doubt in part because of the outraged protests of football fans.

Gipp played his final game on November 20, 1920. Ailing from a shoulder injury and the beginnings of strep throat, he sat out most of the game. When the team's victory was in danger of slipping away, Rockne let him into the game, where he threw a fifty-five-yard pass for the winning touchdown. Gipp was named an All-American player shortly afterward, but he did not live to enjoy it. Due to complications of his strep throat, he caught pneumonia and died on December 14.

Eight years later, Notre Dame was losing to the undefeated Army team when Rockne invoked the Gipper during halftime. He rallied his players by describing the words Gipp had spoken to Rockne on his deathbed: "Rock," he said, "sometime when the team is up against it and the breaks are beating the boys, tell them to go out there with all they've got and win just one for the Gipper. I don't know where I'll be then, Rock," he said, "but I'll know about it and I'll be happy." Notre Dame went on to win the game.

Although some doubt whether George Gipp ever said those exact words, the phrase was immortalized in the 1940 film *Knute Rockne— All-American*. Young actor Ronald Reagan portrayed Gipp in the movie. The nickname "Gipper" stayed with him when he entered politics in later life. Reagan admired the sentiments behind Gipp's famous line. He used it to encourage his vice president, George Bush, at the 1988 Republican convention to "go out there and win one for the Gipper." Reagan's fondness for the slogan helped introduce it to those who were too young to be familiar with the 1940 movie or with George Gipp. The expression is mostly associated with Reagan today. It is often used to encourage people to exert extra effort before some critical task, such as a crucial business meeting.

GIVE A BRONX CHEER.

Express disapproval; reject someone or give the person a negative answer.

A Bronx cheer is really no cheer at all. It's a sound of derision and disapproval—more commonly known as a raspberry—produced by blowing air forcibly out of your mouth with your tongue between your lips. (*Raspberry* is one of the few instances of rhyming slang popular in the United States. It dates from the nineteenth century and is an abbreviation of *raspberry tart*, which rhymes with what the noise sounds like.) Some of the earliest recorded uses of *Bronx cheer* are clearly figurative. A 1929 short story in *Collier's* magazine contains the line "Maxim gave him a Bronx cheer." The context indicates that Maxim expressed disapproval verbally, not with actual sound effects.

Although no direct evidence supports this idea, Bronx cheers have long been associated with the Yankees baseball team, whose stadium is located in the Bronx. Yankee fans show a distinct lack of patience with players who don't perform up to standard. A relevant headline from the May 13, 1946, *San Francisco News* refers to the great Yankee hitter Joe DiMaggio—"Bronx Cheers Hit DiMaggio at Failure to Clout Ball." In the 1940s, Bronx borough president James J. Lyons tried unsuccessfully to dissociate his borough from the cheer, claiming that it had been imported by "vulgar people" from outside the Bronx.

The Bronx cheers given today are usually figurative, except perhaps during ball games. A typical recent example comes from a 2006 posting on the *Hollywood Reporter* Web site concerning a movie by director Steven Soderbergh, claiming that he "got the Bronx cheer at a . . . New York screening of *The Good German.*"

PLAY IN PEORIA.

Appeal to the tastes of the average American.

This expression nearly always appears in the form of a question: *Will it play in Peoria?* It comes from the days of vaudeville, when traveling troupes of performers tested out their acts in Peoria, Illinois. Peoria was thought to typify mainstream America. It is a midsized city located midway between Chicago and St. Louis—between East and West culturally, and between the North and the South historically. If theatergoers there loved your act, it should go over big anywhere in the country. A 1935 article in the periodical *Men's Wear* alludes to this: "Mr. Leary . . . could tell a story about every piece of cloth in the shop and how a suit cut from it helped the wearer to 'lay 'em in the aisles' in Peoria." The expression is believed to have been coined by Groucho Marx as he pondered whether his new act would have a broad appeal. *Will it play in Peoria?* became a catchphrase of Richard Nixon's presidential campaign when his aide John Ehrlichman was overheard uttering it. (Regarding another of Ehrlichman's contributions to American English, see *twist in the wind* in chapter 4, "Politics as Usual.")

The suggestion that some product or idea will play in Peoria is not necessarily flattering. The question can hold a tinge of condescension. It suggests that cutting-edge plays, risqué art exhibits, or bold political theories might appeal more to the sophisticated types in New York than to Peorians. However, Peorians themselves embrace the slogan. The Web site for the Peoria visitors' bureau invites visitors to "see what it means to play in Peoria!" The National Civic League has awarded Peoria the All-America City award three times in the past fifty years.

Chapter 6

WAYS TO TRAVEL

Americans are restless people. From the earliest colonial days, British settlers pushed relentlessly westward, always looking for better land and bigger opportunities. In the late eighteenth century, Kentucky, Tennessee, and Ohio constituted the western frontier. By the 1840s, Americans were streaming across the Mississippi into the Great Plains, and by the end of the nineteenth century, hundreds of thousands had reached California and the Pacific Northwest. In modern times, Americans are still on the move. They take well over two billion long-distance trips a year.

These days, most Americans travel by car. Considering the country's hundred-year-old love affair with the automobile, it's not surprising that various car-related activities have acquired figurative meanings. These include *step on the gas*, *shift gears*, *hit the brakes*, *jump-start a project*, *be blindsided*, *be in the driver's seat*, *put up a roadblock*, and *hit on all cylinders*, discussed below, among others. Before cars, there were trains, giving us the expressions *to railroad someone*, *be on track*, *sidetrack*, *side-swipe*, *derail*, *build up a head of steam*, and *make a whistle-stop tour*, included in "Politics as Usual." Since the 1950s, airplanes have steadily gained ground as the long-distance travel mode of choice. They've also made some linguistic contributions. Besides *bail out*, listed in this chapter, flight-related expressions include *take off*, *fly right*, *go into a tailspin*, and *take a nosedive*.

Several of the expressions in this section rely on low-tech modes of transportation, such as horseback riding and walking. They also involve such unusual moves as skidding downhill, sitting on rails, and hopping on wagons.

RIDE OUT OF TOWN ON A RAIL.

Be summarily expelled from a place or organization; be vanquished or defeated.

In the early United States, the punishment for incurring the mob's anger was swift and brutal. In Nathaniel Hawthorne's short story *The Story Teller*, the townspeople resolve to punish the bearer of false rumors, "only hesitating whether to tar and feather him, ride him on a rail, or refresh him with an ablution at the town pump." During the Revolutionary War, many Tories were subjected to tarring and feathering and riding on a rail—two forms of vigilantism that often went together.

The rail used would have been taken from a split-rail fence. Split-rail fences were made by splitting logs lengthwise into quarters, eighths, or whatever fraction was needed to break them down into a suitable size for fence rails. The rails were then stacked in an interlocking zigzag pattern so they were self-supporting without posts. Sometimes they were stacked directly on top of one another and secured to posts, which made them more permanent but still easy to assemble. Split-rail fences were an excellent use for the timber that had to be cleared from most property during colonial and frontier days. They crisscrossed the countryside, so finding an extra rail would have been no problem whenever some wrongdoer had to be run out of town.

Typically the victim of this punishment was forced to sit astride the sharp edge of the rail, either tied or held down by two men. He was then paraded through the streets before being deposited at the edge of town.

Tarring and feathering was an even more severe form of mob justice. Men (rarely women) were stripped, either to the waist or completely, and daubed with hot tar. Then they were rolled in chicken feathers or anything else that would stick. Although the tar burned the skin, the main purpose of tarring and feathering was public humiliation. Victims of this treatment were expected to leave town in disgrace.

Outbreaks of tarring and feathering occurred immediately before and after the Civil War, when partisan feelings were running high. *An American Glossary* quotes a Mr. Hiram Price of Iowa describing attitudes before the war: "If a citizen of a free State, visiting a slave State, expressed his opinion in reference to slavery, he was treated without much ceremony to a coat of tar and feathers and a ride upon a rail." Isolated instances of tarring and feathering have occurred even in relatively modern times, usually in retaliation for going against the grain of the culture—a French woman becoming mistress to a German soldier in World War II, for instance.

Riding on a rail has not been a literal punishment since rails became scarce. Today, the phrase indicates a violently negative response to unpopular behavior or opinions. A typical example is *When I suggested that the office staff start paying for their coffee, I was practically run out of town on a rail.*

RIDE THE GRAVY TRAIN.

Achieve financial success or the easy life, especially without working for it.

Gravy has meant easy money since the beginning of the twentieth century. It sometimes carries the sense of ill-gotten gains. Eric Partridge's *Dictionary of the Underworld* defines the word succinctly as "loot." Gravy can also refer to an easy job with generous pay. According to the 1933 issue of *American Speech*, to ride a gravy train means "to continue to receive more than one's deserts." The article identifies the phrase as Texas cowboy slang, but it was current in other parts of the country as well. Popular variants during the first half of the twentieth century were *board the gravy train* and *board the gravy boat*, but both have become obsolete in recent decades.

Gravy, a word borrowed from French, has denoted a sauce since late medieval times. Another sense of the term refers to the juices that cook out of meat. In other words, gravy is a desirable culinary by-product gained without special effort. Just pop your roast into the oven and it automatically exudes gravy. It's easy to see how this meaning could be extended to cover money that seeps into your pocket without effort on your part.

The point of *train* is less obvious. Perhaps riding the train is meant as a metaphor for a quick, smooth progression from poverty to riches. This idea is evident in a quote from Adolphe Menjou's 1948 biography, *It Took Nine Tailors*: "Once you get on the Hollywood gravy boat, it is no trick to make money." The phrase could also be influenced by *get a free ride*. Since the 1880s, this expression has meant to gain an undeserved benefit or achieve something at the expense of others.

Besides money, gravy can refer to free goods, such as sample products, or more than you need of something good, such as one more "A" than you need to graduate. A common way of summing up these extra benefits is—*The rest is gravy*.

RIDE HERD.
Guard, control, or supervise a person or group.

Cowboys keep cattle moving together in the right direction by riding at the edge of the herd. Riding herd implies taking control, perhaps forcing the herded animals to move when they would rather be standing still, or to go in a direction they hadn't planned on. Figurative uses of *ride herd* carry these same implications for humans. One of the earliest examples comes from Alfred Henry Lewis's 1897 *Wolfville Days*: "The way them pore darkened drunkards rides herd on each other . . . is as good as sermons." By the end of the nineteenth century, when this phrase first began appearing in print, cattle ranches covered millions of western acres. Most Americans had absorbed some cowboy lore and would have recognized the term.

At least since the mid-twentieth century, *riding herd* has been a standard American colloquialism for close supervision. The expression is most often used in business or government contexts, such as riding herd on a project or on departments under your control. It can suggest paying a little too much attention, or micromanaging—*The boss always rides herd on us during inventory*. The term also continues to carry the literal meaning of riding herd on cattle. *Riding close herd*—making a special effort to keep the cattle close together—is also used figuratively to mean the keeping of a careful eye on some person or situation.

BE TAKEN FOR A RIDE
Be forcibly taken somewhere in a car with the probability that you will be killed; be teased, fooled, or swindled.

This delicate euphemism for finishing off people appeared during the 1920s, the era of high-profile gangsters such as Al Capone. The magazine *Vanity Fair* introduced its readers to the term in a November 1927 article, explaining, "'Taking him for a ride' is underworld for enticing a person to [his] death." *Only Yesterday*, a history of the 1920s published in 1931, describes the practice this way: "Another favorite method [of disposing of a rival] was to take the victim 'for a ride' . . . shoot him at leisure, drive to some distant and deserted part of the city, and quietly throw his body overboard."

By the end of the 1920s, *take someone for a ride* was a familiar American expression. Edward D. Sullivan, in his 1930 exposé *Rattling the Cup on Chicago Crime*, attributes the first use of the phrase to a Chicago racketeer named Timothy D. ("Big Tim") Murphy. Murphy controlled several unions during the teens and twenties. He also had fingers in various criminal pies, which sometimes required taking troublemakers on one-way car trips. Murphy himself never went for a final ride. He was gunned down on June 26, 1928, when he answered the door of his home.

In 1919 the Eighteenth Amendment to the Constitution, prohibiting the "manufacture, sale, or transportation of intoxicating liquors," ushered in the era of Prohibition. The ban on alcohol created a bonanza for organized crime. Americans began relying on bootleggers, rum runners, and other racketeers to provide them with the hard stuff. Millions of dollars were at stake. Turf wars erupted in which rival gangsters or suspected snitches were taken for rides to get them out of the way. As a 1929 article in *Flynn's* magazine remarks, those who step into the backseat of a gangster's automobile "seldom return, even on foot." Another, less fatal way of taking criminals for a ride during this period was to inform on them to the police and get them sent to jail.

Interestingly, *take someone for a ride* could also mean to tease or take advantage of a person. *Dialect Notes* for 1925 defines *take for a ride* as "jolly; josh." It's unclear how such a relatively benign meaning arose in parallel with the more deadly use of the phrase. Today, American gangster culture is not as prominent a part of the American scene as it was during the 1920s. When the expression *taken for a ride* is used now, it usually means that a person has been either swindled or fooled. For instance, a 1993 novel by the British mystery writer W. J. Burley includes the line "His mind told him that the woman was being . . . helpful . . . but he had an uneasy feeling that in some important respects he was being taken for a ride."

WALK INDIAN FILE.
Walk in single file.

This expression first appears in print in the eighteenth century. Like many Native American–related words and phrases, the English first used it to describe what they observed about the natives they encountered. An account of an expedition to the Rocky Mountains published in 1823 includes the description "In a short time [the Pawnees] appeared leisurely in a narrow pathway, in Indian file, led by the grand chief." According to early records, this way of walking was typical of Native Americans marching to battle or traveling through the woods.

Indian file implied more than just walking single file. Walkers stepped into the footprints of the man in front of them, leaving a single line of prints. The last man then scuffed out the prints. This technique camouflaged the exact number of people in the group and made them more difficult to track. By the early nineteenth century, *Indian file* simply meant single file and could be applied to any group of walkers moving in a single line.

Indian file is one of dozens of American English terms that incorporates the adjective *Indian*. British colonists began coining these words soon after arriving in North America. The *Dictionary of American English on Historical Principles*, published in 1938, lists nearly ten pages of *Indian*-related terms, from *Indian corn* to *Indian weed*. A large number of these terms name North American plants not found in England—for instance, *Indian paintbrush*, *Indian turnip*, *Indian bell*, *Indian balm*, and *Indian ginger*. Others encapsulate the colonists' views of Native American culture. These include *Indian giver* (someone who asks for a gift's return, based on the colonists' belief that Native Americans expected a gift equal to what they had given); *Indian summer* (an unseasonably warm spell during autumn, supposedly a time when Native Americans burned grass and underbrush); and the now less familiar terms *play Indian* (behave stoically), *turn Indian* (live off the land), and *put the Indian sign on someone* (hex or curse the person). Expressions of this type, as well as others related to Native Americans—*happy hunting grounds, go on the warpath*—generally reveal more about British attitudes than about Native American cultural traditions. In recent times, many have acquired negative connotations and are becoming obsolete. However, *walk Indian file* is still a familiar term to most Americans.

HIT THE SKIDS.

Deteriorate rapidly, either emotionally, physically, or financially.

A skid is a plank used as a kind of slide over which heavy objects can be pushed. In logging jargon, skids are a set of peeled logs, partly buried in the ground, that form a track for hauling or pushing unfinished logs. In the nineteenth century, skids were commonly used to propel timber into the river. It was then floated downstream to a sawmill or ship. The term *skids* first began appearing in print around the mid-1800s. The *Lumberman's Gazette* of January 1880 provides a good example: "Some of the lumber-men have from 8,000,000 to 10,000,000 [logs] on the skids."

Hit the skids or *be on the skids* has been in figurative use since the beginning of the twentieth century. One of the earliest examples comes from Harry C. Witwer's 1921 book about boxing, *The Leather Pushers*: "Kane Halliday, as the butlers . . . announce[d] him previous to the time he hit the skids." Hitting the skids was often associated with alcohol but could mean any kind of decline—falling apart physically, losing money, or getting in with a bad crowd. It's also possible to put the skids under someone else, causing that person's downfall— *The football team is planning to put the skids under their chief rivals Friday night.*

Skids most likely became associated with down-and-outness because of where they were found—Skid Row. Many people believe that the original Skid Row, first called *Skid Road*, was Yesler Way in Seattle. Yesler Way runs downhill through the downtown Seattle neighborhood now called Pioneer Square, ending at Elliott Bay. During the nineteenth century, Henry Yesler's sawmill sat at the bottom of this road, waiting for logs to be skidded down to it. Unemployed loggers naturally drifted into the area, looking for work or just killing time. Soon the neighborhood south of Yesler Way gained an unsavory reputation as a seedy area of transients' hotels, taverns, and brothels. By the early twentieth century, Skid Road was shorthand for the bad part of town. By 1930 the name had changed to Skid Row and it could mean the bad part of any town. *The Underworld Speaks*, published in 1935, defines Skid Row as the "district in a city where tramps (bums) congregate." The term was often left uncapitalized beginning in the 1930s, indicating that *skid row* had entered the language as an ordinary noun rather than a specific place name.

These days, several large cities around the United States are known for having skid rows. Some, like San Francisco, have a neighborhood officially named Skid Row. More often, the term simply describes that part of any town where the homeless and unemployed gather. Although *on the skids* and *hit the skids* remain common expressions, their original connection to Skid Road has been lost.

HIT THE GROUND RUNNING.

Seize an opportunity without delay; get a head start on an activity; start without preparation.

The first recorded use of *hit the ground running* is literal. It appears in the *Sandusky* (Ohio) *Register* for April 30, 1895: "The bullet went under me. I knew he had five more cartridges so I hit the ground running and squatted low down when his gun barked a second time." Most of the phrase's early uses in print involve actual running, usually after dismounting from a horse or jumping off a train. For instance, the 1925 book *The Trail Drivers of Texas* includes the line "Lambert quit the horse and hit the ground running." However, the expression was also used figuratively from at least the beginning of the twentieth century. *The History of Alabama and Her People* by Albert Burton Moore, published in 1927, says of a local candidate, "In [the 1918] election he 'hit the ground running,' as he was reported to have said."

Hit the ground running is such a natural and useful expression in so many situations that a number of plausible explanations could account for its origin. Several origin stories are in common circulation. The first two listed below appear in William Safire's 1982 *What's the Good Word*, sent in as suggestions to his *New York Times Magazine* column on words and language. Unfortunately they don't stand up to careful scrutiny, as the expression appears in print much earlier than either of the eras in question.

The first proposal suggests that the expression originated with World War II paratroopers who were dropped behind enemy lines. They would have hit the ground running so they could get to cover as quickly as possible. In the same vein, some people have proposed marines who hit the beach from troopships or soldiers who jumped into combat zones from hovering helicopters as the first users of the phrase. Although *hit the ground running* was no doubt used in all these situations, it could not have originated with any of them. Examples appeared in print decades before 1941. Soldiers might easily have brought the phrase home and spread it around the civilian population, causing its figurative use to become more common as well.

Another idea is that *hit the ground running* was originally hobo slang. Hoboes hitching a ride on a freight car often jumped off the train as it neared a station—when it had slowed down but was still moving—to avoid being caught by railroad authorities once it stopped. A *Washington Post* article from June 2, 1935, describes this practice: "The bum dropped off while the train was still travelling at a good speed. . . . He . . . swung down from the ladder at the end of the baggage car and hit the ground running." As with the paratrooper explanation, the timing is wrong for hoboes to have originated the phrase, because a number of examples exist from earlier decades. The *Post* article uses the expression without quotation marks, so it was evidently part of mainstream English by 1935. Glossaries of hobo jargon from the 1930s do not include the term, although they list the phrase *hit the grit*, which carries the double meaning of leaping off a train or starting on a long tramp.

A third possibility gives *hit the ground running* a much earlier origin, with riders of the Pony Express. The Pony Express operated between April 3, 1860, and October 26, 1861, traveling between St. Joseph, Missouri, and Sacramento, California. It guaranteed mail delivery in ten days—about half the time of other overland routes. Riders changed horses every ten miles and the mail pouch changed riders every hundred miles. Riders were allowed two minutes to change horses, but one observer reports that seasoned mail carriers could switch over much faster, often in a matter of seconds. Such a feat would have been impossible unless these riders hit the ground running.

The Pony Express might well have inspired or popularized this colorful colloquialism. The romance of young men galloping across the plains, risking life and limb to deliver the mail, captured the public's imagination. Authors including Mark Twain described the exploits of Pony Express riders in breathless terms. In *Roughing It*, Twain describes crossing paths with a rider while traveling across the plains by stagecoach: "HERE HE COMES! . . . Away across the end-less dead level of the prairie a black speck appears against the sky. . . . In a second or two it becomes a horse and rider . . . sweeping towards us, nearer and nearer . . . a whoop and a hurrah from our upper deck, a wave of the rider's hand, . . . a man and a horse burst past our excited faces, and go winging away like a belated fragment of a storm!"

Hit the ground running could have been in general use in the nine-teenth-century West, where cattle herders, cavalry soldiers, and others would have had reasons for dismounting while on the move. Ameri-cans' fascination with the Pony Express might be responsible for introducing the expression to non-westerners. Once a part of main-stream English, it would have acquired its figurative meaning. *Hit the ground running* fits easily into the American slang vocabulary of rugged individualism. It is only one of several expressions that use *hit* to mean stepping onto a surface then traveling along it—*hit the road, hit the trail, hit the bricks, hit the pavement.*

Wherever *hit the ground running* originated, it is still popular as both a literal and a figurative phrase in English-speaking countries. Two recent examples of figurative uses are the title of the 1998 *Real Life Guide to Life after College: How to Hit the Ground Running after Graduation* and this quote from a June 1, 2007, *Missoulian* article about a Hilton Hotel opening in Kalispell, Montana: "With summer season coming . . . we need to have everything in place so we can hit the ground running." Steer ropers and other rodeo participants still use the phrase literally to describe what they do when they leave the saddle.

HIT ON ALL CYLINDERS.

Operate at the peak of your capacity; be in excellent form.

The cylinders referred to in this figure of speech are those found in automobile engines. The expression *hit on all cylinders* has been a metaphor almost as long as cars have been on the roads. An early example comes from Christopher Mathewson's 1912 baseball book, *Pitching in a Pinch*: "The best infielder takes time to fit into the infield of a Big League club and have it hit on all four cylinders again."

Cylinders are crucial for operating a car because they hold the pistons, which propel the car forward. When powered by gasoline, the pistons slide up and down inside the cylinders, turning the crankshaft and rotating the wheels. If your car's engine is hitting on all cylinders, you'll enjoy a smooth, powerful ride. If not, your trip may be less than optimal.

An interesting feature of this expression is the changing number of cylinders encompassed by the word *all*. As Americans built more powerful automobiles with greater pick-up, engines needed to hit on more cylinders. In the above quote from 1912, the infield only needs to hit on four cylinders to be in prime condition. By 1932, when P. G. Wodehouse wrote his comic novel *Hot Water*, the number of cylinders necessary for optimal functioning was six. One of the book's characters reflects that "[h]is smiling face, taken in conjunction with the bottle of wine which he carried, conveyed . . . the definite picture of a libertine operating on all six cylinders." The main character of Jane Haddam's 2006 novel, *Hardscrabble Road*, needs to hit on even more cylinders to be operating at full power. Realizing that he is exhausted and sleep-deprived, he tells himself that he's not "operating on all eight cylinders."

It's possible simply to say that you are (or are not) *operating*, *hitting*, or *clicking on all cylinders*, without specifying the exact number. When not at your best, you could also say that you're missing hitting some number of cylinders—from a couple to several.

MARCH TO A DIFFERENT DRUMMER.

Be unconventional; be in the minority.

This expression is based on lines from Henry David Thoreau's *Walden*, published in 1854. In the book's conclusion, Thoreau writes, "If a man does not keep pace with his companions, perhaps it is because he hears a different drummer. Let him step to the music which he hears, however measured or far away." This passage was famous within decades of the book's publication. At first, writers quoted the lines directly or at least alluded to Thoreau. Eventually, Thoreau's lines were distilled into the phrases *march to a different drummer*, *march to the beat of a different drummer*, or *march to a different beat*. These phrases began to appear in print without reference to the source.

Henry David Thoreau was a poet and essayist who lived from 1817 to 1862. Most of his short life was spent in Massachusetts. He was a friend of transcendentalist philosopher Ralph Waldo Emerson (see *build a better mousetrap* in "Business Dealings"). On July 4, 1845, Thoreau went to live on land that Emerson owned near Walden Pond, outside of Concord. He built a cabin and led a frugal, self-reliant life there until September 6, 1847, when he returned to his family home in Concord. *Walden, or Life in the Woods* is his account of that time.

Most recent uses of the expression *march to a different drummer* do not treat it as a quote. This typical use is from a 1984 issue of the *New Yorker*: "He's a very intelligent man . . . he just marches to a different drummer."

TELL SOMEONE WHERE TO GET OFF.

Rebuke or scold someone.

The first known appearance of this expression comes from George Ade's *More Fables*, published in 1900: "He said that he was a Gentleman and that no Cheap Skate in a Plug Hat could tell him where to Get Off." Ade, a newspaperman who lived from 1866 to 1940, wrote a series of "fables" in slang during the early years of the twentieth century. Many American expressions appear for the first time, or nearly the first time, in his stories. *Tell someone where to get off* probably dates from at least the late nineteenth century, as most colloquialisms exist in the spoken language for a while before being written down.

The question *Where do you get off?* has also been around since at least the early twentieth century. This form of the expression conveys a slightly different meaning—a demand to know where you got the nerve to offer the speaker advice, as in *Where do you get off telling me how to cook?*

The *Random House Historical Dictionary of American Slang* suggests that *tell someone where to get off* derives from the expression *get off your high horse*. A high horse, also called a great horse, was the animal ridden in medieval battles and tournaments. To say that someone rode the great horse was shorthand for his skill in the practices of warfare. It also implied that he was of a high social class. The figurative expression *ride the high horse*, meaning to behave arrogantly, is first recorded in the late eighteenth century. It originated in England but was used on both sides of the Atlantic. If it is in fact the inspiration for *tell someone where to get off*, there is a gap of nearly a century between the earlier and later expressions.

Another suggestion is that the phrase alludes to streetcar conductors informing people of where to get off for their stop. Streetcars were a common form of transportation in the late nineteenth and early twentieth centuries, the period when *tell someone where to get off* was becoming a familiar expression. On the other hand, it's not obvious why a conductor telling someone to get off at the next stop—that is, doing his job—would have acquired negative connotations. Possibly it referred to the occasions when a conductor had to hustle an unruly passenger off the streetcar at an earlier stop than planned.

Both expressions—*tell someone where to get off* and *where do you get off?*—remain common in modern English. You can also announce that this is where you get off, meaning that you don't feel up to dealing with an issue beyond a certain point.

BAIL OUT.

Abandon a project or plan; leave abruptly.

The first people to bail out were airplane pilots. A 1925 article in California's *Oakland Tribune* places the expression in quotation marks, suggesting that it was new at that time: "A . . . pilot who has to 'bail out' hurriedly from a crippled or burning plane . . ." Probably earlier, the phrase referred to bailing out a leaky boat—throwing water over the side. However, the *Oxford English Dictionary* notes a second possibility. Some early examples spell the term *bale out* rather than *bail out*, suggesting the pushing of a bale, or bundle, through a trapdoor. One such example comes from the 1939 book *Pilot's Summer*: "If you bale out and land in water . . ." The image here is of the pilot dropping straight down out of the plane, like a bale of hay being tossed from a barn's loft.

By the 1940s, *bail out* was being used figuratively to describe those who escaped from unpleasant social situations or onerous responsibilities. In the 1941 play *Meet John Doe*, one character encourages another to leave an awkward situation, saying, "Come on . . . you better bail out." Neil Armstrong's memoir, *First on the Moon*, published in 1970, describes a computer abandoning a calculation: "The computer just bails out and starts over."

Bail out entered youth slang by way of surfing jargon, a common avenue for new slang expressions. The term first described deliberately jumping off a surfboard to avoid injury. Dirt bikers and skateboarders later adopted this usage for when they had to abandon their vehicles to avoid a crash. However, by the time Gary Filosa published *The Surfer's Almanac* in 1977, the term had already acquired a larger meaning (and lost the word *out*). According to the *Almanac*, *bail* meant "leave, depart, exit." The expression going from the surfers to the Valley girls—trendy young teens living in California's San Fernando Valley—was only a short step. In the 1982 *Valley Girl's Guide to Life*, author Mimi Ponds explains to her readers, "When you leave a party, you go, 'Let's bail.'" *Bail* on its own, rather than *bail out*, is now the preferred teenage way of describing a quick exit.

It's unclear whether the "leave" sense of *bail out* is connected with financial bail-outs. Bailing out failed companies comes closer in meaning to the legal term *bail out*, meaning to have someone released from prison. In use since the sixteenth century, the legal *bail out* derives from an Old French word meaning to govern, take charge of, or control. (The "toss water" *bail* comes from the Old French for *bucket*.) Bailing companies out of their financial miseries entails taking charge of them, just as putting up bail for someone under arrest indicates a willingness to be responsible for the person's eventual appearance in court.

GO SOUTH.
Disappear; abscond; fail or break down.

Go south has a convoluted history as a figurative expression. In its most recent incarnation, as a metaphor for complete breakdown or disaster, *go south* has become common only since the 1980s. However, the phrase's other connotations have been around—although evidently rare—since at least the 1890s. The 1903 novel *The Log of a Cowboy* by Andy Adams describes a poker game during which the winning player says, "Before this game ends, I'll make old Quince curl his tail; I've got him going south now." In this context, the phrase clearly means to lose or be defeated. A 1914 issue of *Dialect Notes* lists *go south* as Kansas slang meaning to be baffled or beaten.

An alternative meaning of disappearing, possibly with ill-gotten gains, was current at this time too. The *Word Detective* Web site reports an example of the phrase, discovered by word historian Barry Popik, that appeared in a *St. Louis Post-Dispatch* article about the 1904 St. Louis World's Fair. According to the newspaper, *gone south* was fair slang for "left the town; not heard of; to steal."

One theory of the expression's origin traces it to the traditional belief among the Lakotas (Sioux) and other Native Americans that a dead person's spirit travels south along the Milky Way after death. The general public would have been aware of this belief by the late nineteenth century. A short story in *Harper's New Monthly Magazine* for February 1894 tells readers, "The Dakota tribes believe that the soul, driven out of the body, journeys off to the south, and 'to go south' is, among the Sioux, the favorite euphemism for death." Another widely held idea is that *south* refers to Mexico, then as now a convenient destination for outlaws who want to disappear.

After appearing in print sporadically during most of the twentieth century, *go south* exploded into popularity in the 1980s, but with a new meaning—total disaster, usually either financial or mechanical. The researchers for the *Random House Dictionary of the English Language* report that their earliest citation comes from *Business Week* for September 21, 1974: "The market then rallies, falls back to test its low—and just keeps 'heading South,' as they say on the Street." The quote suggests that *head south* was Wall Street investors' jargon at that time. Whether it is related to earlier versions of *go south* is unclear. Stock prices that drop drastically might be said to disappear. The phrase could also be related to the fact that losses are represented as downward lines on a chart. "South" is often connected with the idea of "down"—as in the bottom of conventional maps.

Computers, cell phones, and other technologies that break down are said to have gone south. Abstract entities like plans and relationships can also go south. *American Speech* recorded several examples from the early nineties that include: "My love affair with baseball has gone south," "[T]he market went south after the President's speech," "You've got two [football] teams heading south." The "abscond" meaning of *go south* that was current in the early twentieth century appears to be obsolete these days.

GO WEST.
To die; to fail.

Go west as a figurative expression for dying was widespread during World War I. *A ticket west* in that war meant a fatal wound. Coningsby Dawson's *Carry On: Letters in War-Time* includes the sentence "Alive or 'Gone West,' I shall never be far from you." By the war's end, *gone west* could also mean disappeared or failed, similar to the modern usage of *gone south*. An example of the "disappeared" meaning appears in *Blackwood's Magazine* for September 1919: "The parcels . . . went persistently 'west.'" The "failed" meaning is evident in this quote from the *New Statesman* of February 4, 1928: "Men of letters will ask you if you had heard that some firm has 'gone west.'"

Some sources attribute the origin of this expression to seventeenth-century London. Criminals of that day were hanged on a gallows known as the Tyburn Tree, which stood in the west London district of Marylebone. However, the association between a western direction and death is much older. Many cultures locate the afterworld in the west. Iroquois, Algonquians, Hurons, and other Native Americans traditionally believed that the land of the dead lay in the direction of the setting sun. The Elysian Fields of Greek mythology and the mythical Irish Islands of the Blest are both found at the western edge of the earth. J. R. R. Tolkien draws on this tradition in his *Lord of the Rings* trilogy, locating "the Undying Lands" of the elves to the west of Middle Earth.

Americans also paradoxically associate the West with new beginnings. Newspaperman Horace Greeley famously encouraged adventurous lads in the nineteenth century: "Go West, young man, and grow up with the country." Greeley's advice appeared in an 1855 *New York Tribune* editorial. He is rumored to have later said that he was inspired by John Soule. According to the *Oxford English Dictionary*, Soule wrote, "Go West, young man! Go West!" in an 1851 article in the *Terre Haute Express*. Mythic ideas of the Old West may be partly a product of the older notion that west was the direction of the afterlife. For nineteenth-century Americans, heading west must have seemed almost like dying. It usually meant permanently taking leave from family, friends, and the life they knew.

Today, *go west* as a metaphor appears to be losing ground to *go south*. However, *go west* is still heard occasionally, usually to mean dying. Riffs on *Go West, young man* are also common, especially in newspaper headlines.

GO ON THE WAGON.

Abstain from alcoholic beverages.

The wagon in question was a water wagon. Water wagons did not carry drinking water. These vehicles, known as water carts in England, were the equivalent of today's street sweepers. They consisted of a barrel or tank mounted on wheels, with numerous small holes punched in its underside. As the water wagon rolled along, it sprinkled the unpaved dirt streets, settling the dust caused by traffic. Water wagons were a common sight in the eighteenth and nineteenth centuries.

The expression *go on the wagon* or *go on the water wagon* apparently arose during the 1890s, when the Anti-Saloon League, the Women's Christian Temperance Union, the Prohibition Party, and other antidrinking organizations were growing. Part of these groups' activism was encouraging drinkers to "take the pledge." Those who swore to abstain from strong drink were promising to stick to a difficult task. They were determined to quench their thirst by drinking from a water wagon if necessary, rather than let alcohol pass their lips. Of course falling off the wagon was easier than climbing on. The expression *fall off the wagon* has been around almost as long as *go on the wagon.*

On the wagon first appeared in print in the United States in a 1904 volume of *Dialect Notes*: "to be on the water-wagon: to abstain from hard drinks." The article indicates that the expression was popular slang in New York State. However, it was probably current elsewhere as well. A 1906 humorous book titled *Extra Dry: Being Further Adventures of the Water Wagon* includes the aphorism "It is better to have been on and off the Wagon than never to have been on at all." A British version of the phrase, *to go on the water-cart*, appeared in print even earlier. Its unlikely venue is Alice Caldwell Rice's *Mrs. Wiggs of the Cabbage Patch*. Mrs. Wiggs, speaking of her tubercular friend Mr. Dick, explains, "He coughs all the time. . . . I wanted to git him some whisky, but he shuck his head, 'I'm on the water cart,' sez he." Gradually the *water* part of *water wagon* was dropped, and people simply said *on the wagon*. Today, going on the wagon can cover abstention from all sorts of activities, including those involving food, drugs, and sex.

BE THERE WITH BELLS ON.
Arrive eager to enjoy yourself.

Often a response to a party invitation, this expression has been current since the beginning of the twentieth century. An early example in print appears in the 1907 novel *Beat It*: "We'll meet you at the pier with bells on." F. Scott Fitzgerald uses the phrase without the final preposition in *The Beautiful and the Damned*, published in 1922: "I'll be there with bells."

Most people, imagining a party-going friend with bells on, would picture something along the lines of jester's bells. However, the most common explanation for the expression's origin involves wagon bells, specifically from a Conestoga wagon.

Conestoga wagons are named for the place where they originated, the Conestoga River Valley of Pennsylvania. German Mennonites in the area are thought to have built the first ones. Conestogas were large, solidly constructed vehicles meant to carry freight. Heavy white canvas stretched over eight or more bent wood bows, which covered the wagons, protecting the goods inside. Besides hauling freight to every corner of the early republic, Conestoga wagons transported all the earthly belongings of settlers headed into the Appalachians or the Ohio River Valley.

The wagons were drawn by teams of six to eight horses or mules. Like other pack animals of the period, Conestoga teams often sported headdresses of bells. These were constructed from a piece of wrought iron shaped into an arch about sixteen inches across. The headdresses were fixed to the animals' collars so the bells hung suspended several inches over their heads. The bells—three, four, or five of them—were different sizes, so they pealed melodiously as the wagon moved forward.

According to George Shumway, author of *Conestoga Wagon 1750–1850*, wagoners took great pride in their bells, often tuning them with files to adjust the sound to their liking. The bells were also an incentive to careful driving. Anyone unfortunate enough to bog down on the dirt roads of that time and require another teamster's assistance would have to forfeit his team's bells to his rescuer. "To arrive at the destination without bells," Shumway writes, "was a disgrace which hurt both the pride and the pocket book. From this early custom we have the fine American expression, 'I'll be there with bells on.'" It was said that some mired drivers would break their wagon tongues, making it impossible for the wagons to be towed out of the mud, rather than risk losing their bells. They wanted to be there with bells on, or not at all.

This explanation of the expression's origin leaves a time gap, as the first recorded use does not appear until about fifty years after Conestoga wagons were replaced with the lighter prairie schooners and other forms of transportation. However, like many slang expressions, it may have existed for quite a while in popular speech before being written down.

Since the middle of the twentieth century, *with bells on* can also be an intensifier, as in this sentence from Robert Leckie's 1960 *Marines*: "The same to you, with bells on." A more recent example comes from an online article in the *Reading (England) Evening Post* for June 20, 2007. Speaking of an ongoing protest against the excessive booting of parked cars, one man "vowed the picket would resume this morning 'with bells on.'" (Traffic police "boot" a car by attaching a device to one wheel that makes it immobile. The car remains stationary until its owner pays delinquent traffic fines.)

※※※

I'll be there with bells on is still a common way to respond to an invitation, either a friendly one—a party, for instance—or an unfriendly one. For example, if two men get into an argument in a bar, one will sometimes invite the other to step out to the parking lot to settle the matter. The second man might respond, "I'll meet you there with bells on!" If things get out of hand, one or both of them might end up in the "slammer."

Chapter 7

COPS AND ROBBERS

Criminal slang, like other types of jargon, is meant to distinguish insiders from outsiders. For that reason, most of it is unfamiliar to mainstream culture. These specialized words and expressions do sometimes make their way into standard English. However, as soon as the jargon of thieves, drug dealers, con artists, and similar types leaks into the larger vocabulary, its original users typically adopt a new language. That way they maintain their secret code.

Americans' knowledge of underworld slang comes chiefly from the hard-boiled novels of the twenties and thirties, such as the classics of Dashiell Hammett and Raymond Chandler, and from books and films about the Mafia, especially Mario Puzo's *The Godfather* and its sequels. Not surprisingly, terms for killing abound. Tough guys who want to get rid of troublemakers can rub out, ice, croak, waste, blow away, hit, snuff, fix, whack, bump off, knock off, or just plain off them. The Mob reputedly targets its victims by giving them the kiss of death. They also provide their enemies with cement boots and send them to sleep with the fishes.

Besides terms for putting people out of the way, Americans are familiar with a number of stock characters from the world of organized crime. These include big shots, mugs, weak sisters, stoolies, punks, molls, hoods, snitches, hit men, the boss of all bosses, and of course, the Godfather. How often any of these words and phrases are used by actual criminals is anybody's guess.

In addition to the expressions in this section, this book's gangster-related terms include *be sent up the river*, *wheel and deal*, *slip someone a Mickey Finn*, and *be taken for a ride*.

GIVE SOMEONE THE THIRD DEGREE.

Interrogate a prisoner using aggressive methods for the purpose of bringing about a confession.

An early use of *the third degree* appears in the *Harvard Lampoon* for February 6, 1880: "He . . . was surprised to receive a clip over the head from one brother's cane. This was followed by a personal chastisement in the third degree." *Third degree* here obviously signifies great intensity, but it's unclear whether the term was connected to police interrogations at this point. Giving someone the third degree had definitely taken on that meaning by the turn of the twentieth century, when *Everybody's Magazine* for November 1900 told its readers, "From time to time a prisoner . . . claims to have had the Third Degree administered to him."

The third degree can indicate the worst level of a thing—such as third-degree burns—or the least serious level—third-degree assault, for example. A common explanation for the origin of *give someone the third degree* is Freemasonry, where the third and highest degree is that of Master Mason. Members are admitted to the degree of Master Mason only after a complicated ritual that involves reenacting a brutal interrogation.

Most people associate the third degree with old-fashioned crime movies. The police in these films shine a hot spotlight into the face of their helpless prisoner, shouting questions at him and threatening to bring out the rubber hoses. Crime stories from as early as the beginning of the twentieth century feature this scenario. The 1909 novel *The Third Degree: A Narrative of Metropolitan Life* includes the following example. After the police discover a murder, the story's innocent hero is held at the scene of the crime for questioning. As the police doctor finishes his examination and prepares to leave, he jokes with the police captain, saying, "You're going to put him through 'the third degree,' eh?" The detectives in this story then proceed according to stereotype. They rough up their suspect, shine a bright light in his face, and shout at him to confess. A 1930 book titled *The Third Degree: A Detailed and Appalling Exposé of Police Brutality* reports, "True or false, juries are coming to believe anyone who accuses the police of using the 'third degree.'"

In recent decades, the expression often refers to a searching inquiry, but not one that actually involves physical violence. People use it half jokingly, as in, *If I'm out past my curfew, my folks give me the third degree about where I've been.* As a serious reference to police interrogation methods, it is not as widely used as it once was, but it is still a familiar expression to most Americans.

COME ON LIKE GANGBUSTERS.
Proceed with great vigor and forcefulness.

From the early 1930s, gangbusters (or gang busters) were law officers who specialized in breaking up organized crime. In the 1947 supplement to *The American Language*, H. L. Mencken claims that the word was invented in 1935 to describe Thomas E. Dewey. Dewey, a prosecuting attorney in New York City during the 1930s, was known for his energetic pursuit of organized crime kingpins such as Dutch Schultz and Lucky Luciano.

Although the label *gangbuster* may have been coined with Dewey in mind, the expression *come on like gangbusters* almost certainly derives from the long-running half-hour radio show *Gang Busters*. The show premiered on July 30, 1935, with the title *G-Men*. It featured dramatizations of real FBI cases. In 1936, the show's creators changed its title to *Gang Busters*, possibly because they judged that this newly popular term would draw a larger audience. If so, the strategy worked. *Gang Busters* aired on various networks from 1936 to 1957. The show opened with a cacophony of sound effects—police sirens, gunfire, squealing tires. Coming on like *Gang Busters* entailed plenty of noise and fanfare.

Although *coming on like gangbusters* implies a pushiness that might be annoying to some people, the expression has also been used positively since the 1940s. *Current History and Forum* for November 7, 1940, defines *coming on like gangbusters* as prison slang for "doing all right." The jazz world also adopted the expression around this time to mean playing very energetically and well.

Going like gangbusters, getting along like gangbusters, and other variants all describe highly successful activities. Garrison Keillor's *Lake Wobegon Days*, published in 1986, includes the sentence "Despite the heat and no rain, gardens came on like gangbusters." People who've just met and are getting along well are said to be hitting it off like gangbusters. *Gangbusters* can also be used alone as an adjective—for instance, *Our business had a gangbuster quarter* or *This spaghetti sauce is gangbusters.*

GET THE BUM'S RUSH.
Be forcibly ejected; be sent on your way in a hurry.

Bum has been a name for a tramp or a derelict since the mid-nineteenth century. Nevada's *Gold Hill News* for April 15, 1864, reports, "The policemen say that even their old, regular, and reliable 'bums' appear to have reformed." By the twentieth century, the word could designate any lazy or worthless type. Eric Linklater's 1931 *Juan in America* includes a classic example of this usage: "I'll fix the dirty bum that framed me!"

Bum is probably short for *bummer*, which in turn comes from the German *bummler*, a lounger or an idler. An article in the January 27, 1855, Portland *Oregonian* provides some evidence for this origin. It features the German-accented quote, "Come, clear out, you trunken loafer. Ve don't vant no bummers here." *Bummer* had been shortened to *bum* by the end of the nineteenth century.

The bum's rush is a way of hustling out an undesirable, usually involving a firm grip on his collar and the seat of his trousers. Glen Mullin's *Adventures of a Scholar Tramp*, published in 1925, offers this vivid description of the technique: "The brawny Louis frequently hopped over the bar to collar some belligerent drunk and rush him breathlessly through the swinging doors into the street, using his knees expertly to propel his victim along. This function Louis referred to with great relish as 'givin' 'em the bum's rush.'"

The bum's rush could also be figurative—an abrupt dismissal—from at least the 1930s. This illustration comes from George Jean Nathan's 1938 *The Morning after the First Night*, about the state of the American theater: "The Gallic drama that consumes two and one-half hours of inordinately mechanized dramaturgy . . . is no longer accepted . . . but is given the bum's rush."

Bum has been a synonym for poor quality almost as long as it has been part of the English language. Beginning in the late nineteenth century, *go on the bum* meant to indulge in a drinking spree. People in the early decades of the twentieth century spoke of *suffering with a bum hip*, *getting a bum steer* (bad advice), and *taking a bum rap* (see *take the rap*, below). In the later twentieth century, a car or a television could be on the bum. Students in the late 1960s who disastrously failed a class said they had bummed out. Later, to be bummed out—bummed for short—meant to feel depressed. A bad experience with a hallucinatory drug was also labeled a bummer. *Bummer*'s meaning eventually expanded to cover any unpleasant situation.

The bum's rush these days is nearly always verbal rather than physical. An example of current usage is *I tried to get in for an interview, but the personnel office gave me the bum's rush.*

PUT THE FINGER ON SOMEONE.

Inform against someone to the police; accuse someone of wrongdoing.

From at least 1899, *to finger* was underworld slang meaning "place under arrest." In *Tramping with Tramps*, published that year, a hobo tells author Josiah Flynt that local police forces "like to finger us." Although an obvious image is the pointing finger of accusation, another possibility is that *finger* in this context alluded to putting a finger under the arrested man's collar to haul him away. (*To collar* was another way of expressing this action.) *Put the finger on*, meaning to identify someone to the police, came into use around the 1920s. Like so many expressions of the kind from this era, it was associated with gangsters and tough guys. A character in Dashiell Hammett's hard-boiled mystery *Red Harvest*, published in 1929, says, "You think I killed them, don't you Dick? . . . Going to put the finger on me?"

J. Edgar Hoover's book of cautionary tales about American criminals, the 1938 *Persons in Hiding*, includes a use of the phrase that means "point out." A kidnapper tries to bribe an undercover FBI man to identify a potential kidnap victim. She says, "I know a job that would bring you in ten thousand dollars, and all you'd have to do would be to finger a certain man for us."

Fingering someone could also involve informing against him to fellow criminals. *The Doorway to Hell*, a 1930 film featuring James Cagney, uses the phrase to mean marking someone out for killing. Putting the finger on people is still a way of getting them into trouble, either with the police or anyone else who wishes them harm.

TAKE THE RAP.
Take the blame or punishment.

Criminals have been *taking the rap* for their misdeeds—that is, serving a prison sentence—since the 1920s. Of course, if they were lucky and a jury found them innocent, they might beat the rap instead. Around that same time, a rap could also refer to the usual sentence for a particular crime. In Ellery Queen's *Spanish Cape Mystery*, published in 1935, a police detective tells his suspect, "You're in a tough spot. Do you know what the rap for blackmail is in this State?"

Earlier in the century, *a rap* was underworld slang for an identification or accusation, such as what might occur during a police lineup. A 1926 *New York Times* article, attempting to educate its readers in what it calls "the bright lexicon of crime," illustrates the meaning of *rap* with this sentence: "When one is singled out from a line of suspects as the dip [pickpocket] who slid the ticktick [watch], one is the victim of a 'rap.'" For some reason, raps are usually pinned or hung on people, as in *The DA pinned a murder rap on Big Joey*. False accusations are bum raps. The police keep track of a criminal's history of charges and convictions with a rap sheet. Although rap sheets have existed for a long time, the term is only recorded in print beginning in 1960.

Rap has been part of the English vocabulary long enough to acquire a host of meanings, some only tangentially related. When the word first appeared in print in the fourteenth century, it signified a severe blow with a weapon, as in a rap with a sword. Later, the meaning softened to something more like a good smack. The British magazine *Spectator* for 1711 describes this incident: "She pulled off her Shoe, and hit me with the Heel such a Rap." A blow administered to a wooden surface, for example, a door, has also been known for a long time as a rap. When spiritualism was a fad during the nineteenth century, those on the Other Side who wanted to communicate with séance participants rapped on the table. A book on the subject titled *Spirit Rappings* appeared in 1853.

More recent meanings of *rap* have to do with sharp verbal blows. Beginning in the nineteenth century, the word indicated an adverse comment or criticism. For example, Cincinnati's *American Pioneer* for January 17, 1777, remarks, "The post master general . . . has lately had a rap, which I hope will have a good effect." In the 1960s, African American vernacular English contributed another meaning of *rap* to the larger vocabulary—lively, verbally clever repartee. Eventually, *rap* in this sense expanded to cover any type of casual conversation but especially one with countercultural overtones. Hippies rapped as they hung out on the streets of San Francisco's Haight-Ashbury district. High schools opened rap centers for their students, while trendy adults who wanted to share their thoughts organized rap sessions. The 1980s saw the advent of rap music, in which lines are spoken rhythmically over a musical background.

Meanwhile, *take the rap* and *beat the rap* continue to be in use. In recent decades, taking the rap can mean being blamed or punished for negative actions less serious than crimes. For example, a March 2002 online article from *Baseball Digest* carries the headline "When Hitters Slump, Coaches Take the Rap." *Take the rap* often implies taking the blame for something that's not entirely your fault. Bottom-tier gangsters who go to jail rather than betray their colleagues are willing to take the rap.

TAKE IT ON THE LAM.

Run away; escape after committing a crime.

Lam first entered the language as a verb. It became part of American underworld slang in the late nineteenth century. This excerpt from Allan Pinkerton's 1884 memoir, *Thirty Years a Detective*, gives an illustration of the word: "After he [the pickpocket] has secured the wallet he will . . . utter the word 'lam!' This means to let the man go, and to get out of the way as soon as possible." *Lam it* and *lam out* were alternative expressions.

Lam turned into a noun soon afterward. *Taking it on the lam* has been a way of escaping the authorities since the early twentieth century. Possibly its first use in print comes from *Life in Sing Sing*, published in 1904: "He plugged the main guy for keeps and I took it on a lam for mine." Fugitives from justice could also *go on the lam, hit the lam*, or *do a lam*. By the 1920s *take it on the lam* was starting to enter mainstream English. *Vanity Fair* for November 1927 tells its readers, "'Take it on the lam' is making a quick getaway or hurried disappearance."

The word *lam* followed a convoluted path from its origins in Old English to the argot of the American underworld. It comes from the Old English *lama*, meaning to lame. Beginning in the sixteenth century, *to lam* meant to thrash soundly or whack, and it was the basis for the more familiar word *lambaste*. How the meaning of *lam* went from "beating" to "escaping" is a puzzle. A possible bridge between the disparate meanings is the expression *beat a path*, meaning to walk along a certain route so frequently that the ground is beaten down. Travelers have been beating paths since around the year 1000.

From the late nineteenth to the early twentieth centuries, a similar Americanism, *beat one's way*, was slang for traveling illicitly. For example, George Peck uses this term to mean hopping a train without paying any fare in his 1882 book, *Peck's Sunshine*: "He started home, beating his way on the trains." This usage naturally led to the shortened form *beat it*, meaning to leave quickly, which has been current since the beginning of the twentieth century. The distance between *beat it* and *lam it*, while not exactly a short step, is not unimaginably far. If *beat* can signify both hitting and travel, why not *lam* too?

While *lam it* has disappeared from modern English, *on the lam* is still familiar. For instance, a 1992 crime novel by Barbara Neely is titled *Blanche on the Lam*. More recently, Fox News for June 13, 2007, reported, "An escaped con . . . was captured Wednesday after six days on the lam." *Take it on the lam* is used less often, but it still appears in print occasionally.

PLEAD THE FIFTH.
Refuse to incriminate yourself.

The Fifth Amendment to the US Constitution provides a number of safeguards for Americans accused of a crime. It specifies that no one can be tried for a capital crime unless first indicted by a grand jury, those accused may not be tried for the same offense twice, and no one may be punished without "due process" of law or deprived of property without just compensation. However, when witnesses on the stand at a trial say they are *pleading the Fifth*, they are referring to the Fifth Amendment's provision that "[n]o person . . . shall be compelled in any criminal case to be a witness against himself." In courtroom dramas, witnesses who plead the Fifth often tell the Court, "I refuse to answer that question on the grounds that it may incriminate me."

Although the Fifth Amendment has been part of the Constitution since 1791, references to it did not appear in print very often until the 1940s. Americans became more aware of the option of taking the Fifth during the much-publicized anticommunist investigations of the House Committee on Un-American Activities (HUAC). HUAC was established in 1938 to investigate German-American involvement with the Nazis. However, the committee soon switched its attention to searching out evidence of communist infiltration, concentrating on labor unions and such New Deal programs as the Federal Theatre Project.

In 1947 HUAC began investigating the alleged pervasiveness of communist propaganda in the movies. Actors, screenwriters, and others in the motion picture industry were subpoenaed to appear before the committee. They were asked if they had ever been members of the Communist Party themselves and to name others who, to their knowledge, had been members. Those who refused to testify could be cited for contempt of Congress. During the first hearings, a group known as the Hollywood Ten—mostly screenwriters—declined to cooperate, citing their First Amendment right to free speech. They were convicted of contempt of Congress and sent to jail. Concerned about bad publicity, Hollywood studio heads agreed to blacklist the Hollywood Ten and anyone else suspected of communist leanings. When the Ten were released from jail, they were unable to get work in films. Throughout this period, the smallest hint that HUAC was interested in an individual's politics resulted in immediate blacklisting. Hundreds of careers were ruined before HUAC and the Hollywood studio system both ran out of steam in the 1960s.

Although those called to testify could do little to escape being blacklisted, they eventually figured out how to avoid naming names without risking contempt charges. They began pleading the Fifth Amendment instead of the First. Using this tactic, witnesses could refuse to answer HUAC's questions on the grounds that the answers might incriminate them.

Today, pleading the Fifth, or taking the Fifth, is a fairly common way of avoiding an open admission of guilt. It's used both in serious legal contexts and in more lighthearted situations, such as pleading the Fifth to avoid having to admit that you ate the last brownie. In spite of the experiences of HUAC's Hollywood victims, most of whom were guilty of nothing except a dislike of being bullied, taking the Fifth is usually interpreted as a tacit admission of wrongdoing.

SING LIKE A CANARY.
Inform the authorities of what you know about criminal activities.

Singing has equaled betrayal since at least the sixteenth century. An adage from that time says, "He that sings once, weeps all his life after," meaning that a man who betrays his companions regrets it for life. Singing was nineteenth-century criminals' cant for snitching to the police, as Sir Walter Scott notes in his 1815 novel, *Guy Mannering*: "To sing out or whistle in the cage, is when a rogue, being apprehended, peaches [tattles] against his comrades."

The term traveled across the Atlantic, and by the twentieth century, singing was also an American criminal activity. Americans added the descriptive detail *like a canary*. *Canary* has been slang for a police informer since the 1920s. Singing can also be akin to blowing the whistle on corporate or government irregularities (see chapter 8, "Playing the Game"), but most often it refers to criminals who sell out their partners in crime. Their usual motivation is the hope of more considerate treatment from the law than they would otherwise get.

Canaries may be related thematically to stool pigeons. The original stool pigeons were passenger pigeons, which were attached to wooden "stools," or perches, with a string and used as hunters' decoys. (*Stool* might also derive from the obsolete word *stall*, meaning a decoy.) Passenger pigeons were among the most common birds in colonial North America. They numbered in the billions when the British first arrived. However, they were extensively hunted for food and went extinct in the early twentieth century.

The first figurative meaning of *stool pigeon* was someone employed as a decoy to entice suckers, for example, to draw them into a betting game. Its first known appearance in print is from 1830. A Newark oyster bar of the time posted a number of humorous advertisements, including one that offered "stool pigeons trained to catch voters for the next Presidency." By mid-century, the meaning of *stool pigeon* was shifting to "police informer." For example, *Banker's Magazine* for August 1849 reports that the senior high constable of Philadelphia had been using a certain individual "as a 'stool pigeon' or secret informer."

Bartlett's *Dictionary of Americanisms*, published in 1848, lists the term *stool-pigeoning*, saying that the police "of olden times" were often accused of it. In stool-pigeoning operations, the police arrested doubtful characters and demanded money or valuables in exchange for their release. Such a system could have led to the criminal passing on information rather than money.

By the twentieth century, stool pigeons were synonymous with canaries. *American Notes and Queries* for 1945 defines *canary* as a "New York City Police Department term for any underworld character who 'sings.'" A possible paraphrase is the expression *to canary to the police*. In spite of all the underworld types who must be out gunning for canaries, they are a flourishing species. A 1984 *New York Post* headline reports, "Mob Canary Sings Again for the Feds."

COP A PLEA.
Admit to a crime in the hopes of mitigating your punishment.

The *Chicago Daily Tribune* for April 10, 1925, gives this definition of *cop a plea*: "to admit one's guilt in a gamble to prevent heavy sentence." Since the early twentieth century, copping a plea usually means making a deal with the prosecution in which the criminal admits to certain lesser offenses in exchange for a light sentence. The deal often entails giving the prosecution incriminating information about one's partners in crime. As a character says in the 1929 book *Let Tomorrow Come*, "No guy that cops a plea is a good guy. An' Greasy copped."

The word *cop* may derive originally from the Latin *capere*, meaning "to seize." In England, *to cop* has meant to capture someone since the eighteenth century. It could also mean to steal something. By the late nineteenth century, *cop it* was British slang for getting into trouble or being arrested. Coppers, later shortened to cops, were the folks who did the copping, or arresting. British thugs, when nabbed by the cops, traditionally surrendered with the words, "It's a fair cop. You got me bang to rights."

The connotation of evading something led to the American slang expression *cop out*, meaning to drop out of conventional society or evade your responsibilities. Originally the phrase belonged to 1940s hipsters—cool denizens of the jazz world. In the sixties it became associated with the counterculture. The University of South Dakota's *Current Slang* for 1968 lists *cop out* with the definition "to quit, give up without trying." A *cop-out* is an excuse, usually a poor one. The "take" sense of *cop* gives us *cop onto an idea* (realize it); *cop a feel* (fondle someone); *cop a nod* (get some sleep); *cop a buzz* (get drunk); *cop an attitude* (get belligerent); and *cop a squat* (sit down).

Since the middle of the twentieth century, copping a plea can simply mean pleading for mercy, even when no prison sentence is involved—for instance, *When Jerry's girlfriend discovered him out dancing with another woman, he tried to cop a plea.* The expression still refers most often to making a bargain with the prosecution.

TAKE A POWDER.
Leave quickly; clear out to avoid arrest.

The first recorded use of this expression appears as the caption to a 1916 *Washington Post* cartoon: "Look at the two birds trying to take a 'run-out' powder on the eats." *Take a powder* was common by the 1930s, especially in stories about gangsters and the underworld. Other versions of the phrase are *run-out powder* and *walk-out powder*. In the forties and fifties, beatniks and other cool cats who had to split from the scene said, "Got to take a fast powder!"

To powder, meaning to leave in a hurry, is centuries old. It first appears in print in the mid-1600s. The 1645 *Narrative of the Siege of Carlisle in 1644–45* includes the sentence "About 800 horse[s] . . . come powdering toward the Cowes so fast." The phrase *with a powder* meant hastily or impetuously, as in *They arrived with a powder*. Both terms were familiar in England until at least the early twentieth century. At that point, *to powder*, meaning to escape, was adopted as underworld jargon. *To powder* might have evolved into *take a powder* following the pattern of *to lam*, explained on p. 141.

Several theories have been proposed to account for this expression. One ingenious suggestion is that *powder* is short for *flee powder*, obviously a play on *flea powder*. Another hypothesis connects the powder with laxative powder—a kind of Mickey Finn (see chapter 5, "People and Places")—that gave people the urge to dash out in a hurry, looking for a bathroom. Laxatives and many other drugs came in powder form during the era when *take a powder* was gangster slang. However, these suggestions don't take into account *powder*'s much earlier use in Great Britain.

A more plausible alternative, suggested by William and Mary Morris's *Dictionary of Word and Phrase Origins*, connects the expression with *dust* or *dust out*, meaning to leave hastily. Like *to powder*, this use of *dust* is first found in the seventeenth century. During the nineteenth century, it was a familiar Americanism. One example comes from the *Mesilla Times* of Arizona for October 18, 1860: "The 'gold seekers' thought prudence the better part of valor and 'got up and dusted.'" Another meaning of *dust* at that time was to gallop past someone on the road. Both uses of the word are probably related to leaving someone in the dust, an expression that is still current. On dirt roads, people moving quickly would kick up dust as they went, whether on foot or horseback.

In early modern English, *powder* was sometimes used as English speakers use *dust* now, for instance, to refer to human ashes. The two words would probably still have been interchangeable when *powder* started meaning "depart in haste."

Although not exactly current, *take a powder* is still fairly familiar to Americans as tough-guy slang. However, the verb forms *powder* and *powder out* appear to be obsolete.

※ ※ ※

Of course a gangster's life isn't all about business. In his leisure hours, he might well indulge in an all-American pastime like poker, another rich source for slang expressions. And if he is a small-time hood, he should be careful when cheating or partaking in con games while at the table—or else be prepared to take a fast powder.

PART 3:
CULTURE AND
AMUSEMENTS

Chapter 8

PLAYING THE GAME

Americans have been great game players since colonial times. Some of those ancestral games would be unfamiliar to modern citizens—for instance, lawn bowling, stick fighting (called cudgeling), and the ancient game of shinny, described under *keep the ball rolling* in chapter 4, "Politics as Usual." Most games were played casually on the public green. Young men with extra leisure time could also be found at the local tavern or inn, betting on cockfights or on bare-knuckled boxing matches.

By the mid-nineteenth century, baseball and football were well on their way to their current popularity as spectator sports. Invented in the 1890s, basketball was meant to provide young men with an indoor game that filled the gap between the fall football season and the first baseball game of spring. Ball games are an especially good source for metaphors—*the ball's in your court, let's see if they'll play ball, somebody dropped the ball, keep your eye on the ball*, and a host of baseball sayings, such as *get a ballpark figure, bat a thousand, touch base, step up to the plate, cover the bases, a whole different ball game*, and *two strikes against.*

Card games that feature bidding and betting have also been a popular American pastime since early days. Most card games are European imports, but poker was invented in the United States. It was first played in New Orleans in the 1820s. Westerners on the post–Civil War frontier played endless hands of poker, often with weapons at the ready. Slipping an extra ace out of your sleeve during a Wild West poker game could result in you cashing in your chips sooner than expected.

HAVE AN ACE IN THE HOLE.

Hold a resource in reserve; have a hidden advantage.

Aces have been desirable playing cards to have in your hand since the sixteenth century. Although in a few card games aces are low, they usually are the cards with the highest value. The lucky possessor of an ace—or two or three—has a distinct advantage over the other players. Sir Thomas More was clearly referring to this fact when he wrote in 1533, "I am as sure of this game as he that hath three aces in his hand."

Aces are so connected to the idea of winning that *ace* has been another word for the best there is since the early 1900s. During World War I, aces were pilots who had downed at least five enemy planes. An ace performer is someone at the top of his or her particular game or skill, whether it's tennis or buying and selling stocks. To ace a test or some other activity is to do supremely well at it.

Americans have boasted about having a metaphorical *ace in the hole* since the beginning of the twentieth century. The expression comes from the version of poker known as five-card stud. In five-card stud, the dealer gives each player one card facedown and one faceup. The facedown card is the player's hole card. Participants then place bets based only on their faceup card. Three more rounds of faceup cards are dealt, and players continue to bet on them, while the hole card remains hidden. After the final round, everyone turns over his or her hole card and the best hand wins. Obviously, a player with an ace in the hole—rather than a two, for example—has a better chance of a winning hand.

Five-card stud originated during the Civil War. *Ace in the hole* seems to have gained its metaphorical meaning soon afterward. Ramon Adams explains in *Cowboy Lingo* that "the shoulder holster . . . was often called an 'ace in the hole.'" This kind of ace in the hole may have come in handy when one of the other players had an ace up his sleeve. Although the popularity of five-card stud has dwindled recently in favor of other versions of poker, the figurative expression remains current. Barbara Kingsolver's 1998 novel, *The Bean Trees*, includes the sentence "All my life mama had talked about the Cherokee nation as our ace in the hole."

HAVE AN ACE UP YOUR SLEEVE.

Have a hidden resource that can be called into play at the right time.

Unlike having an ace in the hole, having an ace up your sleeve is the mark of a card shark rather than an ordinary poker player. Professional gamblers flourished in nineteenth-century America—approximately fifteen hundred of them plied their trade aboard the Mississippi steamboats—and, inevitably, some of them shortened their odds by cheating. A light-fingered player could keep an extra ace tucked into his coat sleeve, to be introduced into his hand when he needed it. The maneuver is akin to the magician's trick of pulling cards and other objects seemingly out of the air. The main difficulty would have been to keep the other players from realizing that the deck had five aces.

The first figurative uses of *have an ace up your sleeve* don't appear until the 1920s. One of the earliest occurs in a book by Francis Coe titled *Me—Gangster*: "The district attorney had another ace up his sleeve." An alternative version of the phrase is *have a card up your sleeve*. The implication is that it's a useful card—an ace rather than a two.

In modern times, having an ace up your sleeve does not necessarily imply cheating. It merely suggests that you have a hidden advantage that you're saving until it's really needed. In George Orwell's *Down and Out in Paris and London*, published in 1933, the unemployed Russian waiter Boris assures Orwell, "Oh we shall find something. I have got a few cards up my sleeve. There are people who owe me money, for instance."

CASH IN YOUR CHIPS.
Give up or quit; die.

You can also hand in or pass in your chips, or pass in your checks—a nineteenth-century word for chips—or simply cash in, with the chips implied. Like many other gambling-based expressions, this one hails from the American West. The first figurative use of the phrase appeared in print in the St. Louis *Missouri Republican* of October 22, 1879: "If you wish to express the demise of a friend . . . in Southern Colorado . . . it would be more elegant to say that he'd 'passed in his chips.'" Another early example appears in this little bit of doggerel, found in *Tramp Poems*: "He / Would not go in / To 'the little church around the corner' / If you or I 'cashed in.'"

Chips have represented money or other assets since ancient times. In the nineteenth-century United States, chips were made of ivory (as they were in Europe) until the cost of that material became prohibitive. By the 1880s, most chips were formed out of clay and finished with shellac. These are the chips that cowboys and forty-niners would have cashed in after their card games. The familiar plastic chip was not manufactured until the 1950s. The word *chip* was also a nickname for money itself in the nineteenth century, giving us the expressions *in the chips*, meaning well-off, and *chip in*, meaning contribute.

Cash in your chips usually suggests a natural death. However, you can deliberately cash in your chips—that is, commit suicide—and you can also cash in someone else's chips—that is, kill the person. The variant *pass in your chips*, once common, seems to be obsolete.

BET YOUR BOTTOM DOLLAR.
Be very confident of some fact.

The first example of *bottom dollar* uses the term literally. A story about an Old West character in the *San Francisco Call* newspaper for January 24, 1857, includes this sentence: "Sometimes, however, luck will run against him, and to use his own expressive phraseology, he 'slips up for his bottom dollar.'" The quotes around the phrase indicate that it was a new one for the article's author. Probably it was also unfamiliar to at least part of his audience. The scene itself, however, was common in nineteenth-century San Francisco. This gold rush boomtown seethed with gambling houses. John James Audubon, visiting the city in 1849, wrote in his journal, "The place [is] full of gamblers, hundreds of them, . . ." The larger houses turned over as much as $200,000 a day, a staggering sum at that time.

Why a "bottom" dollar? One possibility is that it was the dollar at the bottom of a stack of coins. Coins were more common than paper money during this era. Committed gamblers would have stacked up their money and played until they reached the bottom. Probably a substantial number of *San Francisco Call* readers had slid their last remaining, or bottom, dollar across the gambling table at one time or another.

Within a decade of its first appearance in 1857, the expression was being used figuratively. *You may bet your bottom dollar* became a common way of saying that the chances of some particular thing happening were extremely good—so good that you would be willing to risk your last asset on its likelihood. Today, the phrase almost always takes the form *You can* (not *may*) *bet your bottom dollar*.

PASS THE BUCK.
Shift responsibility onto someone else.

Pass the buck originally meant to give someone else a chance. It derives from the frontier poker players' custom of passing a buckhorn knife around the table to keep track of whose turn it was to deal. The expression first became popular during the late 1840s—gold rush days—when a poker game was always in progress somewhere. One song from that era, "Days of 49," includes the line "He'd ante a slug; he'd pass the buck." The verb *to buck* also signified gambling, especially at popular nineteenth-century games like faro (see *play both ends against the middle*, p. 153) and three-card monte, where players bet that they would get a better hand than the dealer.

The 1887 book *Draw Poker* describes a different version of passing the buck. The buck in this case can be any inanimate object, although the book explains that a knife is typically used. Frontier poker players no doubt had knives conveniently available. The knife or other object is added to the jackpot, then temporarily scooped up by whoever takes the pot. When the buck holder's turn to deal comes around, the players must ante up for a new jackpot. (*Ante* is another poker-related word that entered the mainstream vocabulary. It has meant placing your share of the bet since the mid-1800s and now can also mean to pay your share of any expenses.)

A few word historians have questioned whether *buck* really stands for *buckhorn*, noting that buckhorn knives were expensive. Many forty-niners would not have been able to afford them. Charles Funk speculates in *A Hog on Ice* that the term actually refers to buckshot. *Happy Trails: A Dictionary of Western Expressions* suggests that the bucks were silver dollars, assuming that the players used them instead of poker chips. This explanation is improbable, as *buck* to mean *dollar* is not recorded until 1856, several years after *pass the buck* was in wide use. A dollar was also a lot to bet. Slang sometimes circulates orally for years before being written down, so the *Happy Trails* explanation, though unlikely, is not out of the question.

Bucking responsibility to a superior is a time-honored activity in large bureaucracies. This is often accomplished with a *buck slip*, or routing slip, which allows everyone except the last person on the list to pass the problem along. President Truman's famous plaque declaring, "The buck stops here" acknowledged that he was prepared to take ultimate responsibility for whatever problems circulated through his administration. *Pass the buck* as a metaphor for shifting responsibility onto someone else has been in use since at least the first decade of the twentieth century. A 1919 issue of *Yale Law Journal* includes the line "Officialdom can always 'pass the buck.'" Officialdom is still being accused of passing the buck. The phrase is still commonly used in connection with politics and public life generally. This typical usage is from a June 1, 2007, editorial posted online by the *Oshkosh Northwestern*: "[T]he norm seems to be to pass the buck, shrug the blame off on someone else."

PLAY BOTH ENDS AGAINST THE MIDDLE.

Gain an advantage for yourself by pitting people on opposite sides of an issue against each other.

The earliest use of this phrase in print includes a mention of its source. It appears in the 1887 *Recollections of a New York Police Chief,* by G. W. Walling: "He must in gamblers' parlance, 'play both ends against the middle.'" In 1887 the card game that gave rise to this expression, faro, was still one of the hottest gambling games in the country. Walling clearly understood the term's original meaning, as well as its new figurative use. Today, although the expression lives on, the game of faro is almost completely unknown.

The nature of the game explains both its immense popularity in nineteenth-century America and its eventual disappearance. Faro was played at a table (called a faro bank) laid out with images of thirteen cards, ace through king, in two rows. Sometimes actual cards were pasted onto the table. The cards were usually spades, but the suit was irrelevant. All that mattered was the cards' value. The faro dealer took cards from the top of a faceup deck. The deck was placed inside a dealing box, open at the top so the cards could be slid out one by one. Players bet on which card would turn up by putting chips on that card's image. Two cards were dealt for each turn—the first card lost for the player, but won for the bank, while the second card won for the player. Players could bet on a card to lose rather than win by placing a penny or a copper token on the card. They could also bet more elaborately by straddling their chips across two or more cards. If the dealer drew a pair, the bank took half of all the bets on that card. When only three cards remained, players could "bet the turn" by predicting the order in which they would turn up. An abacuslike counting device kept track of which numbers had been dealt.

Originally a European game, faro arrived in New Orleans in 1717.

Soon every riverboat featured a faro bank, and the game quickly spread across the West. It was a favorite of the high-rollers who peopled frontier boomtowns. They were intent on making their fortunes, no matter how, and winning at cards was easier than panning for gold. As an example of the game's popularity, the mining town of Leadville, Colorado, boasted more than one hundred gambling houses in the 1870s, nearly all of them featuring a faro table. For the benefit of newcomers, especially those who couldn't read, houses where a faro bank operated were marked with the sign of a tiger—probably because some early faro decks were backed with a picture of that animal. Playing faro was known as *twisting the tiger's tail*, and trying to beat the house was called *bucking the tiger*. The gambling district was frequently nicknamed Tiger Alley.

Faro's tremendous popularity is partly explained by the excellent odds for players. Except for the rule of giving the bank half of all bets when the dealer turned up a pair, the house had no advantages. Needless to say, dealers soon arrived at a solution to this difficulty—wholesale cheating. Although the dealing boxes were supposed to ensure fair play, dealers invented many ways of slipping out cards in a particular order.

A common trick was to trim the cards so skilled dealers could identify them by feeling the edges. Then, if a heavily staked card was about to turn up, they could slide out another card on top of it. Cards that were trimmed to be convex or concave on one side were known as *both ends against the middle*. Playing a card that was both ends against the middle was thus a way to give the house an unfair advantage. It's unclear how this meaning metamorphosed into the current definition of the expression. Possibly, as faro died out and its terminology became obscure, Americans invented an explanation for *both ends against the middle* that still suggested cheating but made transparent sense.

Crooked faro games were so much the norm in the late nineteenth century that Hoyle's books of card game rules warned readers that honest faro games could no longer be found in the United States. An

American Speech article for 1986 titled "Cheating Terms in Cards and Dice" lists no fewer than thirty-three cheating terms specifically applying to faro. As the West became less wild, citizens put pressure on state governments to outlaw these scams. By 1907 faro banks had been shut down in every state except Nevada. Those eventually closed as well when casinos learned what old-time faro dealers had always known—honest faro doesn't make enough money for the house.

Play both ends against the middle now has a meaning closer to *playing someone for a fool*, another nineteenth-century Americanism. Its original reference to playing cards has been lost. Further obscuring the original meaning, the phrase is sometimes given as *play both sides against the middle.*

PLAY HOOKEY.

Skip school or another activity without permission.

Also spelled *hooky*, this term for delinquency has been around since the mid-nineteenth century. Several possible sources have been proposed. Some are more persuasive than others. One suggestion relates *hookey* to the old-fashioned card game called blind hookey. In blind hookey, players pass a deck of cards around the table and each player cuts four or more cards from the top of the deck, depending on how many people are playing the game. When the cards are all dealt, players bet "blindly," without looking at their hands. Whoever beats the dealer wins the amount of his bet. *Playing blind hookey* was sometimes used figuratively to mean taking a risk, or jumping blindly into an unpredictable situation. According to proponents of the "blind hookey" explanation, this idea could have expanded to cover the risky business of skipping school, although no recorded evidence connects the two. An alternative explanation links *hookey* with other slang words popular at the time, such as *hookey-crookey* or the still-current *by hook or by crook. Hookey-crookey* was an adjective used to describe sneaky or underhanded maneuverings, as in this quote from an 1833 magazine: "They manage to keep themselves by hookey-crookey gambling ways." *By hook or by crook*—that is, by any means necessary—doesn't work as well as *hookey-crookey*. In fact, linking either of these terms to *play hookey* requires an uncomfortable stretch of meaning.

A more likely candidate along these lines is the expression *to go off on your own hook*, slang for doing something on your own initiative. This phrase was current in both the United States and England throughout the nineteenth century. It was occasionally heard as late as the 1940s. One early example is from the ubiquitous slangster Davy Crockett, who writes in his 1836 book, *Col. Crockett's Exploits and Adventures in Texas*, "I start anew upon my own hook." Schoolboys who played hookey were going off on their own hook. A related slang term—*hook it*—meant simply to leave. When boys got bored with school, they hooked it.

The linguist John Sinnema has proposed an intriguing explanation for *play hookey* that takes its etymology in an entirely different direction. In a 1970 *American Speech* article, Sinnema argues that the expression derives from the Dutch game *hoekje-spelen*, or hide-and-seek. The game of *hoekje* (pronounced "hook-yah") was popular in the Dutch colony of New Netherland, which became the British colony of New York in 1664. (See *beat the Dutch* in chapter 5, "People and Places.") Although New York officially belonged to the English long before the advent of the term *play hookey*, the territory remained home to a large number of Dutch speakers. Children no doubt continued to play *hoekje* for generations before the game gradually changed into hide-and-seek.

The Dutch term might have disappeared at that point, according to Sinnema, if not for the fateful hand of the New York State government. New York passed the first compulsory school attendance laws in 1853. *Play hookey* gained new life as a specialized term for hiding. Delinquent children played hookey by hiding from the truant officer who was on the lookout for them. The expression could easily have spread across the country as other states passed attendance laws similar to New York's. *Play hookey* to mean evading school first appears in print in 1848, five years before New York's truancy law. However, this explanation could still work. The issue of nonattendance was surely being discussed long before the law came into effect, and the term could easily have arisen as soon as the behavior it described became an issue. *Hookey*'s new meaning might have been reinforced by its similarity to *hook it* and *go off on your own hook.*

Today, not only children but also adults can play hookey. In the twentieth century, the expression broadened to mean any escape from duty. We can all play hookey from school, work, meetings, church, or anywhere else we don't want to be.

CALL THE SHOTS.
Make all the decisions; take control of an enterprise.

This expression originated with pool, or pocket billiards, a part of American culture since the eighteenth century. Pocket billiards was very popular in colonial America. Most well-furnished houses included a billiards table—both Thomas Jefferson and Alexander Hamilton were enthusiastic players. (The name *pocket billiards* indicates that the table is built with six pockets, or openings into which players hit the balls. Billiards played on an unpocketed table is called carom billiards.) As Americans moved west, they carried the game with them. In the 1830s, Bent's Fort in Colorado featured a billiards table among its amenities.

Americans started calling pocket billiards *pool* in the early nineteenth century. The name may have come from the pool rooms—off-track betting shops where bettors wagered a pool of money on horse races. These establishments often provided billiards tables for their customers. Although billiards players tried to dissociate themselves from the betting connection, the term *pool* is now much more common than *billiards* in the United States.

In certain pool games—for instance, some versions of eight-ball—players must call each shot, saying which ball they intend to hit into which pocket. Fifteen balls are set up in the middle of the pool table.

Each is numbered and is easily identifiable because of its distinct color, either solid colored or white with a colored stripe. As long as players make their shots, they can continue playing. When they miss a shot, the next player takes a turn and the previous player is no longer calling the shots.

The figurative use of *call the shots* is relatively recent. The *Oxford English Dictionary*'s earliest example dates from 1967, although the phrase would certainly have been in use before that. The example comes from a book about street corner gangs called *Tally's Corner*— "Gloria was calling the shots in this relationship." Today, the phrase is often used in a business context, where whoever is in charge, especially whoever controls the money, gets to call the shots.

GET BEHIND THE EIGHT-BALL.

Get in serious trouble; be in a difficult situation.

Being *behind the eight-ball* has been a problematic position since the early decades of the twentieth century. Most sources attribute it to the pool game called eight-ball, described in the above entry. Among the billiards balls is a black ball numbered eight. Players aim to hit either all the solid colored or all the striped balls into pockets, avoiding the eight-ball until

last. If a player prematurely pockets the eight-ball, he or she forfeits the game. When the eight-ball is positioned directly in front of the ball that a player wants to hit—in other words, when the object ball is behind the eight-ball—the situation gets tricky. To keep from being penalized, a player must strike the object ball without also hitting the eight-ball, usually a difficult shot.

An alternative explanation attributes *behind the eight-ball* to the game of kelly pool. In kelly pool, each player is randomly assigned a specific ball, which must be pocketed in numerical order. Whoever succeeds in pocketing his or her assigned ball first wins the game. The game can potentially include as many as fifteen players, one for each billiard ball. Those numerically behind the eight-ball—assigned to play the nine-ball or higher—have little chance of winning. A player with a lower number is almost certain to successfully pocket a ball first.

Proponents of this explanation argue that figurative uses of *behind the eight-ball* were fairly common by the early 1920s, although the game of eight-ball itself did not become popular until 1925, when the Brunswick-Balke-Collender Company publicized the game under the name B. B. C. Co. Pool. Although the first version of eight-ball was invented around 1900, it used unnumbered balls. Against this explanation is the arbitrariness of choosing numbers higher than eight as likely losers. Why not say *behind the nine-ball*, *behind the ten-ball*, or any other high number?

A 1926 dictionary of criminal jargon defines *eight-ball* as bad luck. Other early examples place an unlucky victim behind the notorious ball. A typical quote comes from the 1936 Ellery Queen novel, *Halfway House*, spoken by a young lawyer in trouble: "I'll probably finish behind the eight-ball, pleading small claims cases." Although *behind the eight-ball* reached its peak of popularity in the 1930s and 1940s, it is still in occasional use. The phrase has been incorporated into the titles of several recent books.

As with a multitude of other English nouns, *eight-ball* can also be used as a verb. Beginning around World War II, a marine could be eight-balled for causing trouble—that is, he could be transferred to an out-of-the-way base. Eight-balling someone can also mean to thwart the person, as in this line from the 1970s television program *Kojak*: "We been eight-balled, baby!"

HAVE SOMETHING ON THE BALL.
Be unusually alert, talented, or intelligent.

The first ones to have something on the ball were pitchers. To a pitcher, having something on the ball means throwing a curveball, slider, sinker, knuckleball, change-up, or other pitch that deceives the batter into swinging at the ball, but not hitting it. Sports writers as early as 1912 were using the term literally, although they usually wrote about players who did not have something on the ball. A *San Francisco Call* reporter writes in 1913, "Confidence is great stuff, but the pitcher must put something else on the ball." More colorfully, *Collier's* magazine says of one unfortunate player, "Swede didn't have a thing on the ball but the maker's name."

Americans were playing a game known as "base-ball" in the eighteenth century. The game probably evolved from rounders, an English game with similar rules. The earliest mention of base-ball appears in a 1791 Pittsfield, Massachusetts, statute, which forbids play within eighty yards of the town's meetinghouse. Presumably this rule was passed to protect the meetinghouse windows—some things never change.

A Manhattan engineer named Alexander Cartwright is credited with inventing the modern game. He organized the Knickerbocker Base Ball Club in 1845, naming it after the Knickerbocker fire station, where he worked. The following year, the first recorded game took place between the Knickerbockers and the New York Nine. The Knickerbockers lost 23 to 1 in four innings.

By the 1930s, *on the ball* was being used to mean alert, intelligent, or capable. In modern times, the phrase is usually shortened to *be on the ball*. Baseball players are still spoken of as literally having some particular kind of throw on the ball—or not.

PULL A BONER.
Make a foolish mistake.

This expression dates from the beginning of the twentieth century. A few etymologists have suggested that *pull a boner* refers to the minstrel show character Mr. Bones. Minstrel shows, an early form of vaudeville, usually featured two characters called Mr. Tambo, who played a tambourine, and Mr. Bones, who played a bone castanet. Between numbers, these two joked and traded straight lines with the master of ceremonies. According to this theory of *boner*'s origin, Mr. Bones's increasingly ridiculous responses were known as boners. Eventually, any remark of the type was called pulling a boner. While this hypothesis is plausible, there is no linguistic evidence to support it. As far as anyone has discovered, *pull a boner* was not used in conjunction with Mr. Bones during the minstrel show era—at least, no examples appear in print. (For more about minstrel shows, see *whistle Dixie* in chapter 9, "Great Performances.")

A more probable theory derives the term from baseball. According to this alternative, *boner* is short for *bonehead play*. *Bonehead* describes someone whose brain is lacking because his head is solid bone. The word has been around since the beginning of the twentieth century. A 1903 issue of *Smart Set* includes the line "You bone-headed fool!" *Dialect Notes* for 1918 gives the sentence "He pulled a bonehead all right," showing an early combination with *pull*. The first examples of *boner* in print refer to baseball, as in this 1913 judgment from *American Magazine*: "Got his signals mixed and pulled a boner."

The *Dickson Baseball Dictionary* describes an incident that many people believe popularized the expression. It took place on New York's Polo Grounds on September 23, 1908, in a game between the New York Giants and the Chicago Cubs. The teams were contending for first place in the National League. In the bottom of the ninth inning, the game was tied 1–1. New York had two outs, with men on first and third bases. When the Giants player at bat hit the ball into center field, the man on third base ran home, for what should have been the winning run.

Unfortunately, the man on first, a player named Fred Merkle, neglected to complete his run to second base. Apparently believing that the game was over when his teammate crossed home plate, he turned and headed for the clubhouse. As a result the Cubs were able to tag him out. Merkle's out invalidated his teammate's run, so the Giants lost. After a great brouhaha, the president of the National League decided that the game should be replayed. This time Chicago won the game, along with first place in the National League. New York fans seized on the recent slang term *pull a boner* as a satisfying way to express their wrath. Merkle never lived down his mistake. When he died in 1956, the AP obituary was titled "Fred Merkle, of 'Boner' Fame, Dies."

By 1920 *pull a boner* could mean a stupid mistake in any situation, not just baseball. A George Ade story written that year includes the sentence "Before he had a chance to pull a Boner . . . the Card Tables were whisked away." The expression is still current with that meaning. *Bonehead play* is also still used in sports contexts.

BE OUT IN LEFT FIELD.

Have an extreme opinion or unorthodox approach, which is probably wrong; be away from the center of activity.

In baseball *left field* refers to the part of the outfield that is left of center field from the perspective of someone standing at home plate. Why left field should have inspired a metaphor for being on the extreme periphery is something of a puzzle. If anything, left fielders are apt to see more action than right fielders. The majority of batters are right-handed, so they tend to "pull" toward the left when they hit, sending the ball out into left field.

Way out in left field has been a way of saying that someone was slightly wacky since at least the 1930s. The *San Francisco Chronicle* for April 19, 1937, writes that Lefty Gomez, a Yankees pitcher known for his offbeat sense of humor, is "'way out in left field without a glove' in baseball jargon. In other words, he is as proficient at whipping over a smart crack as a sizzling strike." This quote shows that the figurative meaning was at least current among baseball players and probably known to fans as well.

Several explanations have been proposed for this counterintuitive metaphor. One claims that the expression got started when Babe Ruth was playing right field for the Yankees during the 1920s. Anyone wrongheaded enough to buy tickets for seats overlooking left field—on the opposite side of the ballpark from the Great Bambino—must indeed have been not too bright. (Ruth batted left-handed, so presumably he would have hit the ball into right field as well.)

A number of sources hypothesize that *out in left field* originated at Chicago's old West Side Grounds, where the Cubs played from 1893 to 1915. This derivation claims that the park's left field shared a property line with the University of Illinois's Neuropsychiatric Institute, so anyone playing near the left field fence was getting close to mingling with psychiatric cases. The main problem with this etymology is timing. The Neuropsychiatric Institute did not exist during the years when the Cubs played ball at the West Side Grounds. The university's medical school bought the Grounds after the Cubs moved to what is now Wrigley Field and, in 1939, built the Neuropsychiatric Institute on the former site of left field. During the ballpark's glory days, left field faced a block of apartments. The Neuropsychiatric Institute's presence on what used to be left field could not have inspired *out in left field*, even if people had remembered the ballpark's old location, because the expression predates the institute's 1939 construction.

A more likely explanation for the slang use of *out in left field* relies on the shape of early ballparks. At the turn of the twentieth century, parks were commonly designed to fit inside a long city block so they would not cross the streetcar rails, which ran parallel with the streets. The result was that left field went slightly deeper than right field, putting left fielders comparatively farther away from the center of the baseball diamond. Chicago's West Side Park was one such example, with a right field of 316 feet, but a left field of 340 feet.

Left field is now the location of extreme behaviors and opinions, especially political opinions. The term is sometimes used to refer specifically to the political left, with the implication that it's far away from the center of opinion. The variation *out of left field* can also mean to come out of nowhere, as in *Volunteers just seemed to come out of left field*. The negative cultural associations of *left*, as in left-handedness, could also have influenced this expression's development.

BE CAUGHT FLAT-FOOTED.
Be unprepared.

In the nineteenth-century United States, being flat-footed was a good thing. It meant to stand firm and resolute, as in this 1846 quote from the *New York Herald*: "Mr. Pickens of South Carolina has come out flat-footed for the administration." However, by the twentieth century, the meaning had shifted to being unprepared, unskilled, or tactless, as in a flat-footed compliment. More specifically, to be caught flat-footed means to be standing still when you should be moving.

Sources agree that flat-footedness in this sense was originally a sports term but differ on which sport should claim it. The earliest use in a baseball context seems to carry the old meaning of resoluteness. It comes from an article in the New York *Daily Telegram* of August 5, 1908: "Frank Chance, who is a member of the joint rules committee of the major leagues, is flatfooted against the 'spit ball.'"

According to the *Dickson Baseball Dictionary*, the modern term *flat-footed* describes a batting stance. The batter swings while keeping both feet on the ground, as opposed to balancing on the balls of his feet. A flat-footed stance is considered a good position for hitting a sacrifice fly, since being quick off the plate doesn't matter. However, if a player has to run, being flat-footed adds a few extra seconds to his start.

Football players can also be caught flat-footed. As a metaphor for unpreparedness, *caught flat-footed* works even better for football, where being ready to run at a moment's notice is more critical. Yet another suggestion is that the phrase comes from horse racing. When the jockey is not ready for the start of a race, his horse is said to be caught flat-footed. Because the animal is not poised to pick up its feet, it wastes precious time with all four hooves on the ground while other horses are already moving. In fact, flat-footedness seems to be a common problem in sports. Possibly the expression *to be caught flat-footed* started in one sport and was adopted by others.

Today, being caught flat-footed often implies being unprepared in a public situation. For example, politicians are said to be caught flat-footed by a reporter's question, or by an unexpected event. Business-people who can't answer a client's question, or public speakers who don't respond well to questions from the audience, are also caught flat-footed.

BLOW THE WHISTLE.

Expose wrongdoing, especially of a superior; put a stop to a questionable activity.

Blow the whistle was evidently a familiar colloquialism by 1934, the date of *Oxford English Dictionary*'s first example of the phrase. It appears in P. G. Wodehouse's novel *Right Ho, Jeeves*: "Now that the whistle had been blown on his speech, . . . there was no longer any need for the strategic retreat which I had been planning." Wodehouse uses the expression to mean "make a revelation." Examples of the phrase with the specific meaning of "exposing scandals" don't begin appearing until decades later. This typical example comes from Paul Sann's 1967 *Fads, Follies, and Delusions of the American People*: "Herb Stempel . . . blew the whistle on [the game show] Twenty-One when he was shoved aside to make way for Charles Van Doren."

The most commonly suggested sources for blown whistles are the police and sports referees. No direct evidence connects either profession with early uses of *blow the whistle*, but most etymologists vote for the referee's whistle. Its purpose—signaling a violation of the rules and calling a halt to play—is closer to the expression's current meaning. However, the police also blew whistles to alert the public to violations—in this case, the misdeeds of fleeing criminals. In the earlier, broader sense of drawing attention to a situation, either origin could work equally well.

The term *whistleblower* first appears in 1970. The *New York Times* of March 23, 1970, contains this use: "When they reflect more fully on how the majority leader handled a whistle-blower and protected their interests . . ." Today, whistleblowing is nearly always connected to government or corporate scandals and misuses of power.

SHOOT THE WORKS.

Go to the limit or to an extreme of an activity; risk everything.

This expression probably originates with the venerable American dice game called craps. Craps is the modern version of the European game hazard, first played during the Middle Ages. Both games involve throwing two dice and betting on the outcome. The player rolling the dice in the American version of the game is called the *shooter*, and the game itself is usually known as *shooting craps*. (*Craps* may be a corruption of *crabs*. The lowest throw at hazard—two ones—was known as *crabs*, or *turning up crabs*. In craps games, this throw is called *snake eyes*, something those living in frontier America may actually have confronted on occasion.)

Like poker and faro (see *play both ends against the middle*, p. 153), craps was first played in New Orleans. A New Orleans native named Bernard de Marigny introduced the game sometime during the 1840s. In an 1848 exposé of gambling in America titled *An Exposure of the Arts and Miseries of Gambling*, author Jonathan Green describes craps this way: "This is a game lately introduced into New Orleans and is fully equal to faro in its vile deception and ruinous effects."

In spite of its ruinous potential, the game was highly popular. It soon spread from New Orleans to the rest of the country. Part of the appeal of craps was that it didn't require a casino. The game could be played informally by any two or more people who happened to have a couple of dice. That made it the perfect game for those who enjoyed gambling but were stuck out on the range or otherwise cut off from big-city entertainment. Another appealing aspect of craps for gamblers was that spectators, as well as the shooter, could place bets on which numbers would turn up. Avid gamblers were ready to bet *the works*— slang for "everything" since the beginning of the twentieth century— on a throw of the dice.

Shoot the works has been a metaphor for going to an extreme since at least the 1920s. Eugene O'Neill uses the expression in his 1922 play, *The Hairy Ape*. The character Yank, speaking with an old-fashioned Brooklyn accent, says, "Can't youse see I belong? . . . I'll stick, get me? I'll shoot de woiks for youse."

The modern use of the phrase often signifies a serious cash outlay. People planning a wedding or a special party say they've decided to shoot the works—go all out financially to stage a memorable event. The expression can also mean putting your best effort into an activity. For example, *The Dodgers: 120 Years of Dodgers Baseball* by Glenn Stout and Richard A. Johnson, published in 2004, includes the sentence "On the last day both clubs [the Dodgers and the Astros] shot the works," meaning they played their hardest.

GO FOR BROKE.
Make a strenuous effort; risk everything.

The 442nd Regimental Combat Team is credited with introducing this expression during World War II. The 442nd was made up of Japanese Americans, many of them from Hawaii, and the phrase is sometimes described as Hawaiian pidgin slang or Nisei (first-generation Japanese American) slang. Pfc. Larry Sakamoto describes the evolution of *go for broke* in *The Stars and Stripes Story of World War II*, published in 1960 by the military newspaper *Stars and Stripes*. "Our main slogan," he says, "is 'go for broke.' That means the same thing as 'Shoot the works' in American slang. The fellows first started to use the expression in a crap game, and they used it so much . . . that we became known as the 'Go for broke' boys."

Go for broke obviously began life as a gambling term. *Go* was a common word for betting during the nineteenth century. An 1842 *Spirit of Times* newspaper contains the line "They went their entire pile." It especially meant to agree to a wager, as in *I'll go you five dollars that your horse loses. Broke* meaning "bereft of funds" has been around since the eighteenth century. Willingness to "go," or bet, to the point of being broke meant making a serious commitment.

By 1960, *go for broke* was part of mainstream American slang. Murray Burton Levin uses the expression in his 1962 book, *The Compleat Politician*: "On the basis of the poll the Peabody brain-trusters . . . decided not to . . . 'go for broke.'" The 1951 movie *Go for Broke*, about the 442nd Regimental Combat Team, no doubt helped popularize the expression.

GO THE WHOLE NINE YARDS.
Do everything possible; go all out; indulge yourself to the limit.

The whole nine yards is one of those mysterious expressions that stimulate the creative juices of language enthusiasts. Several etymologists have noted that they receive more inquiries about this puzzling phrase than any other idiom. Unfortunately, although theories of origin proliferate, few of them stand up to any sort of scrutiny. About the only things word researchers know for sure is that the expression is fairly recent and the earliest examples in print are connected with the Vietnam War.

Elaine Shepard's 1967 novel of soldiers in Vietnam, *The Doom Pussy*, uses the phrase several times, including in this reference to a Danang barber: "Most Americans enjoyed getting the full nine yards that is included in the French barber's repertoire." Shepard spent time in Vietnam as a reporter before writing her book and probably picked up the expression there. Another citation from the sixties is found in the military newspaper *Pacific Stars and Stripes* for November 13, 1967: "Ann-Margaret . . . she dances, sings, acts—the whole nine yards." The April 1970 issue of *Word Watching* lists *the whole nine yards* with the definition "the entire thing."

Many people think first of football when they hear the phrase, since that's a game where yards count. However, the crucial number of yards for making a first down is ten, not nine. It has been suggested that the use of *nine* is ironic, implying that whoever ran the whole nine yards did not go quite far enough, but this interpretation is difficult to reconcile with the expression's actual usage. Since *the whole nine yards* first appeared in print, it has always signified "the whole thing" or "the limit," and has not had ironic overtones. Also, there is no record of the expression being used in sports writing—usually fertile ground for new slang terms—until it was already an established part of the language.

Other popular theories include the number of yards on World War II machine-gun ammunition belts; the volume of cement that a cement mixer holds; the amount of cloth required to make a suit, a kilt, or a shroud; the amount of cloth found on an uncut bolt; and the number of yardarms on three-masted sailing ships. All of these explanations have problems.

In a February 14, 2002, posting on the American Dialect Society's discussion list, Michael Quinion, author of the Web site *World Wide Words*, passed on some relevant information about the length of machine-gun belts. He received the information from British journalist John Morrish, who made inquiries at the Imperial War Museum in Cambridgeshire. The museum's curators told Morrish that the belts for the Browning machine guns on display there were exactly twenty-seven feet—nine yards—long. However, subsequent ADS postings, especially by Dave Wilton, as well as facts found elsewhere, indicate that the explanation is not so clear-cut. Different models of World War II fighter planes carried varying amounts of ammunition. Ammunition belts can be any length, and most of those used during the war were much shorter than nine yards. Another argument against this explanation is that ammunition is never referred to in terms of belt length but rather in number of rounds. This story also fails to account for why *the whole nine yards* first appeared in the 1960s among American soldiers, rather than in World War II England, where these ammunition belts were used.

Several of the other alternatives share this same weakness. Cement mixers do not necessarily carry nine cubic yards of cement. According to various sources, cement mixers in the 1960s held about four-and-a-half cubic yards. Modern cement trucks typically have a capacity of around eight cubic yards. Likewise, an uncut bolt of cloth measures thirty yards or more. Suits, depending on the size of the person and the width of the fabric, might require anywhere from three to six yards of cloth. Modern kilts typically call for six to eight yards. Even if any of the measurements in question did equal nine yards, it's difficult to imagine how the specialized jargon of the cement or tailoring industries could have found its way into mainstream English, especially if it arrived via Vietnam vets. The "ship's yardarm" explanation can be dispensed with on similar grounds. Although some fully rigged sailing ships have three masts, each with three yards (horizontal cross-pieces that hold the sails)—making nine yards in all—other ships have four or five masts and more than nine yards. Sailing ships are no more likely to have contributed to 1960s slang than cement mixers or kilts.

Interestingly, nine yards of cloth does appear to be a standard measurement for shrouds in some regions, such as the Appalachian Mountains. The poem "Nine Yards of Other Cloth" by M. W. Wellman appeared in the November 1958 *Magazine of Fantasy and Science Fiction*: "I'll weave nine yards of other cloth / For John to have and keep / He'll need it where he's going to lie, / To warm him in his sleep." However, bridging the meaning gap between shrouds and going all out is a bit of a stretch.

Another story of military origins, posted on Barry Popik's Web site *The Big Apple*, comes from Cmdr. Richard Stratton. Stratton recalls first hearing the expression during the 1950s at the Navy

School of Preflight. It figured as the punch line of a racy story about a fictional Scotsman named Andy McTavish and his sweetheart, Mary Margaret. This long shaggy dog story, which involves some confusion concerning Andy McTavish's private attributes and a long knitted scarf, ends with the punch line "What? The whole nine yards?" This story is interesting because it indicates that the expression was familiar in military circles as early as the 1950s. However, the story itself is unlikely to be the origin of the phrase. Punch lines that rely on a figure of speech are not funny unless that expression already has some significance for the audience. *The whole nine yards* would have been a known slang phrase when the joke was being told.

Some sources suggest that the expression is related to the nearly obsolete idiom *to the nines*, meaning "to perfection" or "to the ultimate." This phrase is still occasionally heard, as in *dressed to the nines*. An example of an earlier use comes from the 1719 *Familiar Epistles between William Hamilton and Allan Ramsay*: "How to the nines they did content me." *The nines* is said to be an allusion to the fact that the number nine signifies completion or perfection in some systems of numerology.

The number nine might have made the expression more appealing to people because of its mythic weight. Dante's *Divine Comedy* describes nine circles of hell and nine spheres of heaven. Greek mythology has nine muses, and Germanic mythology describes nine realms of existence. Cats have nine lives, and wonders last for nine days.

The theory that comes closest to connecting Vietnam is the idea that *yards* refers to the Montagnard (pronounced mawn-tin-YARD) hill tribes. The Montagnards, now known as Hmong, cooperated with the US military during the war. American soldiers working with them often shortened their name to "Yards." In 1970 Robert L. Mole published a book titled *The Montagnards of South Vietnam: A Study of Nine Tribes*. Some word historians believe *the whole nine yards* refers to this title. Alternatively, some veterans of the war claim that Special Operations Group teams were made up of three soldiers and nine

Montagnard tribesmen. Either way, this etymology faces some of the same problems as the others that have been proposed. Normal English usage would refer to people as *all (nine Montagnards)* rather than *the whole*. It's also very difficult to wring anything like the phrase's figurative meaning out of American interactions with Vietnam's hill tribes. Despite its shortcomings, this solution is more probable than others in some ways—it does hit the target area in terms of time and place.

Unless new print evidence comes to light—an unlikely contingency, considering the number of etymologists who have already made exhaustive searches—the exact origin of this intriguing phrase will remain a mystery. *Go the whole nine yards* continues to be a popular way of describing extravagant behavior. In recent years, younger speakers have shortened the original phrase to *go the whole nine*.

Going the whole nine yards and other extravagant behavior wasn't always acceptable in America. The grand gestures of acting and the theater were at one time highly suspect, and even considered immoral.

Chapter 9

GREAT PERFORMANCES

The theater was slow to gain a foothold in the British colonies, since it was hampered by Puritan disapproval. In areas with a strong Puritan presence like New England, attending plays was forbidden for most of the eighteenth century. However, British touring companies began arriving in less Puritanical regions such as Virginia by 1750, offering Shakespeare and other tried and true theatrical chestnuts. By the 1830s, Americans were writing their own plays. These plays often featured characters such as Nimrod Wildfire, the hero of *The Lion of the West*, by J. K. Paulding. In the play, Wildfire puts a characteristically American spin on his description of himself: "half horse, half alligator and a touch of the airthquake." He was a tough backwoodsman who could "outrun, outjump, throw down, drag out and whip any man in all Kaintuck."

In spite of linguistic fireworks such as these, American theater has not been a hotbed of figurative expressions. As with underworld lingo, the jargon of the stage and other entertainment venues is meant for insiders only. Little of it has entered mainstream American English. Vaudeville has contributed *slapstick, ad lib, cornball, one-liner, knock 'em dead, schmaltz*, and *schtick*. From P. T. Barnum's big top we get *ballyhoo, jumbo, dog and pony show*, and *three-ring circus*. Movie words and phrases that have entered the larger vocabulary include *flashback, close-up, star, fade-out, subtitle, mob scene, casting couch, back at the ranch, lights-camera-action*, and *Mickey Mouse* as an adjective.

The theatrical term *play in Peoria* is discussed in chapter 5, "People and Places."

JUMP ON THE BANDWAGON.

Join a currently popular cause; align yourself with what appears to be the winning side.

Before the days of mechanized floats, parades featured bandwagons—large, sturdy horse-drawn wagons, slowly towing brass bands through the streets as they played. The earliest example of the word in print is found in showman P. T. Barnum's 1854 autobiography: "At Vicksburg we sold all our conveyances excepting four horses and the 'band wagon.'" *Pictorial History of the American Circus* by John and Alice Durant shows a publicity illustration of P. T. Barnum's circus parade. Among the procession of elephants, bareback riders, caged tigers, and sideshow "freaks" is an elaborately decorated carriage pulled by a string of horses. Band members are shown seated inside in facing rows, playing their instruments.

Bandwagons gained popularity in political circles during the 1848 presidential campaign of Zachary Taylor. One of Taylor's supporters was a well-known circus owner and clown named Dan Rice. Rice sometimes invited Taylor onto his bandwagon and paraded him through town to meet and greet potential voters. According to the story, other politicians from Taylor's Whig Party, seeing the resulting publicity, vied to be taken up on the bandwagon too. Bandwagons soon became a necessary part of any campaign. The *New York Evening Post* for October 21, 1905, describes one candidate's bandwagon moving through the streets, saying, "It bears on its sides announcements of . . . mass meetings."

By the 1890s, jumping on, hopping on, climbing on, or otherwise boarding the bandwagon meant latching onto a winner. Theodore Roosevelt wrote drily in an 1899 letter, "When once I became sure of the majority they tumbled over each other to get aboard the band wagon." Horse-drawn bandwagons had disappeared by the 1920s, and *jump on the bandwagon* was being used in nonpolitical contexts. Figurative bandwagons were beginning to carry social theories or trends.

Predictably, *bandwagon* turned into a verb. *Bandwagoning* means joining a popular movement or embracing the latest fad. It can also suggest copycat criminal behavior. The *bandwagon effect* describes people's tendency to follow the crowd. Once a trend catches on, it has appeal simply because other people have adopted it. One example is the inclination to vote for someone you think will win, based on polls showing that he or she already has strong support.

CHEW THE SCENERY.
Overact; be melodramatic.

This term has been used figuratively since at least the late nineteenth century. Mary Hallock Foote's 1895 book about miners, *Coeur d'Alene*, includes the line "Lads, did ye hear him chewin' the scenery, givin' himself away like a play-actor?" By the time western miners were saying it, *chewing the scenery* (or *chewing up the scenery*) must have been a well-established term.

Chewing the scenery was obviously never a literal activity. Actors might have been hard on the scenery and props in other ways though, while energetically interpreting their roles. Stock melodramas performed by touring companies were enormously popular in the nineteenth century. These intensely dramatic, action-filled plays traditionally included the scheming villain, the damsel in distress, the pure-hearted hero, and a couple of comic characters included for light relief. Good always triumphed over evil, but not until the damsel had gotten herself into a number of hair-raising situations. Melodramas begged for over-the-top, scenery-chewing performances.

Hollywood later adopted this classic format in such film series as *The Perils of Pauline*, the probable source of *cliffhanger*. To draw the audience back for the next installment, the movie always ended with the unfortunate Pauline hanging from a cliff or in some other desperate plight. Later, the early sixties television cartoon *The Rocky and Bull-*

winkle Show parodied old-time melodramas. One segment of the show was a satire featuring heroic Mountie Dudley Do-Right, his sweetheart Nell, and the villain Snidely Whiplash.

In recent decades, *chew the scenery* has become a staple cliché for reviewers. Examples of its use abound. An early one from a Dorothy Parker review, written in 1930, describes an actor this way: "More glutton than artist . . . he commences to chew up the scenery."

LAY AN EGG.

Fail, especially publicly; take part in a failed theatrical production.

This expression appears most famously in the *Variety* headline of October 30, 1929: "Wall Street Lays an Egg." This news item describes the stock market crash the day before, a financial catastrophe that ushered in the Great Depression of the 1930s. *Variety* obviously considered the crash a failed performance of a spectacular sort, writing, "The most dramatic event in the financial history of America is the collapse of the New York Stock Market."

Curiously, although *Variety* clearly expected its readers to understand the figurative meaning of *lay an egg*, the 1929 headline marks its first appearance in print, except for a line in J. P. McEvoy's *Hollywood Girl*, also published in 1929: "Boys, it looks like we laid an egg." In the entertainment world that formed *Variety*'s audience, the term must have been a familiar one. However, it could not have been in wide circulation or it probably would have appeared elsewhere in print. The headline itself may have introduced *lay an egg* to a more general audience.

Variety—a weekly magazine first published in 1905 covering the New York theater world—is known for its creative use of showbiz jargon, especially abbreviations and word shortenings. Part of the reason for the magazine's characteristic short, zippy stylings is to pack a lot of information into the space of a headline. One example is "Sticks Nix Hick Pix." This headline, famously quoted in the musical *Yankee Doodle Dandy*, conveys the information that rural audiences are rejecting movies set in the countryside. Like all jargon, *Variety*'s version is mainly directed at show biz insiders. However, *Variety* coinages do occasionally escape into the mainstream vocabulary. Three examples are *deejay* (disc jockey), *sitcom* (situation comedy), and *pix* (pictures).

It's unclear how *lay an egg* came to mean flop publicly. The *Random House Historical Dictionary of American Slang* speculates that it might be related to the metaphorical meaning of *turkey*—a failed play. This sense of *turkey* has been in use since at least the 1920s. (It does not appear to be connected to *talk turkey*, a much older expression.)

The theatrical sense of *lay an egg* is apparently unrelated to the World War I fighter pilot slang *lay an egg* or *lay eggs*, meaning "to drop bombs." In this case, *egg* is almost certainly a straightforward reference to the shape of the bombs and the fact that they are dropped from the belly of the plane. *Lay an egg* is also unconnected to the slang term *bomb*, meaning "to fail" or a show that failed, which didn't come into circulation until the 1960s.

Laying an egg is now possible in many different entertainment venues, and even in everyday life, such as during an unsuccessful date. A recent example from the National Football League Draft Site blog is this December 26, 2006, headline: "The Cowboys Lay an Egg on Christmas." The blogger is referring here to the Dallas Cowboys' 23–7 loss to the Philadelphia Eagles.

WING IT.
Improvise.

This term first began appearing in the late nineteenth century. The magazine *Stage* for August 21, 1885, says that *wing it* "indicates the capacity to play a *rôle* without knowing the text, and the word itself came into use from the fact that the artiste frequently received the assistance of a special prompter who . . . stood . . . [and was] screened . . . by a piece of scenery or the wing." The past tense used here suggests that the expression was already considered an old one in theatrical circles.

A slightly different explanation of the origin comes from Philip Godfrey's 1933 book, *Back-stage*: ". . . 'winging it' . . . refreshing his memory for each scene in the wings before he goes on to play it." In this version, no prompter is involved.

Wing it was evidently a theatrical term for several decades before the general public started using it. The phrase doesn't appear in nontheatrical contexts until around the 1950s. *Esquire* magazine for November 1959 thought it necessary to define *wing* for its readers as "do something without preparation." Today, *wing it* can be used for any kind of improvisation, although it often has something to do with a public appearance, as in *I forgot my notes for the speech, so I had to wing it*. The expression can also mean making up strategy as you go along, for example, *We'll just see how the client responds and then wing it*.

HAM IT UP.

Show off; overact; dramatize yourself.

Ham, as in ham acting, comes from an older term, *ham-fatter*. George Sala first put the word into print in his 1879 book, *America Revisited*. He writes, "Every American who does not wish to be thought 'small potatoes' or a 'ham-fatter' or a 'corner loafer' is carefully 'barbed' and fixed up in a hair-dressing salon every day." According to tradition, ham fat was part of the equipment of old-time jazz musicians. A 1966 *New Yorker* piece on Louisiana music alludes to this claim: "Most of the musicians playing in these clubs are old men. . . . They're hamfat musicians. In the old days, the rough musicians kept pieces of ham fat in their pockets to grease the slides of their trombones." By the time Sala used the word in his book, it had become synonymous with a third-rate performer or other low-class person.

The word *ham-fat* is thought to have entered the vernacular through a popular minstrel song called "The Hamfat Man." Most early uses of the term refer to musicians, such as a group calling themselves the Harlem Hamfats. A story from an 1882 issue of *Illustrated Sporting and Dramatic News* seems to confirm the musical connection: "'Banjo Hams' are held up to scorn. . . . One writer proudly describes himself as 'no ham, but a classical banjo player.'"

By the end of the nineteenth century, *ham-fat* had been shortened to *ham* and it meant a third-rate actor or vaudevillian. An article in the March 13, 1881, *Washington Post* says, "The 'variety' player is looked down upon by the legitimate actor and is called a 'ham.'" In the twentieth century, the term began to refer to any overdramatic presentation, such as an unpersuasive sob story. A character in Raymond Chandler's 1942 *High Window* says, "Don't feed me the ham. I've been in pictures. I'm a connoisseur of ham." Hamming it up now covers any sort of showing off, as in *The kids started hamming it up as soon as their mother pulled out her camera.*

TAKE A BRODIE.

Take a serious fall; in show business, flop spectacularly.

Early examples of *brodie* are often spelled with a capital letter, indicating that the word originated with a personal name—that of Steve Brodie. Steve Brodie was a bookmaker and all-around self-promoter in late nineteenth-century Brooklyn. He claimed to have leaped off the 135-foot-high central span of the Brooklyn Bridge on July 23, 1886, saying he did it to win a two-hundred-dollar bet. No one saw him jump, and in fact he probably didn't. A few months earlier, an intrepid swimming instructor named Robert Odlum had attempted the same feat and died of internal injuries. Brodie, on the other hand, performed his stunt injury free. Skeptics concluded that he had a friend throw a bolster off the bridge while he waited below in the water until the rescue boats appeared on the scene.

Nonetheless, the publicity paid off. Whether they believed in it or not, newspapers gave the event wide coverage. Brodie was able to parlay his fame into a successful vaudeville career, performing in shows where he re-created his famous daredevil leap. He also opened a Bowery saloon and packed in the customers by mounting a "jump" exhibit. Displays included the clothes he was wearing and an affidavit from the rescue boat captain. Best of all, Brodie earned a spot in the American slang lexicon.

The first figurative use of *brodie* appears in the 1899 *Billy Baxter's Letters* by George Kountz: "K. C. . . . did a Brodie out of his chair and lit on his eye." An alternative meaning, current from the early twentieth century, is to take a large risk, on par with jumping off the Brooklyn Bridge. The 1926 *Wise-Crack Dictionary* defines *do a Steve Brodie* as take a chance. It could also mean taking a gamble or a guess. For example, someone might say, *I took a brodie on a start-up company*.

Yet another meaning is to fail utterly in the entertainment world. This use of *brodie* does not refer to Steve Brodie's business acumen—after all, he was a show-business success—but to the idea of taking a painful flop. An early use comes from the *New York Times* of December 23, 1917: "They 'did a Brodie' up at the Royal." A brodie is more than an ordinary failure. It is a complete, unmitigated disaster. *Brodie* can also be a verb in this context, as in *If my next show brodies, I think I'll retire.*

As the heyday of Steve Brodie recedes into the past, the word is most often spelled with a lowercase *b*. It is sometimes incorrectly spelled with a final *y* (*brody*) instead of an *ie*. You can do a brodie as well as take one.

FACE THE MUSIC.

Confront danger; accept adverse consequences of your own making.

In the nineteenth century, *music* could mean trouble or danger, especially gunfire. The *Congressional Globe* for March 1850 contains the exhortation "There should be no skulking or dodging . . . every man should 'face the music.'" Later, as the Civil War got under way, many men did just that. E. H. Rhodes describes the scene in his 1865 book,

All for the Union: "The air is full of bursting shell. The Rebels are replying, and we have 'Music in the air.'"

Linguist Maximilian Schele de Vere offers two origins theories in his 1872 book, *Americanisms: The English of the New World*: "*Face the music:* derived, according to J. F. Cooper, from the stage, and used by actors in the green-room, when they are nervously preparing to go on the boards and literally face the music. Another explanation traces it back to militia musters, where every man is expected to appear fully equipped and armed, when in rank and file, facing the music." *Music* in the second explanation is a specialized military term meaning the troops who sound signals on a musical instrument, for instance, a bugle.

The earliest print appearances of *face the music* are all connected with facing battle or gunfire. However, by the end of the nineteenth century, the phrase could mean to face any kind of unpleasant consequences. *New England Magazine* for September 1893 includes the sentence "His 'sober second thought' decided him to face the music, confess his fault and make the best of it." These days, facing the music usually means getting an unpleasant ordeal over with, as in *I'm on my way to the supervisor's office to face the music.*

Another kind of unmelodious nineteenth-century music was *chin music*. Chin music meant chatter beginning in the 1830s. By the 1880s, the meaning had narrowed to denote baseball players' chatter, as well as all the crowd noises that accompany a game. Very recently the meaning has shifted again. Sports announcers now refer to a ball pitched high or close to the batter's head as chin music. Probably inadvertently, they are once again using the word *music* with its nineteenth-century implications of trouble or danger.

WHISTLE DIXIE.
Make an empty boast or irrelevant statement.

This expression is virtually always used with *not*—*You're not just whistling Dixie* (or more colloquially, *You ain't just whistlin' Dixie*). It means that the speaker is not just mouthing empty words but has said something significant and true. The phrase began appearing in print around the 1940s—Pierre Berton, writing in *Adventures of a Columnist*, claims to have heard it first in a Daffy Duck cartoon around 1941. However, the expression could well be much older. The word *Dixie* itself has been widely familiar since the Civil War.

The exact origin of *Dixie* is an intriguing question. Its first known appearance in print is in the song titled "Dixie's Land," written in 1859 by Dan Emmett. Emmett wrote the song for a minstrel show, an early form of vaudeville. Minstrel shows featured white musicians appearing in "blackface"; that is, they smeared their faces with burnt cork to appear as Southern black characters. Players typically performed a folksy mix of jokes, dances, and songs meant to be reminiscent of the Old South. Although minstrel shows now seem like a bizarre form of entertainment, they were popular in all parts of the country during most of the nineteenth century. Toward the end of the century, African Americans produced their own versions of these shows, performing for both white and black audiences. Emmett wrote "Dixie's Land" as a "walk-around," to be sung during the part of the performance when the troupe wandered among the audience.

Where Emmett found the term *Dixie* is unclear. Various etymologies have been put forward. One that is highly unlikely but often cited claims that the original Dixie was a kindly slave owner living on a large tract of land in Manhattan. When antislavery sentiment forced him to sell some of his slaves (or to move South with them, depending on the version of the story), his former workers discovered that other locales were not as ideal as "Dixie's land." They often wished they were back in their old Dixie home. Eventually the term entered the language as a synonym for a desirable place. Aside from the absurdity of this story as whole, it fails to explain how the name of a Northern slave owner could have been transposed into a term for the South. No evidence exists that *Dixie* or *Dixie's land* were ever used to refer to a specific plantation, either in Dixie's supposed original home of Manhattan or in the South.

Another suggestion is that *Dixie* comes from the ten-dollar notes issued by the Louisiana Citizen's Bank before the Civil War. Supposedly they were called dixies from the word *dix*, French for ten, which was printed on their reverse side. This idea is more plausible than the first. However, the word with this meaning does not appear in any print sources of the time.

A third possibility is that the word derives from the Mason-Dixon line. This boundary line, surveyed by Charles Mason and Jeremiah Dixon in the 1760s, runs between Maryland and Pennsylvania. By the nineteenth century, it was commonly considered a dividing line between the North and the South. Some support for this origin comes from an 1862 magazine article by Henry Hotze, reprinted in *The Confederate Reader*. Hotze claims that the refrain "I wish I was in Dixie" is much older than Emmett's tune. He writes, "The word 'Dixie' is an abbreviation of 'Mason and Dixon's line.' . . . Years before I heard the tune I have heard negroes in the North use the word 'Dixie' in that sense." Hotze comments further, "It is marvellous with what wild-fire rapidity this tune . . . has spread over the whole South . . . it now bids fair to become the musical symbol of a new nationality, and we shall be fortunate if it does not impose its very name on our country."

Hotze's fears were realized—Dixie soon became a universal nickname for the Confederacy. As the United States careened toward the Civil War, Southerners embraced Emmett's song, with its catchy melody and rousing chorus of "I wish I was in Dixie, Hooray! Hooray! In Dixieland I'll take my stand to live and die in Dixie . . ." Southerners wrote patriotic verses to the tune, such as those by Confederate Brigadier General Albert Pike, which begin, "Southrons, hear your country call you! Up, lest worse than death befall you!" The song was also well known in the North. Parodies appeared there with lyrics such as "I wish I was in Baltimore, I'd make Secession traitors roar . . ."

The expression *not just whistling Dixie* remains popular. Today, newspaper headlines often use it with a double meaning for articles concerning the South. For example, a July 7, 2007, story about presidential hopeful Rudy Giuliani's trip to Savannah posted on the *South Georgia Liberal* blog was headed "Giuliani Whistling Dixie." The headline is mainly a reference to Giuliani's visit to "Dixie," but it also implies a negative opinion about his public appearances.

GO TO TOWN.

Accomplish a task with great energy; enjoy yourself unrestrainedly.

Go to town originated in the 1930s as a jazz term. A 1935 issue of *Stage* defines *go to town* as to "play hot." *Swing That Music*, published in 1936, says, "That phrase 'goin' to town' means cuttin' loose and takin' the music with you." Robert S. Gold suggests in *Jazz Talk* that the expression alludes to the excitement of rural folks going up to town for the day.

By 1940, *go to town* had expanded to cover activities unrelated to jazz. An early example comes from *Variety* for July 15, 1936: "At last those three ace fun makers . . . get a chance to go to town in a big time laugh hit of their own." Another typical use appears in J. B. Priestley's 1946 *Bright Day*: "The only writer who ever made . . . Gruman pay him a royalty on the gross. . . . And did we go to town with it."

Going to town can also mean cutting loose in a negative way, for instance, *The reviewers really went to town on his last novel.* The online *Urban Dictionary* gives the expression a modern definition of "action(s) performed in a hardcore manner," with examples of beating someone up, making love, and dancing.

CUT TO THE CHASE.

Get to the point.

This expression originated in the early days of film. It first appears in print as an editing direction in J. P. McEvoy's *Hollywood Girl*, published in 1929: "Jannings escapes. . . . Cut to chase." Chase scenes have always been a popular feature of movies. The first Western,

1903's *The Great Train Robbery*, includes a thrilling chase scene as the posse tracks down the bandits. Although the phrase is often associated with Westerns, most of which feature more than one scene of the good guys chasing the bad guys (or vice versa), other kinds of chase scenes are popular as well. No modern action movie would be complete without a car chase. *Cutting* in the film world means editing. To create a fast-paced movie, film editors must cut the boring, slow scenes and quickly get to the exciting action scenes.

Cut to the chase was familiar as an editing direction for decades before it entered the language as a figure of speech. By the late forties, the expression was beginning to appear in print. An early example comes from Frank Scully's 1955 autobiography, *Cross My Heart*: "I am the sort who wants to 'cut to the chase.' As far as I'm concerned we can read the instructions later." The phrase grew more popular beginning in the 1980s and is now part of colloquial English.

※※※

Besides cutting to the chase, early Westerns also immortalized the shoot-out. Expertise with guns was a prized skill on the American frontier, and gunslinglers had their own unique vocabulary.

Chapter 10

MARKSMANSHIP

Words and expressions related to guns and shooting are an integral part of the American language. Hunting was more than a sport in the early days of the country. Settlers relied on wild game for a large part of their diet. Men hunted often in groups, sometimes bagging hundreds of animals a day. Guns were also handy for protection from dangerous wildlife, as well as any human varmints who might be about. Frontiersmen kept their skills honed with shooting matches. These were family events that included picnics, as well as prize competitions for the best marksmen.

Americans are familiar enough with firearms to make the origins of most shooting-related expressions seem obvious. Phrases incorporating *gun* include *be gun shy, go gunning for someone, bring out the big guns, go great guns*, and *stick to your guns*. Guns also figure in *lock, stock, and barrel, trigger-happy, quick on the draw, shoot down an idea, shoot yourself in the foot, give it your best shot*, and *dodge the bullet*. A shot can be *a shot in the dark, a long shot*, or *scattershot*. If we don't succeed at a task the first time, we can always *take another shot at it*.

Listed below are several expressions whose origins are less obvious than most.

GET THE DROP ON SOMEONE.

Gain an advantage over someone.

In the days of the Wild West, getting the drop on someone meant having the chance to shoot before your opponent could raise his weapon, a clear advantage in a gunfight. The earliest known example of this expression appears in Alexander McClure's *Three Thousand Miles through the Rocky Mountains*, published in 1869: "So expert is he with his faithful pistol . . . rogues have repeatedly attempted in vain to get 'the drop' on him." McClure's use of quotation marks suggests the phrase was still recent.

How did a man get the drop on his enemies? Probably by grasping the stock, or "handle" of his weapon, the wooden part of a pistol or shotgun that attaches to the barrel. The *Dictionary of American English on Historical Principles* lists *drop of stock* as a nineteenth-century term for "the bend or crook of the stock below the line of the barrel." When pulling a pistol out of its holster, a shooter would likely grasp the drop of stock. The trick to surviving shoot-outs would be to get the drop before your trigger-happy foes did.

Nineteenth-century uses of *get the drop* refer literally to firearms, but the phrase was being used figuratively by the early decades of the twentieth century. British novelist Nicholas Blake used it that way in his 1940 *Malice in Wonderland*: "He suspects Miss Thistlethwaite . . . of having got the drop on him." *Get the drop* is still used literally in situations that call for it, as in a May 23, 1970, *New Yorker* article that describes FBI agents trying to sneak up on a hijacker to "get the drop" on him. Now the expression is more often used in its figurative sense.

SHOOT FROM THE HIP.

Speak or act impulsively; speak frankly, without regard for the consequences.

One way to get the drop on an opponent was to shoot from the hip. This figure of speech comes from the act of firing a handgun immediately after pulling it from its holster, without stopping to take aim. Americans are familiar with this maneuver from Western films. No classic Western is complete without a gunslinger who can whip his six-shooter out of the holster and fire before his unlucky opponent even realizes the gun is drawn.

Although many historians believe this scenario is exaggerated, the technique was genuinely in use in the nineteenth century. An early literal example of *shoot from the hip* comes from the magazine *Galaxy* in March 1869. *Galaxy* instructs its readers, "Point your pistol quickly with your forefinger along the barrel; don't stop to take aim, but shoot at once from the hip." Guns were considered a necessity on the western frontier for protection against outlaws and other hazards. Many people—both men and women—carried revolvers made by Colt, Smith & Wesson, or Remington. In his 1854 *Journey through Texas*, Frederick Olmsted remarks, "There are probably in Texas as many revolvers as male adults."

Shoot from the hip has been used figuratively since around the mid-twentieth century. For example, the *American Economic Review* for 1951 includes the sentence "Very often, the executive has to shoot from the hip." *Shoot-from-the-hip* is also used as an adjective. This sentence from the February 17, 1975, issue of *Business Week* is a typical example: "Some observers think the claim is a shoot-from-the-hip guess."

TAKE A CHEAP SHOT.
Make a wounding or an unfair remark.

Aiming sharp words at someone has been known since the nineteenth century as *taking a shot*. *The shot went home* indicates that an insult hit its target. Other versions are a *parting shot*, fired off as you're leaving the room, and the nineteenth-century expression *Parthian shot*. Parthian shots were named for the ancient Parthians, who had a habit of firing arrows backward over their shoulders as they retreated.

It seems likely that cheap shots are related to the well-aimed insults of earlier times. However, this particular kind of shot appeared suddenly in the 1970s and was first used in sports. It didn't refer to speech but to unsportsmanlike actions. Although some etymologists speculate that the term derives from boxing matches, the first known examples come from football. The *Second Barnhart Dictionary of New English* gives as its earliest citation these lines from the December 19, 1967, *New York Times*: "Davidson since has had a reputation among the Jets as a 'cheap shot' performer. In pro football jargon, a cheap shot is an unnecessary tackle or block when an opponent is defenseless."

Almost immediately after *cheap shot* entered the sports vernacular, it moved to cover politics as well. In this case, the phrase meant figuratively knocking down an opponent when he or she wasn't expecting it or was in a weak position. Any remark that succeeds in breaching a politician's armor is invariably labeled a cheap shot. Newspapers who report scandals or failures are accused of taking cheap shots. A letter to the editor of the *New York Times Magazine*, published on October 10, 1976, begins, "Bruce Porter's article . . . contains one omission and two cheap shots which call for a response."

Sports players and others who are especially good at bringing down their foes are called *cheap-shot artists*. And of course the term has been verbed, as in this quote from the *New York Times Magazine* for December 8, 1991: "[Hockey player Brett] Hull . . . is a practicing pacifist on the ice, refusing to fight and even proclaiming himself loath to cheap-shot an opponent."

TAKE A POT-SHOT.
Criticize someone, especially randomly or opportunistically.

Pot-shot has been current since the mid-nineteenth century to mean shooting at an animal with the intention of killing it for food, without regard for the rules of sportsmanship—shooting a sitting duck, for example. Pot-shots can also be random or careless shots, or shots aimed at whoever happens to be within range. A correspondent to the

Daily News, writing in 1877, describes a recent adventure when "a Russian sentry took a steady pot-shot at us." *Pot* is short for *pot-shot* in sentences like this one from a 1914 letter by Rudyard Kipling: "Every available male in England [is] scuttling into the ranks in order to get a gun to have a pot at the Germans." In sports, pot-shots are an opportunistic individual's attempt to score, as opposed to a play set up by the team.

Verbal pot-shots are an American invention. *Christian Century* for July 7, 1927, includes an early example of this use: "Let him take lusty potshots . . . at some poor, prostrate ghost of bygone years, and he is hailed as brilliant, erudite, and—curiously—daring!" Figurative pot-shotters have been around since mid-century. The 1942 *American Thesaurus of Slang* identifies this type as "a careless person." Pot-shotting is also possible, as in, *The author pot-shots his opinions, only hitting the target occasionally. Take a pot-shot* is still used both literally and figuratively.

JUMP THE GUN.
Act prematurely.

The *gun* in *jump the gun* belongs to sports rather than hunting. It's the starter's gun fired to signal the beginning of a race. In field sports, jumping the gun can have serious consequences. One incident earns the runner a warning; a second means disqualification.

Variations on the phrase are *beat the gun* and *beat the pistol*. An early sports use appears in the British *Rowing and Track Athletics* for 1905: "False starts were rarely penalized . . . 'beating the pistol' was one of the tricks which less sportsmanlike runners constantly practised."

By the 1930s, *jump the gun* was an Americanism meaning to act before the appropriate time. A typical example appears in a July 27, 1964, *Newsweek* advertisement for life insurance. Two proud parents chatting at the dinner table imagine their three-year-old son becoming president one day. Eventually, the prodigy's father comments, "I think we're both jumping the gun in talking about his chances." In recent decades, the figurative *jump the gun* has become part of mainstream English, usually used to suggest overeagerness that may bring a penalty. *Jump the gun* is also still used technically in racing. The alternatives *beat the pistol* and *beat the gun* appear to be obsolete.

From the mistake of jumping the gun we get another metaphor—*make a false start*. The false start to a race occurs when one or more of the participants moves before the signal has been given and then must return to the starting line. A figurative false start—in activities from singing to choosing a career—requires the person to begin again with a different approach. A typical use is the sentence *After one or two false starts, Carrie decided to major in architecture*.

BE LOADED FOR BEAR.

Be very well prepared, especially for a fight; be drunk.

This expression has been current since at least the 1880s when the *New York World* for October 19, 1888, reported, "Ewing was loaded for bear and was just spoiling for a chance to catch somebody on the bases." The *Dictionary of Slang, Jargon and Cant* from 1890 indicates that the "drunk" definition was current at the same time: "loaded for bears [plural] . . . signifies that a man is slightly intoxicated, enough to feel ready to confront danger." *Loaded for bear*, both then and now, could describe anyone bristling with indignation and hoping for a fight. It also describes someone thoroughly prepared for any emergency.

North America teemed with black bears and grizzlies when the first British settlers arrived. They were hunted for both meat and sport. Shooting bears requires heavy-duty ammunition. *The Hunter's Encyclopedia*, discussing how to hunt the Alaska brown bear, says, "Every experienced hunter has emphasized the need for extremes in bullet weight, velocity, and long-range accuracy for his hunting." Bear hunting carries a certain mystique—Theodore Roosevelt, among others, hunted bears then wrote about the experience.

Today, *loaded for bear* can refer literally to being very well armed, especially in the context of military operations. *CBS This Morning* reported on December 9, 1992, that the marines who landed in Somalia "hit the beach loaded for bear." More often, the expression means being fully prepared for a confrontation or challenge, as in Stan Pottinger's 2004 novel, *The Final Procedure*: "Melissa was loaded for bear when she entered the courtroom." It can also still mean "drunk," although *loaded* on its own is more common.

PRAISE THE LORD AND PASS THE AMMUNITION.
Let's combine piety with practicality.

United States Navy chaplain Howell Maurice Forgy is credited with introducing this maxim on December 7, 1941, during the Japanese attack on Pearl Harbor. Here is the story according to the *Athens (AL) Limestone Democrat*, published on February 26, 1942: "During a lull in the firing this man of God was heard to intone: 'Praise the Lord and pass the ammunition, I just got one of the s— of b—.'" Over time this story passed into legend. Various versions made the rounds of the military, and other chaplains besides Forgy were credited with inventing the saying.

Praise the Lord and pass the ammunition became a catchphrase in 1942 when composer Frank Loesser wrote an inspiring wartime song with that title. The first verse imagines the incident: "Down went the gunner, a bullet was his fate / Down went the gunner, then the gunner's mate / Up jumped the sky pilot, gave the boys a look / And manned the gun himself as he laid aside The Book, shouting / Praise the Lord and pass the ammunition!" Kay Kyser and His Orchestra recorded a version in 1943 that reached the top of the charts.

The Web site *Pearl Harbor Remembered* offers a different, although no less inspiring, version of the episode, provided by Henry Wristen, president of the USS *New Orleans* Reunion Association. He reaffirms that the expression's originator was indeed Howell Maurice Forgy. In this recollection of the event, Rev. Forgy walked along the

USS *New Orleans* ammunition line, encouraging the men by saying, "Praise the Lord and pass the ammunition." A lieutenant who was there remembers that "he was patting the men on the back and making that remark to cheer them and keep them going."

The expression is still a cultural reference. The *Times* of London for July 31, 1982, includes the question "Can we leave unchallenged those who believe it possible to praise God and pass the ammunition?" The phrase is also sometimes used as a general shout of encouragement.

RIDE SHOTGUN.
Accompany someone as a protector.

During much of the nineteenth century, mail, money, and people traveled west by stagecoach. The stage was the surest and fastest way to transport goods, but hauling gold or other valuables was a dangerous business. Bandits haunted the roads, looking to relieve stagecoaches of their treasure. For this reason, stagecoach drivers were nearly always accompanied by a shotgun messenger. These armed messengers rode next to the driver, keeping an eye out for trouble and ready to shoot if the need arose.

As far as anyone can discover, the shotgun messenger's job was never actually referred to as *riding shotgun*. The expression apparently arose in the twentieth century, invented by writers of dime novels and Hollywood Westerns. The Web site *The Straight Dope* has discovered the earliest print usage to date. It appears in the March 27, 1921, issue of *Magazine of Fiction*, published by the *Washington Post*. A story of the Old West titled "The Fighting Fool" includes this dialogue: "That's the man—Lum Martin! He's ridin' shotgun for Wells Fargo."

By the mid-twentieth century, *ride shotgun* was being used figuratively to mean go along in a protective role, either armed or not. One example of this use comes from B. S. Johnson's *Travelling People*, published in 1963: "And if you want anyone to ride shotgun for you, just you let Henry know." Also beginning around this time, riding shotgun could refer to sitting in the front passenger seat of an automobile. Children racing out to the car still shout, "I call shotgun!" *Ride shotgun* can also be completely figurative, as in riding shotgun on a piece of legislation making its way through Congress.

HOLD A SHOTGUN WEDDING.

Get married in a hurry, probably because the bride is pregnant; make a forced compromise or form an ill-considered alliance.

The term *shotgun wedding* conjures up an image of rough-and-ready pioneers or mountain folk at an impromptu wedding ceremony. The minister unites the tearful bride and uneasy groom in a hasty service. The bride's daddy sternly brandishes his shotgun until the ceremony is safely over. Whether or not such an episode ever really took place, its cultural underpinnings are solid enough to make it sound authentic. In Sinclair Lewis's 1927 novel, *Elmer Gantry*, which includes one of the earliest examples of the phrase *shotgun wedding*, no actual shotgun is involved. However, the bride's father and a cousin frog-march the unwilling Rev. Gantry to his engagement party after threatening him with a beating.

Shotgun wedding is also applied to forced alliances of other kinds. The *Baltimore Sun* for October 29, 1946, mentions charges that the United Nations' veto system was "a 'shotgun wedding' forced upon the small nations." An interesting use of the phrase as a verb appears in the October 23, 1995, edition of the *Birmingham News*: "The committee was questioning . . . on charges he had 'shotgun married' a Colorado power co-op to the Western Colorado Power Company." More recently, a 2003 *New York Times* article comments on an ill-advised culinary combination: "Kobe beef with potato-leek pirogi and a lush Perigueux sauce seems like a shotgun wedding." *Shotgun wedding* is also still used to describe hurried weddings, especially when a baby is thought to be on the way. Another version of the phrase is *shotgun marriage*.

※※※

Even in the rush of arranging a shotgun wedding, the bride will probably take time to put on her best outfit. Americans prefer to dress well for all occasions, and particularly on their wedding day.

PART 4:
THE HOME FRONT

Chapter 11

DRESSING WELL

American fashions of the eighteenth and nineteenth centuries generally followed those of England and other European countries. Until the 1840s, most clothing was made at home, except for people wealthy enough to afford tailors and dressmakers. Homemade outfits were called *homespun*. The best of them—say, a dress made of silk rather than of calico—served as Sunday go-to-meeting clothing. Outfits purchased at dry goods stores, known as *store clothes*, gradually replaced homespun after the Civil War. A German immigrant named Levi Strauss owned one such store, where he began selling blue jeans to San Francisco miners in 1853.

Occasionally Americans showed themselves to be fashion innovators. Around the middle of the nineteenth century, daring young ladies began appearing on the street in bloomer suits. These consisted of a close-fitting, short-skirted dress over a pair of bloomers—loose, full trousers gathered at the ankle. Amelia J. Bloomer, a social reformer, was responsible for popularizing the outfit. She believed a bloomer suit was healthier and more comfortable for active women than the voluminous skirts usually worn at this time. Unfortunately, the outfit never really caught on. Female trousers struck most people as slightly scandalous.

Mountain men were another fashion-forward group. They adopted buckskin clothing from Native Americans, who made the fabric by pounding deer hides until supple. A suit of buckskins was frequently topped off with a coonskin cap. Frontiersman extraordinaire Davy

Crockett is credited with introducing this look. Cowboys working the range preferred ten-gallon hats. Their eventual adoption by eastern dudes and tenderfeet gave rise to the description *all hat and no cattle*. Other commonly heard hat expressions include *keep it under your hat*, *I'll eat my hat*, *arrive hat in hand*, *wear many hats*, *throw your hat in the ring* (found in chapter 4, "Politics as Usual"), and an eighteenth-century synonym for being drunk, *got on his little hat*.

TALK THROUGH YOUR HAT.

Spout nonsense; exaggerate; bluff.

The first recorded use of this curious phrase comes from the May 12, 1888, issue of *New York World*. The paper quotes an interview subject saying, "Dis is only a bluff dey're makin'—see! Dey're talkin' tru deir hats." If the New Yorker on the street was using the expression so casually that the newspaper presented it without comment, it must have been fairly well established by this date. *Dialect Notes* for 1896 identifies *talk through one's hat* as a Northeastern regionalism, and it may have originated there. However, it was common everywhere in the country by the turn of the twentieth century.

What this expression originally alluded to is anybody's guess. Surprisingly, in spite of its bizarre imagery, the phrase has not inspired much in the way of imaginative origins theories. Evan Morris, author of *The Word Detective* column, lists a few of the possibilities. One theory claims that the phrase refers to men in church holding their hats in front of their faces while pretending to pray. Another suggestion connects the meaning with the emptiness of the hat crown perched above the wearer's head. In this case, the phrase could be a version of talking off the top of your head or, as the British say, talking through the back of your neck. The idea would be that you're talking through some part of your head other than the part that includes your brain.

Talk through your hat is still a familiar colloquialism. Modern uses lean more toward the "nonsense" meaning of the phrase rather than the "bluffing" or "lying" connotation—for example, *Experts are enthusi-*

astic about the future of the economy, but I think they're just talking through their hats.

BE READY AT THE DROP OF A HAT.
Be ready instantly.

Word historians widely assume that this expression originated with nineteenth-century conventions governing fistfights. For instance, *Brewer's Dictionary of Phrase and Fable* claims that "the expression alludes to the American frontier practice of dropping a hat as a signal for a fight to begin, usually the only formality observed." Many of the earliest examples in print do refer to hostile encounters. *The Western Avernus*, a travelogue of the American West published in 1887, includes the line "Ready to quarrel 'at the drop of a hat,' as the American saying goes." However, the *Oxford English Dictionary*'s earliest citation shows the phrase in another context. It comes from *Life of a Country Merchant*, published in 1854: "You said you'd marry me at the drop of a hat!" If the phrase originated with fighting, it's surprising that the earliest recorded use by several decades refers to an unrelated topic.

It's possible that the expression had originated elsewhere but appeared frequently in connection with fighting because sudden, casual bouts of fisticuffs were common in the Old West. Frontier-style tall talk usually included an offer to take on any and all comers "at the drop of a hat." Another possibility is that the drop of a hat did signal the beginning of a fight but was also a more general way of starting any kind of contest. For example, the typical starting signal for horse races during the nineteenth century was the downward sweep or wave of a hat. (References to starting pistols do not appear in print until the twentieth century. In any case, they would probably have been reserved for only the most official occasions.) In the context of a horse race, being ready to go at the drop of a hat would simply mean being poised for a quick start as soon as the signal was given.

Modern uses are compatible with a general meaning of fast action.

At the drop of a hat implies any kind of quick or impulsive behavior—not necessarily fighting. Recent newspaper mentions of the phrase connect it with travel plans, abrupt changes in work regulations, quickly cooked meals, improvised comic routines, and sudden shifts in the weather.

KEEP YOUR SHIRT ON.
Be patient; keep calm.

Whether or not unplanned boxing matches started with the drop of a hat, they were almost certainly preceded by removal of the participants' shirts. However, no direct evidence connects this expression with fighting. Its earliest appearances in print are all about showing patience. The first is a folksy example from the *Spirit of Times* for November 4, 1854: "I say, you durned ash cats, just keep yer shirts on, will ya?"

Some evidence that the phrase refers to picking a fight comes from the existence of a related figure of speech that was popular around the same time—*get your shirt out* or its variant, *get shirty*, meaning to lose your temper. Getting your shirt out, or untucking it from your trousers, is an obvious prelude to removing it entirely so it won't be ruined while you're brawling. Although unfamiliar to most Americans, the slang word *shirty* was common in England as late as the mid-twentieth century and is still more or less current there.

These days, *keep your shirt on* is usually said to encourage someone to be patient, or to advise the person against forming a snap judgment or taking premature action. Its potential for double meanings also tempts headline writers. Recent articles on sun exposure, menswear, and appropriate tourist behavior, among other topics, are headed with some variant of *keep your shirt on.*

THROW A NECKTIE PARTY.
Conduct a hanging, especially a lynching.

A sign posted in the wild frontier town of 1882 Las Vegas, New Mexico, informs "Thieves, Thugs, Fakirs and Bunco-Steerers" that if found inside the city limits after 10:00 p.m., they will "be invited to attend a Grand Neck-tie Party." Another 1882 mention of necktie parties occurs in *Hands Up, or Twenty Years of Detective Life in the Mountains and on the Plains*, written by D. J. Cook, founder of the Rocky Mountain Detective Association. Cook describes the citizens' methods for controlling rampant lawlessness in newly established towns of the West: ". . . numerous warnings to offenders to leave these places, and many 'neck-tie parties' as well, at which no 'duly-elected' judge sat . . . but where justice was seldom, as in other courts, blind . . ."

Neckties themselves had only been common as menswear since around the 1850s. Before this time, American men wore cravats—soft rectangular lengths of cloth that could be arranged around the neck with a variety of folds and knots. Cravats gradually evolved into modern neckties. By the 1860s, *necktie* was slang for a hangman's rope. Many denizens of the nineteenth-century West who attended necktie parties would not have worn neckties themselves. This fashion accessory was reserved for professionals. Ranch hands and other workers typically wore neckerchiefs.

A number of crimes could result in becoming the guest of honor at a necktie party, also called a *necktie sociable, necktie social,* or *necktie frolic.* Murder was one, of course. Crimes against property, such as robbing trains or stagecoaches, stealing horses, and rustling cattle, were also considered hanging offenses. A story in *Harper's Magazine* for November 1871 recounts the tale of "Mr. Jim Clementson, equine abductor," who was "made the victim of a neck-tie sociable."

A perception that the established forces of law and order were inadequate to deal with frontier lawlessness encouraged leading townspeople to take matters into their own hands. They frequently organized into groups known as vigilance committees, or vigilantes. William Drannan describes the activities of one such group in his 1900 memoir, *Thirty-one Years on the Plains and in the Mountains.* He recalls forty or fifty armed men gathering in Virginia City's main street one morning shortly after breakfast. The men began walking through town, in search of four known outlaws. By midafternoon all four men had been rounded up and locked in an empty cabin. A large crowd gathered to watch the next step of the proceedings. Four hanging ropes were thrown over a joist, and four dry goods boxes were lined up underneath them. The condemned men were made to stand on the boxes while the nooses were fixed around their necks. Members of the vigilance committee then completed their summary justice by kicking the boxes out from underneath the men. Drannan remarks, "[A]fter this little hanging-bee, everything was quiet until near spring."

The term *necktie party* is familiar today only from the many movie Westerns that feature such an event. One of the most famous is *The Ox-Bow Incident,* a 1943 movie starring Henry Fonda and Dana Andrews. Adapted from a 1940 novel by Walter Van Tilburg Clark, *The Ox-Box Incident* tells the story of three innocent men who are lynched for alleged murder and cattle rustling. The Library of Congress has selected this film for preservation in the National Film Registry as a culturally important work.

DIE WITH YOUR BOOTS ON.
Die violently; keep active until the end of your life.

Victims of necktie parties were said to have died with their boots on. *Die in your boots* or *die in your shoes* has been slang for dying violently since at least the eighteenth century. It first appeared in England, where it often referred to executions, but it could also mean dying suddenly from any cause. Today, the expression is strongly associated with the American West.

At first, Americans used *died with his boots on* specifically to refer to hanging. An example comes from an 1871 tourist guide to the West written by George Crofutt: "Slade's . . . wife . . . had ridden . . . thirty miles for the avowed purpose of shooting Slade to save the disgrace of having him hung, and she arrived . . . with revolver in hand, only a few minutes too late to execute her scheme—the desperado was dead and he died with his boots on." However, the phrase soon took on the meaning of any violent death. Western chronicler Joaquin Miller, writing in 1873 in *Life amongst the Modocs*, defines the term as "the poetical way of describing the result of a bar-room or street-battle."

The many frontiersmen who died with their boots on gave rise to another tradition—burial on Boot Hill. Boot Hill cemeteries are scattered throughout the West. The most famous is located in Dodge City, Kansas, former home of Wyatt Earp and the fictional sheriff Matt Dillon, among others. Dodge City's Boot Hill operated as a cemetery for only six years, from 1872 until 1878. It is now a museum. Although the bodies have been relocated, several of the grave markers are still in place. According to the museum's Web site, those who were laid to rest on Boot Hill include Jack Reynolds, victim of the first recorded killing in Dodge City, who was shot six times by a railroad worker, and two men who were shot by the Dodge City Vigilance Committee while visiting the town's dance hall.

Gradually, dying with your boots on acquired positive connotations. It began to mean dying bravely in battle or in a shoot-out with the bad guys. One example of this use is the 1941 movie titled *They Died with Their Boots On*. Starring Errol Flynn and Olivia de Havilland, the movie is an admiring portrait of General George Armstrong Custer, including his last stand at Little Bighorn. Presumably the title refers to this battle.

In recent decades, people who talk of dying with their boots on mean they want to continue being active until the last minute. Often the expression describes a desire to postpone retirement as long as possible.

KNOCK SOMEONE'S SOCKS OFF.

Beat someone up; amaze or impress someone.

Socks are a very old item of footwear, mentioned in writing as early as the fourteenth century. Knocking them off people seems to have been an American innovation. Originally this nineteenth-century expression meant hitting the person hard enough to cause him to rise out of his footwear. Although obviously an exaggeration, the threat *I'm going to knock your socks off* did convey an intention to do serious physical damage. Soon the phrase was also being used to mean defeat someone soundly. An early example in print comes from a letter written by Charles Beecher, describing members of his congregation cheering him on against a rival: "'Beecher you must put in your best licks today!' 'You must knock the socks off those Old School folks!' And so they stood by to see me fight."

At some point during the late nineteenth or early twentieth century, knocking people's socks off turned into a good thing to do. *Dialect Notes* for 1905 lists the phrase as slang for "surpass," for example, *He can knock the socks off me at marbles.* It can now also mean to outcompete an opponent. In a 1979 example from the *Arizona Daily Star*, a spokesman for the Atchison, Topeka & Santa Fe Railway says, "Trucks have been beating our socks off, but now we have a chance to get some of the business back." This expression is only one of many examples to suggest that flooring people is a good thing—for instance, *put on a blockbuster show, make a big hit, deliver a real punch, knock 'em dead, knocked me for a loop,* and *really knocked me out.*

SOCK MONEY AWAY.

Amass savings.

This expression dates from the early twentieth century. A typical use is found in Ellis Lucia's 1962 biography of Kitty Rockwell, *Klondike Kate*: "Instead of gambling a fortune away at the wheels . . . [Kitty] was wisely socking it into the bank." Several writers also talk about their sock (usually figurative) when they mean their savings. For example, in *Lady Sings the Blues*, singer Billie Holiday says, "I opened Café Society as an unknown; I left two years later as a star. But you couldn't tell the difference by what I had in my sock."

Most etymological sources attribute the expression to the bygone habit of saving money by stuffing it into an old sock. However, another possibility is that it derives from one of the meanings of *sock* that refers to closing up or hiding. In the sixteenth and seventeenth centuries, to sock or sock up a shroud was to sew the corpse into it. This practice was the usual way to prepare a corpse for burial at that time. Records note the paying out of certain sums for socking up a relative. In the eighteenth century, *sock* could also be slang for a pocket, which may be related to the "shroud" meaning. Items can be hidden or enclosed in a pocket. The modern American weather term *socked in*—that is, shrouded in fog—could be connected as well.

Another use of *sock* with money is to sock down money, meaning to pay for some item, especially to pay a lot. Those reeling from unexpectedly high prices sometimes complain of getting socked for a bundle. This use is probably related to the "hit hard" meaning of *sock*, dating from the 1700s, rather than to stockings or pockets.

Today, *sock money away* usually means to deposit it in a savings account. However, the phrase is used occasionally to mean hiding it, either in a sock or some other obscure place, such as the back of a dresser drawer.

WAIT FOR THE OTHER SHOE TO DROP.

Expect further trouble; wait to find out the end of the story.

The earliest recorded use of this phrase known so far, posted on the American Dialect Society's online discussion list, comes from a piece in the *Chicago Tribune* for April 16, 1905. The writer of the *Tribune* article says, "At one time we lived under another couple for months. The man came home 'loaded' half the time and Mark Twain's story about waiting to hear the other shoe drop was borne in upon me." The story in question is no doubt the old anecdote about the boardinghouse lodger who comes home a little tipsy. As he staggers around getting undressed, he carelessly pulls off one shoe and lets it drop noisily to the floor. Then, belatedly remembering that his fellow boarders are sleeping, he removes his other shoe much more quietly. Some time later, as he's dropping off to sleep, he hears a shout from the cranky little man in the room below: "Well, aren't you going to drop the other one? I can't get to sleep, waiting for you to drop the other shoe!"

This joke must date from vaudeville days, if not earlier. It was already considered a cliché when a 1921 *New York Times* article posed the question "If nine out of ten of us hadn't heard that 'drop the other shoe' chestnut and molded our lives accordingly for the sake of the neighbor below us, what would be the end of us?" By the 1930s, the expression was being used figuratively to mean waiting for the inevitable result or logical conclusion of an event. And people are never waiting for good news. A typical use is the sentence *The boss has called an emergency meeting of all employees tomorrow, and now I'm just waiting for the other shoe to drop*. Generally, the sound of that other shoe signals disaster.

News writers lately have taken to using *other shoe* as a synonym for bad news. This slight redefinition has led reporters to ask questions such as "Do you expect many more shoes to drop?" Whereas once the downstairs tenant could relax and go back to sleep after hearing the second shoe, now it seems that any number of shoes could eventually hit the floor.

BUCKLE DOWN.
Apply yourself seriously to a task.

Buckle down, meaning "to get to work," first appears in the 1865 volume of *Atlantic Monthly*: "If he would only buckle down to serious study." Most etymologists believe the expression refers to the act of buckling on armor before a battle. Plate armor of the type worn by medieval knights "in shining armor" was uncommon after the seventeenth century, which leaves a gap of well over one hundred years before *buckle down* made its first appearance as a figure of speech. However, *buckle down* is almost certainly related to the earlier British expression *buckle to*. Edmund Burke uses the phrase to express settling down to work in a 1746 letter: "I have shook off idleness and begun to buckle to." The gap between buckling on armor and buckling to is not as wide—only fifty years or so.

A well-known instance of *buckle down* is the song "Buckle Down, Winsocki," first heard in the 1941 musical *Best Foot Forward*. The song cheers the fictional Winsocki military school's football team on to victory. People can buckle down to any number of tasks. The expression is still used frequently in connection with "serious study," as mentioned in the 1865 quote above. One recent example of encouraging a student to buckle down comes from Walter Mosley's 2000 novel, *Walkin' the Dog*: "He [the vice-principal] said you got to buckle down if you wanna get good grades."

※ ※ ※

After buckling down to work and achieving your goals, it's time to relax—perhaps over a good meal. Donning your Sunday best and sitting down to a tasty dinner is an American tradition.

Chapter 12

EATING WELL

E nglish settlers in the Plymouth and Jamestown colonies would have starved before the first winter was out had the natives not shared part of their corn harvest. This North American staple crop was called *maize* in Europe, but the English called it *Indian corn*, or simply *corn*. It was soon central to the colonists' diet. Renderings of the first Thanksgiving feast are incomplete without golden sheaves of corn piled high around the table. Terms for bread made with cornmeal include *corn pone, corn dodger, batter cake, hoe cake, corn fritter, spoon bread*, and *johnny cake*. (For cornmeal pancakes, see *sell like hotcakes*, p. 222). The abundance of corn also inspired that all-American drink, bourbon. Although this chapter does not include any expressions that directly incorporate *corn*, several highlight the fact that corn is a traditional American staple.

Beans, another important food for the colonists, were also introduced by Native Americans. The combination of cornmeal and beans is a venerable one, especially when served with that other iconic American food, pork. Two bean-related expressions are listed here. For more about pork, see *live high on the hog* and *go the whole hog* in chapter 2, "Behaving Like an Animal," and *ham it up* in chapter 9, "Great Performances." Turkeys are also covered in "Behaving Like an Animal." This chapter features two favorite American snacks as well—hot dogs and Kool-Aid.

TAKE THE CAKE.

Win the prize; be an extreme example.

The first people to take the cake were the winners of dance contests called cakewalks. Cakewalks were originally walking competitions, held among slaves in the antebellum South. The walk itself, performed by couples, was basically a smooth, gliding step. Struts and other flourishes were added as the dance developed. The couple with the most stylish walk won the cake (probably a cornmeal cake or something similar, rather than a fancy layer cake). Cakewalks were meant to satirize the grand processions that took place during the plantation owners' formal balls. The owners themselves often judged these events, with the best dancers traveling to neighboring plantations to compete.

After the Civil War, cakewalks continued to be performed as entertainment. They were a regular part of many late nineteenth-century minstrel shows. In the early 1900s, a version of the cakewalk went mainstream in the form of a popular ballroom dance.

At the same time as the first cakewalk contests were being held, the phrase *take the cake* was also being used as a general term for winning a prize. *A Quarter Race in Kentucky*, published in 1847, includes this description of a horse race: "They got up a horse and fifty dollars in money aside. . . . The winning horse [would] take the cakes." Alternative versions of the expression were *take the cakes* and *rake the cakes*.

By the 1860s, *take the cake* referred to the most egregious example of something. It was often used ironically, as in these tongue-in-cheek lines from the 1894 book of cowboy poetry *Git Along Dogies*: "At punching cows I know I'll shine; / I'm sure I'll take the cake." People who take the cake usually are impressive for having a bad trait rather than a good one—for instance, *Of all the bubble-headed flakes I've ever encountered, Candy Sue really takes the cake.*

The word *cakewalk* also shifted in meaning during the later years of the nineteenth century. Originally, boxers used the term to describe a fight that would be a "walkover." Then it began to mean any easy task or easily accomplished feat, as in this 1894 quote from a critical essay by Mark Twain: "This Shelley biography . . . is a literary cake-walk."

Cakewalking as a dance craze had pretty much disappeared by the 1920s and *cakewalk* has also disappeared as a word for a simple task. The modern equivalent is *piece of cake*. However, the expression *take the cake* is still current.

NOT AMOUNT TO A HILL OF BEANS.
Be worthless or unimportant; be a disappointment.

Not worth a bean, meaning of small value, has been a figure of speech since the thirteenth century. However, Americans were the first to talk about "hills" of beans. The earliest recorded figurative use is found in the 1863 novel *My Southern Friends*: "[I] karn't take Preston's note— 'taint wu'th a hill o' beans."

Planting beans in hills was a typical Native American farming method. Several early colonial observers mention the process in their records. One is Mark Catesby, whose *Natural History of Carolina, Florida, and the Bahama Islands* was published in 1771 but written much earlier. Catesby explains that corn is first planted in mounds. After the cornstalks reach their full height, "there are drop'd into every hill two or three beans." The cornstalks support the bean vines as they grow. Hills of growing beans would have been a familiar sight to the colonists.

Although Native American haricot beans were different from the fava beans grown in England, they looked and tasted similar enough to make them an easy food choice for the British colonists. Boston baked beans and succotash are two traditional dishes adopted from Native Americans.

Beans have always been plentiful and cheap. That fact is apparent from their status as a synonym for worthlessness. The expression *not know beans* has been in use since the nineteenth century. It includes many elaborations. The periodical *Dialect Notes* for 1905 lists *not know split beans from coffee* and *not know beans when the bag's open*. William Safire's *New York Times Magazine* column for August 7, 1983, reports the results of a survey taken by the *Dictionary of American Regional English*. They discovered several alliterative versions of the expression, including *doesn't know beans from barley, buttons, bats, apple butter, bullfrogs,* and *baloney*. A related American expression is *not care beans*, also current since the nineteenth century. About the only positive use for beans is to be full of them, meaning bursting with energy and pep. *Bean* denoting a person's head has given us *bean ball*, a baseball thrown dangerously close to a batter's head.

Perhaps one of the most famous uses of this expression occurs near the end of the 1942 film *Casablanca*. The hero, played by Humphrey Bogart, is trying to persuade his lost love, Ingrid Bergman, to board a plane with her husband. He tells her, "I'm no good at being noble, but it doesn't take much to see that the problems of three little people don't amount to a hill of beans in this crazy world." The expression *not amount to a hill of beans* is still common. It is always used with a negative. Saying that someone amounts to a hill of beans would not be much of a compliment.

SPILL THE BEANS.

Reveal the truth; blurt out a secret.

This expression dates from the beginning of the twentieth century. An early example comes from T. K. Holmes's *The Man from Tall Timber*, published in 1919: "'Mother certainly has spilled the beans!' thought Stafford in vast amusement."

Etymologists disagree about the probable origin of *spill the beans*. One widely repeated theory is that the expression derives from the ancient Greek practice of electing members to secret societies by dropping beans into a jar. A white bean signified a "yes" vote and a black bean a "no" vote. If someone accidentally knocked over the jar, spilling the beans, the whole process came to a halt.

It's unclear where the ancient Greeks would have acquired black and white beans, as the multicolored beans of the Americas were unknown to them. They ate fava beans, the only kind that grew in Europe at that time. Favas are green when fresh and turn brown when dried. In any case, an ancient Greek voting procedure is unlikely to have led directly to a twentieth-century American figure of speech. However, it's worth noting that early colonial records mention beans being used to cast votes. William Williamson's *History of the State of Maine* describes a vote taken around 1650, conducted using beans and corn. Beans meant "yes" and corn "no."

A more probable explanation for the phrase is that *spill the beans* derives from the "divulge" sense of *spill*, which has been a possible meaning since the sixteenth century, although uncommon. The twentieth-century Americanism *spill it* means "provide information." *Brewer's Dictionary of Modern Phrase and Fable* suggests that the beans in question are being figuratively regurgitated. *Brewer's* compares the phrase to expressions such as *spit it out*, *cough it up*, and *spill your guts*.

During the early decades of the twentieth century, *spill the beans* was gangster slang that referred specifically to betraying your colleagues under pressure. In recent times, the expression implies telling any kind of secret or sharing information that you were planning to keep under wraps.

CUT THE MUSTARD.
Come up to standard.

This expression first came into vogue around the turn of the twentieth century. A 1905 issue of *Dialect Notes* defines *cut the mustard* as "to succeed," giving the example "But he couldn't cut the mustard." This figure of speech usually occurs in the negative, although O. Henry's 1907 short story "Cupid à la Carte" includes the line "So I looked around and found a proposition that exactly cut the mustard." In the early 1900s, to be *the mustard* meant to be sharp and full of pizzazz. *That's the mustard* was slang for the real thing. *The Log of a Cowboy*, published in 1903, includes the sentence "For fear they [the dogs] were not the proper mustard, he had that dog man sue him in court for the balance, so as to make him prove the pedigree." In America, *mustard* could also mean "courage" or "spirit."

The most likely explanation for these figures of speech is that they refer to mustard's sharp, tangy properties. Although a paste made of crushed mustard seed and water has been known since ancient times, the commercial premixed mustards that add zip to modern sandwiches have been produced only since around 1870. When these *mustard*-related expressions were being coined, the condiment was still a novelty. Bottled mustard was featured at the 1904 St. Louis World's Fair, and some Americans probably tasted it there for the first time. (Hot dogs were also reportedly served. For more on that perfect mustard vehicle, see below.)

The *cut* part of the phrase is probably being used in its meaning of "outdo" or "excel." An example of this use, current around the late nineteenth century, comes from *Referee* magazine for April 13, 1884: "George's performance . . . is hardly likely to be disturbed for a long time to come unless he cuts it himself."

Some sources offer the alternative theory that *cut the mustard* is a corruption of *pass muster*, originally a military term meaning to pass inspection. By the eighteenth century, *pass muster* had acquired the figurative meaning of coming up to standard. While the meanings of *pass muster* and *cut the mustard* are similar, no particular evidence connects the two. The first, much older term is originally British, although it is used in the United States as well. *Cut the mustard* is an Americanism that arose separately and did not replace the earlier expression.

Can't cut the mustard is still used in modern American English. In some circles, the meaning has narrowed to refer to an older man's failings in the romance department. The expression *can't cut it*, meaning that a person can't successfully complete a task or reach a benchmark, is probably more common today. *Can't cut it* is an Americanism that was first heard around 1900.

HOT DOG IT.

Show off; display exceptional skill, especially at a sport.

Human hot dogs first appeared in the 1890s. They were mainly found on college campuses. The November 1995 issue of *Comments on Etymology* offers this example of 1897 collegiate humor: "Brown's a hot dog, isn't he?" "Yes, he has so many pants." *Dialect Notes* for 1900 defines a "hot-dog" as "one very proficient in certain things." *Hot dog* could be a genuine compliment, but it often implied a show-off, someone who was good, but too self-congratulatory.

The verb *to hot dog* does not appear in print until the 1960s, although it was almost certainly being used earlier. Usually it referred to a superior but flamboyant surfer, skateboarder, or skier. A *Life* magazine article on surfers from September 1, 1961, describes this scene: "Almost every wave carries a 'hot dogger' doing tricks or . . . dressed in outlandish garb." A hot-dog board is a short surfboard, more easily maneuvered on the waves than longer, heavier models. Around the same time that *hot dog* became a common surfing and skateboarding term, baseball players also began calling their grandstanding teammates *hot dogs*.

A hot dog is also, of course, a sandwich of sorts. Sausage sandwiches arrived in the United States with the nineteenth-century influx of Germans and other Central Europeans. They were popular with non-Germans as well. Numerous beer gardens sold them, and by the 1860s, vendors in many American cities sold sausage sandwiches from street carts. In 1871 Charles Feltman opened a sausage stand on

Coney Island, a place that has since become synonymous with hot dogs. Sausages in those days were called frankfurters (from Frankfurt) or wienerwursts (Vienna sausage), sometimes shortened to wieners.

Hot dog as a name for a sausage on a bun dates from about the same era as *hot dog* to mean a show-off. Until recently, myth and speculation obscured the origins of the term. Word historians Gerald Cohen, David Shulman, and Barry Popik discovered its true beginnings, publishing their researches in a 2004 book called *Origin of the Term 'Hot Dog.'*

The usual story of how *hot dog* was coined attributes the word wrongly to cartoonist and sports writer Thomas A. Dorgan, known as TAD. TAD is credited with inventing or popularizing numerous slang expressions of the early twentieth century, among them *twenty-three skiddoo*, *you tell 'em*, and *drug-store cowboy*. According to this story, he was attending a 1901 Giants' game at New York's Polo Grounds when a concessionaire named Harry Stevens first sold hot dogs to the crowd. As the legend goes, Stevens had his employees pitch their wares by shouting, "Get your red hot dachshund sandwiches!" (Although the reason for calling them dachshunds is not spelled out, presumably the sausages reminded him—as they do many other people—of these sausage-shaped "wiener dogs.")

Supposedly Dorgan drew a picture of the little sausages with feet and wanted to caption it "hot dachshunds," but he didn't know how to spell the word. Instead he labeled the little creatures "hot dogs." The next day New York's cartoon-reading public was introduced to yet another piece of TAD slang.

Cohen, Shulman, and Popik have demonstrated that this story cannot be true. Among other problems, Dorgan did not arrive in New York City until 1903, two years after the event that the story relates. His first known use of *hot dog* is a December 12, 1906, cartoon illustrating the scene at a six-day bicycle race at Madison Square Garden. In 1926 Harry Stevens admitted to a newspaper that neither he nor Dorgan had much to do with introducing *hot dog*. He told the reporter that his son Frank first had the idea of selling hot dogs at the Madison

Square Garden bicycle race. Stevens argued that ham and cheese would be more popular, but eventually his son persuaded him to give the new snack a try. It turned out that Frank was right. (It's tempting to connect Frank with *franks*, but they were definitely named for Frankfurt.) Spectators loved the dogs, and Dorgan recorded the fact in cartoons printed on December 12 and 13. Dorgan may have popularized the term, but he didn't invent it.

In fact, referring to sausages as *dogs* goes back much further than either 1901 or 1906. Sausage meat was known as *dog's paste* as early as 1859. This figure of speech came about because it was widely believed (possibly with some truth) that sausages of the time could include ground-up dog meat. A number of stomach-turning examples of this belief made their way into print during the late 1800s. In an 1845 *New Orleans Picayune* piece, court reporter Dennis Corcoran quotes an outraged Cockney visitor who claims to have been sold a sausage that included a dog's tail, "hair and all." He tells the court that he has noted in his diary, "New Orleans is a wery wile, wicious place. They . . . retails . . . [dogs], tails and all as sassenger meat." *Peck's Bad Boy*, published in 1883, includes this remark: "I hope to die if there wasn't a little brass padlock and a piece of . . . dog collar embedded in the sausage."

In spite of their unsavory reputation, sausages were a popular snack food by the middle of the nineteenth century. However, people must have remembered the stories, because by the 1890s sausage was jokingly known as *hot dog*. As with the "show-off" use of *hot dog*, the first references appear on college campuses. Some of the earliest are from the *Yale Record*. A story from October 19, 1895, describes "[h]ow they contentedly munched hot dogs during the whole service." Another story from the same year, announcing a proposed boycott of the lunch wagon, enjoins readers, "Let us eschew the dog wagon." By 1900 *Dialect Notes* reported that *hot dog* was college slang for a hot sausage in at least thirteen states.

How the various meanings of *hot dog* are related is not obvious. *Hot dog* the flashy human and *hot dog* the culinary item began appearing at essentially the same time, both on college campuses. The exclamation *hot dog!* (and the more fervent *hot-diggity dog!*), expressing enthusiasm or approval, dates from about 1906. How the sausage got its nickname is transparent enough. The transfer of the term to high-achieving, if showy, people is more mysterious. *Hot* has been slang for energetic, exciting, or trendy for hundreds of years, but why *dog*? One possibility is that several slang expressions already referred to people as dogs—*sly dog*, *clever dog*, *lucky dog*, and others. Beginning in the 1870s, a *gay dog* meant a young man who enjoyed a busy social life. The expression *put on dog*, meaning to dress ostentatiously, was another piece of college slang heard on the late nineteenth-century Yale campus. In this context, it's not too much of a stretch to imagine that a showy young athlete could have been labeled a hot dog.

In recent decades, hot dogging is usually associated with sports. For example, *Bronx Zoo*, a 1979 book about the New York Yankees, includes the line "Tito Fuente . . . has been one of the most renowned hot dogs in baseball history." A *New York Times* article from January 30, 2005, talks about older snowboarders who "aren't hot-dogging down the mountain." People are also still dogs, thanks to hip-hop slang, only now it's spelled *dawg*.

CHERRY-PICK.
Select only the best or most useful of a thing.

Railroad workers were probably the first to use this expression metaphorically. The April 1940 issue of *Railroad Magazine* defines *cherry-picker* as slang for a railroad switchman, so-called because of the red lights used at switch stands to signal oncoming trains. A secondary definition extends the term to "any railroad man who is always figuring on the best jobs and sidestepping undesirable ones (alluding to the expression 'life is a bowl of cherries')."

The second slang meaning of the word may be unrelated to the first. Far from being a bowl of cherries, the switchman's job entailed a certain amount of stress. Switchmen operated the railroad switches—rails that could be shifted from place to place. These were set temporarily at the junction between two railway lines to allow trains to roll from one set of tracks to another. Correctly operating the switches was crucial for train safety. Setting them wrong, or failing to clearly indicate which lines were open, would result in a train wreck. Another railroad metaphor, *asleep at the switch*, has passed into the mainstream vocabulary as a term for negligence on the job. *Cherry-picker* may have started as a reference to switchmen, then broadened to include other workers when someone thought of the old adage about the bowl of cherries.

The figurative verb *cherry-pick* evolved from *cherry-picker*. By the 1960s, the expression was being used in both the United States and England to mean selectively choosing from the available options. The options in question were often consumer goods. For example, an article in the April 19, 1975, issue of *Business Week* contains the sentence "Many customers . . . are doing more 'cross-shopping,' . . . cherry-picking the specials." However, the most desirable items of any group could be cherry-picked, as in cherry-picking only the most talented people from a company's staff for some specific task or benefit. In recent years, the verb is often used with *evidence* to mean selectively accepting only the facts that support your argument and ignoring any information that seems to contradict it.

CHEW THE FAT.
Chat; trade news and gossip in a leisurely fashion.

In the nineteenth century, this expression was British slang for complaining or grumbling. A related phrase, now obsolete, was *chew the rag*. By the beginning of the twentieth century, *chew the fat* had crossed the Atlantic and acquired the meaning of casually chatting. The 1911 book *Power* describes a typical occasion for indulging in this activity: "An assortment of salty looking characters sat around, chewing the fat while smoking and drinking coffee." The expression often occurs with *sit around, lie around, hang around,* and similar verb phrases.

Words could be chewed over as early as Shakespeare's time. In the 1603 play *Measure for Measure*, the character Angelo muses on his ability to mouth empty prayers while thinking about something else: ". . . heaven in my mouth, / As if I did but only chew his name, / And in my heart the strong and swelling evil / Of my conception . . ." The motion of the jaws while chewing a piece of fat is reminiscent of cows chewing their cud, an action that has long been a metaphor for brooding. It has also given us the word *ruminate*, which means thinking over some issue, but it can suggest talking it over as well.

Other Americanisms that equate talking with chewing are *chew someone out*, *chew over an idea*, *chew somebody's ear off*, and *chewing match*—which meant a loud argument in the 1950s and 1960s. *Chew the fat* to mean engage in casual conversation is current in most English-speaking countries.

SELL LIKE HOTCAKES.

Sell very quickly or in large volume; be a product in great demand.

An early example of this expression is found in *The Adventures of Harry Franco*, published in 1839: "'You had better buy 'em Colonel,' said Mr. Lummocks, 'they will sell like hot cakes.'"

Hotcakes themselves—small corn cakes or pancakes—have been a favorite food since early colonial days. William Penn, founder of Pennsylvania, writes about them as "hot cakes of new corn . . . which they [Native Americans] make up in a square form in the leaves of the stem, and bake . . . in the ashes." Dutch settlers made pancakes of wheat flour. Later, Scandinavian and eastern European immigrants brought their own versions of this popular dish to the United States. *Winters in the West*, a collection of letters from 1830s Illinois, describes the "usual settlers' dinner of fried bacon, venison cutlets, hotcakes, and wild honey, with some tolerable tea and Indian sugar [maple sugar]."

Hotcakes have been big sellers since the late nineteenth century, when the first pancake houses opened. Even before that, Americans and British ate pancakes in large numbers on the Tuesday before the beginning of Lent, known as Shrove Tuesday in England and Mardi Gras in the United States. Making pancakes was a way of using up butter, milk, and other rich ingredients before Lenten fasting started. Churches have traditionally organized pancake breakfasts or pancake suppers on this day. Pancake suppers are also a popular way to raise money at other times of the year.

The word *hotcakes* is mainly reserved these days for fried cakes made of cornmeal. Americans in most parts of the country say *pancake* when they mean the variety made with flour. Other regional terms are *slapjacks, flapjacks*, and *griddle cakes*. However, the figurative *selling like hotcakes* is common throughout the country. Recently, computer programs, cell phones, novels, automobiles, frozen fruit, and concert tickets, among other things, were all reported in newspapers to be selling like hotcakes. Hotcakes still sell like hotcakes too. The August 10, 2007, edition of the *Register-Guard* for Eugene, Oregon, features an article on a local Scandinavian festival's Swedish pancake booth. Writing about the booth's opening, the paper tells readers, "Their wares sold like . . . well, you know the rest of the cliché."

DRINK THE KOOL-AID.

Follow blindly; commit yourself unquestioningly to a set of beliefs.

Nebraskan Edwin Perkins invented Kool-Aid in 1927. He developed the powdered drink mix from an earlier liquid concentrate version when the cost of shipping the bottled liquid began to rise. In 1953, Perkins sold the product line to General Foods, and it is now owned by Kraft. Since the middle of the twentieth century, American children have downed countless gallons of this fruit-flavored beverage.

Drinking Kool-Aid took on a darker significance in 1978, when more than nine hundred members of the People's Temple religious cult committed suicide by drinking poisoned Flavor Aid, a beverage similar to, but not, Kool-Aid. Their leader, Jim Jones, founded the People's Temple in 1955 in Indianapolis. His stated purpose was to further the causes of social justice and racial equality. The People's

Temple was notable at the time for its inclusive attitude toward African Americans. Although the church was nominally affiliated with the Disciples of Christ, the charismatic Jones preached his own brand of theology.

In 1965, Jones, his family, and about eighty church members relocated to California's Redwood Valley, which Jones believed would be one of the few places to survive a nuclear holocaust. In California, the membership swelled to about one thousand. In the 1970s, Jones came under pressure from the Internal Revenue Service, as well as from disillusioned former members who had organized into a group called Concerned Relatives. The group accused Jones of brainwashing and other cultish practices. To get away from these troubles, Jones and his followers moved to Guyana in 1977, where they established Jonestown in the middle of a vast tract of jungle.

Complaints about the People's Temple continued to mount. Although Jones kept a tight rein on church members, rumors spread of brutality, forced labor, and murder. Former members also spoke of being put through rehearsals for a mass suicide. Matters reached a crisis in November 1978. Congressman Leo Ryan, a Democrat from San Francisco, flew to Guyana, along with several media representatives and members of the Concerned Relatives group. He intended to investigate stories that people were being kept in Jonestown against their will and that a mass suicide plan was in place.

Overcoming numerous attempts to block their visit, Ryan and his team at last managed to enter Jonestown. When they left, they took fifteen or twenty disaffected members with them. As the group reached the airstrip and began boarding their two small airplanes, several men loyal to Jones drove up to one of the planes and opened fire. They killed Congressman Ryan and five others.

Meanwhile, Jones called together church members and announced another "white night," which was his name for previous suicide rehearsals. This time it was not a rehearsal. A doctor, a nurse, and several others began passing out paper cups of Flavor Aid laced with cyanide and Valium. According to reports, families lined up to receive the poison together. As the word spread that real poison was being distributed this time, some people hid or fled into the jungle. Others who chose not to cooperate were apparently forcibly injected with the poisonous dose. Altogether 909 people died, including well over 200 children. Jones himself was found with a bullet in his right temple, although it is unknown whether he committed suicide or was killed.

Soon afterward, references to drinking metaphorical Kool-Aid began to appear in print. (The Kool-Aid brand is better known than Flavor Aid, which no doubt accounts for its substitution in references to the Jonestown tragedy.) A *Washington Post* article for January 14, 1979, contains the sentence ". . . if he [Hess] had ordered the SS to pass around the Kool-Aid [at the Nuremberg rally], all those crewcut Nazis would have tossed it back with the same fervor with which they cheered Hess' ravings." *Kool-Aid* here obviously suggests an unthinking acceptance of extreme beliefs. A later citation that uses the exact expression *drink the Kool-Aid* appears in the September 23, 1985, edition of the *Washington Post*: "What he didn't want [Rep. Foley said] . . . was 'what I call the politics of Jim Jones, that "let's drink the Kool-Aid" kind of downer.'" By this time, Kool-Aid drinking was clearly established as a metaphor for blindly obedient behavior that leads to severely negative consequences.

Drink the Kool-Aid is most often used to refer to the true believer's wholehearted commitment to a political or social cause. However, *Kool-Aid* can refer to any kind of questionable claim or bogus argument that the hearer is expected to swallow. It frequently appears in print in connection with the stock market, for example. *Don't drink the Kool-Aid* is a way of warning friends against being too gullible. Since the early twenty-first century, the doctrinal flavor of the *Kool-Aid* is sometimes specified. In a *New York Times* column for August 5, 2007, Frank Rich includes the line "Washington [DC] never drank the Nixon Kool-Aid."

COOK WITH GAS.

Perform a task supremely well and with great vigor; be on the right track; play inspired jazz.

Cooking with gas would certainly have been an improvement on cooking with old-fashioned coal or wood stoves. Instead of having to shovel fuel into the belly of the stove, cooks could simply turn a switch and the fuel came up to the burner through a pipe. Heating up a pan was much easier and much faster. Although gas stoves were made beginning around the 1880s, few kitchens could boast one before the twentieth century.

Cooking with a gas stove first became common just before World War I. Scattered uses of *cook with gas* as a figure of speech appear a few years later. Volume 15 of the wartime *Information Journal* warns citizens to keep their gas masks handy with this jingle: "It's all right to 'cook with gas'/ But who wants to croak with it? Get that mask on *Quick!*" Another example of the expression comes from a seventy-six-year-old man reminiscing about that same era. He is quoted in the *Random House Historical Dictionary of American Slang* saying, "We'd see these old worn-out planes. . . . We'd say look at that old crate. But when a new, fast-flying plane went over, we'd say, 'Now they're cookin' with gas! Now that's a *plane!*'" If you were cooking with gas, then you were doing the smart thing.

Beginning in the 1940s, the expression was widespread but frequently applied to jazz musicians. *Encyclopedia of Jazz* defines *cook* as "play with rhythmic inspiration." An article in *Down Beat* for October 31, 1956, reports, "Big Nick Nicholas had the band there . . . and it always came up cooking." Other possibilities were *cooking on the front burner* or *cooking with both burners*. *What's cooking?* was the jive talkers' way of asking what was going on.

Now that electricity is so prevalent, *cook with gas* has an old-fashioned ring. Musicians are still said to cook, although usually without the source of fuel being specified.

Chapter 13

AROUND THE HOUSE

E veryday items around the house sometimes have a moment of glory as the inspiration for a striking metaphor. However, what constitutes a typical American household object has changed over the years. Axes, hatchets, and stakes, which feature in several early figures of speech, were much more common around eighteenth-century homes and farms than they are now. They were needed for taming the tree-covered wilderness that British colonists faced when they arrived in North America. Squatters (a term first used around 1775) who wanted to claim a piece of property were required to make at least minimal improvements. Called *tomahawk improvements*, these usually consisted of whacking down a few trees and building a primitive dwelling out of the resulting logs.

The importance of clearing and fencing off land is also reflected in Americans' many "fence" expressions, including *sit on the fence* and *mend fences* (both found in chapter 4, "Politics as Usual"), *be on the right side of the fence*, *rush your fences*, and *make a Virginia fence*, an obsolete expression for drunken staggering. Making repairs was another never-ending chore on early farm settlements. This fact may explain the ubiquitous use of the verb *to fix* in colonial America, discussed below in *fix someone's wagon*. Some of the expressions listed here feature items still found in modern American households—cans (including cans of paint), towels, and clocks.

PULL UP STAKES.
Move, with the implication of leaving a place where you're settled.

Stakes figure prominently in the early settlement of New England. Colonial records mention them in several places. Capt. John Smith reports in *The General History of Virginia, New England, and the Summer Isles*, written in 1624, that the colonists chose individual properties by drawing lots. They then marked off their newly acquired territory with stakes. Another early mention comes from a 1639 instruction to Connecticut settlers: "Every man shall set a sufficient stake with the two first letters of his name."

An early version of *pull up stakes* was *pluck up stakes*. Thomas Lechford, a London lawyer who lived in Boston from 1638 to 1641, wrote to a friend back home, "I am loth to hear of a stay, but am plucking up stakes with as much speed as I may." *Pull up stakes* begins appearing in settlement records around 1700. By the nineteenth century, the phrase was used to cover all the activities that moving entails. Variants are *move stakes* and the truncated *up stakes*. The expression *stick stakes*, now obsolete, was used in the eighteenth and nineteenth centuries to mean settling down.

The American linguist Maximilian Schele de Vere, collecting Americanisms in the 1870s, writes about the established method of staking a claim on the western frontier: "Having secured his lot . . . the newcomer begins by staking out the ground for his cabin and kitchen garden. The stake plays, hence, a prominent part in the Western man's speech."

Restless Americans pulled up stakes frequently. To early immigrants who came from the crowded countries of western Europe, the sparsely populated North American continent appeared to have endless open space. Between the Louisiana Purchase of 1803 and the end of the nineteenth century, the United States government gradually claimed about three million square miles of land between the Atlantic and the Pacific. A series of federally supervised land giveaways encouraged easterners to relocate to the vast area west of the Mississippi. Americans acquired the habit of pulling up stakes and moving west whenever a more promising parcel of land became available.

The expression *pull up stakes* continued to be used as a metaphor for moving, long after literal stakes were no longer necessary. The 1974 *Super Tour* by Marilyn Allen contains the line "I'm assuming you're in a position to pick up stakes in a hurry." Pulling up stakes is still a common American activity. According to the 2005 census (the most recent one available), nearly 15 percent of the population moved from one house to another that year, with a large proportion of those people moving to another town as well.

FLY OFF THE HANDLE.
Lose your self-control; lose your temper.

One the earliest uses of this expression appears in *The Attaché, or Sam Slick in England*, an 1843 collection of humorous stories by Thomas C. Haliburton, a Nova Scotia judge: "He flies right off the handle for nothing." The character Sam Slick was a stereotyped version of the nineteenth-century American yokel. This example is only one of a number of colorful North American words and expressions that he introduced to the reading public.

The *handle* of *fly off the handle* is an axe handle. Axes are constructed in two parts, with a handle usually made of wood and a sharp-bladed axe head. Axes were familiar tools in early nineteenth-century America, where a large proportion of residents were farmers. Many who did not farm still used axes to chop the wood needed for fireplaces and stoves. Both groups of axe users would have been familiar with the frightening phenomenon of a loose axe head flying off its handle in mid-swing. Not only was it dangerous, but it was sudden and startling—like an explosive temper.

A paraphrase of this expression was *go off the handle*. However, *go off the handle* or *slip off the handle* could also mean to die. Sam Slick offers an early illustration of this expression also, saying, "If Old Cranberry was to slip off the handle, I think I should make up to [his daughter]." Throughout the nineteenth century, *fly off the handle* was considered countrified speech and was usually represented that way, as in this quote from the March 16, 1844, *Spirit of Times*: "Oh, don't fly off'n the handle that way." A similar example comes from the 1825 *Brother Jonathan* by John Neal: "How they pulled foot when they seed us commin', most off the handle . . ." (*Pull foot* is another early Americanism, now obsolete. It means "to hurry.") In the twentieth century, *fly off the handle* became part of standard speech. It is frequently used in news stories about people who lose their tempers with bad consequences.

GET A HANDLE ON THINGS.
Understand some issue or gain control over a situation.

Get a handle or *have a handle* dates from around the mid-twentieth century. Unlike the case of *fly off the handle*, exactly what the handle in this phrase is attached to is unclear. Some of the expression's earliest uses come from baseball and refer to getting a grip on the ball. For instance, the announcer for a 1970 game between the Yankees and the Red Sox told his audience that a fielder "can't find the handle! He drops the ball!" However, the phrase also shows up in other contexts at around the same time, as in this quote from an October 14, 1972, *New Yorker* article: "I don't think people have any idea of how tough it is for anyone in this job to get a handle on anything." *Get a handle* does not seem to be related to *get a grip*, a much older expression going back as far as the seventeenth century.

Although the expression is modern, *handle* itself has been used for several centuries to mean anything people can figuratively grasp. This line from a 1716 sermon illustrates a typical use of *handle*: "Hope and Fear are the two great Handles, by which the Will of Man is to be taken Hold of." Typically, a handle indicates a fact, idea, or situation that someone can use to gain a strategic advantage, as in the sentence *He was careful not to give her any handle against him.*

Between the seventeenth and twentieth centuries, noses were jokingly called the handle of the face. An 1887 issue of the magazine *Modern Society* includes a description of "a restless . . . old lady, with an immense handle to her face." A handle can also be a nickname, especially the on-air name of truckers and others who operate CB radios. In England, an aristocrat with a title is said to have a handle to his name.

A variant of this expression that began appearing in the mid-1980s is *have a handle on something*—for example, *The police seem to have a handle on the gang problem.* Both forms of the expression are in common use today. Baseball announcers also still talk about players getting a handle on the ball.

FIX SOMEONE'S WAGON.

Punish or get even with someone; bring about a person's downfall; injure or kill a person.

The exact origins of this expression are mysterious. The phrase appears in what may be its earliest recorded use in a short piece by journalist Joseph Mitchell called "The Cave Dwellers." Although published in 1945, Mitchell's essay tells of events that happened in 1933. He describes a woman on trial for stabbing her husband to death because he stole her Christmas savings to buy gin. "I sure fixed his wagon," she said. The expression appears in one or two other pieces of writing from the 1930s and then more frequently beginning in the 1950s. From the 1960s, the alternatives *fix someone's little red wagon* or *fix someone's little red fire engine* were also heard.

Picturesque Expressions speculates that the phrase may have originated in the days of covered wagons, when "fixing" or damaging someone's wagon could have meant disaster for the owner. Other sources suggest that the expression refers to the Radio Flyer Company's wagons for children, the first versions of which were made in 1917. Both of these explanations leave a time gap. Covered wagons were an ancient memory by 1933, the date of the earliest known use of *fix someone's wagon*. A multidecade gap also stretches between the first Radio Flyer wagons and *fix someone's little red wagon*, first heard in the 1960s.

An early version of this expression, current from around 1830 to the late nineteenth century, was *fix someone's flint*. Once again, Sam Slick offers an example of its usage in *Sam Slick in England*: "Take it easy, Sam," says I, "your flint is fixed; you are wet through." Sticklers for correct language considered the expression a vulgarism. Nonetheless, it was widespread. The flint in question may have been a reference to the chip of flint used to ignite the powder in flint-lock muskets.

Nineteenth-century Americans used *fix* as an all-purpose verb. British travelers often commented on it with puzzlement. The novelist Frederick Marryat, visiting the United States in 1837 and 1838, wrote in his diary, "The verb 'to fix' is universal. It means do anything." Americans fixed their clothes, their hair, a piece of broken furniture, a wounded man, and their hats on their heads. If they were cold they fixed a fire in the fireplace. They fixed meals, which might include chicken with all the fixin's. Occasionally, they found themselves in a fix. In that case, they could try to fix the jury, just as modern Americans can.

The verb phrase *fix it* meant to arrange it. Like *fix his flint*, it was considered backwoods talk. It often appears in books as part of a nonstandard dialect, as in this quote from the 1844 novel *Major Jones's Courtship*: "The master . . . axed them the hardest questions he could find in the book, but he couldn't stump 'em no how he could fix it."

Sometime in the early twentieth century, *fix someone's flint* became obsolete and people started using the simplified phrase *fix someone*. *I'll fix you good* was a typical threat. As with fixing someone's wagon, fixing a person could cover a range of activities, from intimidating to killing. The expression's ambiguity is illustrated in this dialogue from P. G. Wodehouse's 1942 novel, *Money in the Bank*:

"Don't you worry. I'll fix him."
"How do you mean, fix?"

"Just fix."

"You wouldn't croak him?"

Mrs. Molloy laughed merrily at the whimsical thought.

Both *fix someone* and *fix someone's wagon* are common in current English. Although the expressions' exact derivations and purposes remain unclear, they generally carry a threat of violence—although probably not to the extent of croaking the person.

GET CANNED.
Be fired from a job.

Getting canned has been a possible way to lose your job since the beginning of the twentieth century. A 1905 issue of *Dialect Notes* records the term, giving the example sentence "Jim . . . got canned for two weeks." *Can it*, meaning "stop it," also entered the language at around the same time. Helen Green's 1908 book, *Maison de Shine*, features the line "You can that stuff!"

The expression probably derives from an earlier one, to *tie the can to someone*. This expression was in vogue around the end of the nineteenth century. It refers to the cruel trick of tying a can to a dog's tail and chasing him down the street. As the can rattles behind it, the dog runs faster. The logic apparently is that if you tie a can to someone, he or she will run away. An early example that explicitly refers to this idea occurs in a 1908 novel by Robert Lee Durham titled *The Call of the South*. The book features a rowdy scene at a political rally, during which the crowd shouts down a heckler. Cries of "Shoot the dog! Tie a can to his tail!" are heard.

Probably the earliest figurative use of the phrase appears in George Ade's *Forty Modern Fables*, published in 1901: "She had tied a can to [Husband] No. 2." The baseball world also adopted the term to mean trading or firing players, as in this example from the 1911 short story collection *The Big League*: "I got a notion to tie the can on you for the rest of the season."

Although tying a can to someone is becoming obsolete, getting canned unfortunately still occurs. For instance, Anthony Bourdain wrote in his 2000 autobiography, *Kitchen Confidential*, "I got canned from the Mexican place, for which particular reason I don't know." *Can it* is also still heard, usually as a directive to someone to be quiet.

GET DOWN TO BRASS TACKS.
Discuss basic details; get down to business.

This expression and its variant *come down to brass tacks* have been used since the turn of the twentieth century. The artist Frederic Remington wrote in an 1895 letter, "How little I know . . . when you get down to brass tacks." Another early example comes from the November 28, 1903, edition of the *New York Sun*: "This bold sister was the first . . . to get down to brass tacks in a discussion of the scandal."

One of two theories is usually suggested as the origin of the phrase. The first traces it to nineteenth-century country stores, where fabric was cut from bolts and sold by the yard. The counters in these establishments featured two rows of brass tacks exactly one yard apart. When a customer decided which fabric she wanted and exactly how much, the clerk measured it out according to the brass tacks along the counter. Getting down to the brass measuring tacks meant that hesitation and small talk were over. The serious business of buying had begun.

An alternative explanation hypothesizes that the phrase refers to chairs of the period, which were upholstered using brass tacks. When a chair had to be reupholstered, the first step was stripping off the old covering and padding, revealing the underlying brass tacks. The brass tacks were a basic, although usually hidden, detail of the chair.

Some sources speculate that *brass tacks* originated as Cockney rhyming slang for the word *facts*. However, all the earliest citations of *get down to brass tacks* are from American English. In any case, the phrase is more about focusing on details than facing the facts. Today, *get down to brass tacks* is current in England, as well as most other English-speaking countries, but *brass tacks* on its own does not appear to have separate status as rhyming slang. The phrase is also unconnected to *big brass*, which is an allusion to the brass insignia worn by senior military officers.

CLEAN SOMEONE'S CLOCK.
Punch someone in the face; defeat someone by a wide margin.

This expression also goes by the short form *to clock somebody*, meaning to punch a person. *Clock* has been a slang term for the face since the beginning of the twentieth century. (The British version is *dial.*) The first known use in print appears in an O. Henry short story titled "A Chaparral Prince," in the form *fix his clock*: "I reckon we'll fix your clock for a while." In the story, the subject of this threat is tied up and kept out of the way for a while, but not punched. One of the earliest uses of *clean someone's clock* also refers to a figurative, rather than a literal, beating. It comes from the *Trenton Evening Times* for July 28, 1908: "It took the Thistles just one inning to clean the clocks of the Times boys."

The comparison of faces with clocks makes sense, but why clean? Possibly the verb is meant to suggest wiping the smirk off someone's face or rearranging his features. Part of the answer probably lies in English speakers' appreciation of alliteration and rhyme. Many slang expressions display one or the other—for example, *fix his flint, wheel and deal, blow your buffer, knock someone's socks off, talk turkey.*

To clean the clock in railroad jargon means to apply the air brakes suddenly. This action is also known as *wiping the gauge*, presumably because the needle on the pressure gauge swings back to zero. The reference is obviously to the needle sweeping around, or "wiping," the dial.

Clean someone's clock is still widely used, both to mean literal punching and to mean defeating or vanquishing someone. A recent example of the phrase to mean punching comes from Richard Russo's 1997 novel, *Straight Man*: "I heard Gracie cleaned your clock this afternoon." Those who win elections or ball games by a wide margin are often said to have cleaned their opponents' clocks.

THROW IN THE TOWEL.
Quit; concede defeat.

The first version of *throw in the towel* was *throw up the sponge*, a term that originated in England in the early days of prize fighting. During professional matches, fighters kept sponges handy to wipe the sweat and blood off their face. When a fighter wanted to quit, or when his manager decided he'd had enough, someone in his corner would signal the fact by throwing the sponge into the ring. By the 1860s, *throw up the sponge* was being used figuratively to mean "give up."

Using towels instead of sponges was evidently an American innovation. *Throw in the towel* is first found in the writings of Jack London, describing the same tradition as throwing up the sponge. When a fighter was ready to concede defeat, he threw his towel into the ring. One reference to this practice occurs in London's 1913 novel, *The Valley of the Moon*: "Just then the gong sounds, an' I can see the Terror startin' for me. 'Quit,' says Bill, makin' a move to throw in the towel. 'Not on your life,' I says. 'Drop it Bill.'"

By the 1920s, *throw in the towel* also meant conceding defeat or abandoning an activity. P. G. Wodehouse includes a variation of the expression in his 1923 novel, *The Inimitable Jeeves*: "He had found the going too hard and had chucked in the towel." The term is still used in boxing. This line appears on the *Yahoo! Sports* Web site for October 7, 2007: "[U]nlike 2003, when his corner threw in the towel, this time Barrera hung on."

CARRY A TORCH.
Feel a lingering attachment to a lost love.

The pangs of unrequited love have been described as *carrying a torch* since the early decades of the twentieth century. The November 1927 issue of *Vanity Fair* explains this new piece of slang to its readers: "When a fellow 'carries the torch' it doesn't imply that he is 'lit up' or drunk, but girl-less. His steady has quit him for another." The same article explains the origin of *torch song*: "'Sing a torch song' is commonly used in Broadway late-places as a request for a ballad in commemoration of the lonesome state. [Twenties nightclub singer] Tommy Lyman is said to have created the slang and he announced one night: 'My famous torch song: "Come To Me, My Melancholy Baby.'""

The exact origin of *carry a torch* (or *carry the torch*) is unclear. One suggestion is that it derives from the torchlight procession that was part of a wedding ceremony in classical Greece. Participants lit a torch at the bride's old home and carried it through the streets to her new home, where it was used to kindle the hearth. However, this custom conveys almost the opposite of the modern meaning of *carry a torch*. Carrying the torch to the bride's new home signifies a new beginning rather than the sad ending of a romance.

Another possibility is that the expression is related to the figurative use of *torchbearer*, someone who loyally supports a cause, a meaning that has been around since at least the mid-nineteenth century. In the case of romantic torchbearers, their cause would be a lost one. Alternatively, the torch might simply be a search aid. Broken-hearted lovers could be using the torch to light their path as they seek their former romantic partners.

A final suggestion is that the torch provides heat rather than light. To torch something is to set it on fire, in this case the faithful lover's heart. As long as he or she carries a torch, the flame of love still burns.

PAINT THE TOWN RED.
Celebrate boisterously.

Red has been the color of sprees since the 1880s. In an early use of the phrase, the July 27, 1883, edition of the *New York Times* reports that Mr. James Hennessy, attending a meeting of local Democrats, "offered a resolution that the entire body proceed forthwith to Newark and get drunk. . . . Then the Democrats charged upon the street cars, and being wafted into Newark proceeded, to use their own metaphor, to 'paint the town red.'"

The expression originated west of the Mississippi, where frontier towns always seemed to need another coat or two of metaphorical red paint. *Echoes from the Rocky Mountains* by John Clampitt, published in 1888, describes the bandits who periodically descended on these rough new towns: "Sometimes buildings would be burned and valuable lives would be lost, when resisting the efforts of these lawless pirates to 'paint the town red,' as was their favorite expression when engaged in making such a raid." However, any sort of excitement or unusual amount of noise in western towns was known as painting the town red.

Etymologists speculate that the paint color might be a reference to the red-light districts that sprang up in all frontier towns. Along with the brothels, which advertised their business by burning a red light in the window, saloons were usually located in the red-light districts. Cowboys in search of a good time would most likely head for this part of town.

The color red has long been associated with excitement, sensuality, and powerful emotions. It symbolizes fire and blood, among other things. *Red-blooded* has meant full of life and vigor since at least the late nineteenth century. Red is also the color of sin. In *The Scarlet Letter*, Hester Prynne wore a scarlet *A* as punishment for committing adultery. It is the logical color to choose if you are in a riotous mood.

By the end of the nineteenth century, the expression *paint the town red* was part of standard English. These days, refinements of the color are often mentioned, such as painting the town vermilion. James Joyce's novel *Ulysses* contains the line "And there he was at the end of his tether after having often painted the town tolerably pink." Sometimes the expression is truncated to *paint the town*, with the color red being implied.

And what better way to celebrate, after fixing wagons, cleaning clocks, and otherwise taking care of the old homestead? Painting the town red is one of the few chores that's actually fun.

AFTERWORD

When it comes to inventing fresh ways of expressing themselves, Americans are always pushing the envelope and thinking outside the box. Ingenious new figures of speech continue to show up in newspapers and on television. These days, they are posted online almost as soon as they are coined. Some future edition of *Let's Talk Turkey* could include recent expressions such as *to prairie dog*, meaning to pop your head over your cubicle wall to chat with a colleague; *jump the couch*, invented after Tom Cruise's 2005 appearance on *The Oprah Winfrey Show*, to describe excitable behavior; *shut up and color*, an injunction to mind your own business; *pull a heart muscle*, to withdraw from a competition or obligation; and *throw someone under a bus*, to betray someone.

These examples are only a few of the dozens of new slang expressions that American English absorbs every year. Like the more established figures of speech listed in this book, they arose out of the trends and activities that captured our collective imagination. Some may find a permanent place in the vocabulary. Others will no doubt go the way of *make a Virginia fence* (stagger drunkenly), *put on the dog* (dress flashily), *do a Dutch act* (disappear), and all the other sayings that made our great-grandparents chuckle. Meanwhile, these colorful expressions characterize and preserve the passing scene for our enjoyment. They are a lively, sometimes humorous, shortcut way of expressing the cultural experiences that we modern Americans often relish and share.

SELECT BIBLIOGRAPHY

Historical Dictionaries

Cassidy, Frederic G., ed. *Dictionary of American Regional English*. 4 vols. (A–Sk). Cambridge, MA: Belknap Press, Harvard University Press, 1985–. Fieldworkers gathered data for this dictionary from more than one thousand urban and rural communities in every part of the United States. The dictionary lists words and phrases found only in certain regions, as well as American folk usages. Entries include dated citations.

Craigie, William A., Sir, ed. *A Dictionary of American English on Historical Principles*. 4 vols. Chicago: University of Chicago Press, 1938–1944. Words of American origin, or with some significant connection to the United States, are included here. Most entries provide dated citations, especially for the earliest uses. Some also include notes on a word's origin or usage.

http://www.dictionary.oed.com. The *Oxford English Dictionary* online comprises the second edition of the *Oxford English Dictionary*, published by Oxford University Press in 1989, plus a three-volume additions series and quarterly updates. Its publishers rightly call it "the definitive record of the English language." It traces the history of more than half a million words from everywhere in the English-speaking world. Detailed entries list meanings in chronological order, with dated citations supporting each definition. Etymologies are included wherever known.

Lighter, J. E., ed. *Random House Historical Dictionary of American Slang*. 2 vols. (A–O). New York: Random House, 1994–. A comprehensive guide to American slang past and present, this dictionary features dated citations for each definition, as well as etymological and usage notes. Expressions are listed under their main term. Oxford University Press recently acquired the project, and a third volume is forthcoming under the title *Historical Dictionary of American Slang*.

Mathews, Mitford M. *A Dictionary of Americanisms on Historical Principles*. 2 vols. Chicago: University of Chicago Press, 1955. This dictionary covers words that originated or acquired new meaning in the United States. Some entries include etymological information. Example citations often overlap with Craigie.

Specialized Dictionaries

Ammer, Christine. *The Facts on File Dictionary of Clichés*. New York: Checkmark Books, 2001. This work defines more than thirty-five hundred British and American expressions. It also includes the history and theories of origin for each entry, but with few supporting citations.

Bartlett, John Russell. *Dictionary of Americanisms: A Dictionary of Words and Phrases, Usually Regarded as Peculiar to the United States*. 1848; reprinted, with a foreword by Richard Lederer. Hoboken, NJ: John Wiley & Sons, 2003. Nineteenth-century American colloquialisms, slang, and dialectal words are collected here for the first time in dictionary form. The book includes words and expressions that originated in England but were common in the United States. Entries frequently include illustrative quotations.

Brewer, Ebenezer Cobham. *Brewer's Dictionary of Phrase and Fable*. Revised by Ivor H. Evans. London: Cassell, 1970. A grab bag of biblical and literary allusions, place names, eponyms, proverbs, and the like, which features a number of words and expressions with interesting histories. Entries include some etymological information.

Chapman, Robert. *New Dictionary of American Slang*. New York: Harper & Row, 1986. This updated and expanded version of Wentworth and Flexner (listed below) includes some etymological and usage notes, but most entries are very brief.

Green, Jonathon. *Cassell's Dictionary of Slang*. London: Weidenfeld & Nicholson, 2005. Brief definitions include the approximate date of an entry's first use. The book includes more than seventy-four thousand words and expressions taken from all over the English-speaking world. It covers the sixteenth through twentieth centuries.

Grose, Francis. *A Classical Dictionary of the Vulgar Tongue.* 1796. Edited by Eric Partridge. Reprint, New York: Barnes & Noble, 1963. This eighteenth-century dictionary includes colloquialisms, popular slang, and criminals' cant, mainly from England. The editor has added origins and usage notes to many entries.

Hendrickson, Robert. *The Facts on File Encyclopedia of Word and Phrase Origins.* New York: Facts on File, 1987. Definitions and theories of origin, including some labeled "doubtful," are provided for approximately seventy-five hundred entries. Only a few entries have supporting citations or the date of a word's first appearance.

———. *Happy Trails: A Dictionary of Western Expressions.* New York: Facts on File, 1994. This collection of both obsolete and modern speech of the American West features about thirty-five hundred terms. Most entries are very brief, but some feature etymological notes.

Knowles, Elizabeth, ed. *Oxford Dictionary of Phrase and Fable.* Oxford: Oxford University Press, 2000. This book lists "words, names, and phrases with cultural resonance." Figurative expressions often include some etymological information or illustrative quotations.

Morris, William, and Mary Morris. *Dictionary of Word and Phrase Origins.* 3 vols. New York: Harper & Row, 1962–1967. This dictionary features short essays on the histories of common slang expressions, figures of speech, regionalisms, and cultural allusions.

Palmatier, Robert A., and Harold L. Ray. *Sports Talk: A Dictionary of Sports Metaphors.* New York: Greenwood Press, 1989. Entries give a brief definition of the term, followed by the sport that inspired it and the dictionary or other source where the authors found the word or expression listed. An index organizes the terms by sport.

Partridge, Eric. *A Dictionary of Slang and Unconventional English.* 8th ed. Edited by Paul Beale. New York: Macmillan, 1984. This collection of slang, catchphrases, and colloquial expressions focuses on British English, but some American terms are listed also. Entries include the date of first use, and some include etymologies or example citations as well.

Room, Adrian, comp. *Brewer's Dictionary of Modern Phrase and Fable.* London: Cassell, 2000. This twentieth-century version of *Brewer's* features literary allusions, adages, familiar expressions, and references to popular culture. Most of the slang-related entries include etymological notes.

Safire, William. *Safire's New Political Dictionary: The Definitive Guide to the New Language of Politics*. New York: Random House, 1993. Current political terms, metaphors, slogans, catchphrases, and nicknames are included here. Entries usually feature the history of the term with illustrative quotations.

Urdang, Laurence, editorial director; Walter W. Hunsiger, editor in chief. *Picturesque Expressions: A Thematic Dictionary*. 2nd ed. Detroit: Gale Research Co., 1985. More than seven thousand entries are arranged by topic. Besides definitions and theories of origin, most entries provide an approximate date of first use. Some include supporting citations. An index lists entries alphabetically.

Wentworth, Harold, and Stuart Berg Flexner, eds. *Dictionary of American Slang*. New York: Crowell, 1975. This dictionary includes words and expressions commonly used in the United States, including those that originated outside the country. The emphasis is on current slang. Most entries are short, but some include usage or etymological notes.

Books about American English

Funk, Charles Earle. *Heavens to Betsy! And Other Curious Sayings*. New York: Harper, 1955.

———. *A Hog on Ice and Other Curious Expressions*. New York: Harper, 1948. These two collections explore the histories of dozens of colorful American expressions. The style is anecdotal, with sources not cited. An entertaining read, but many of the etymologies are now outdated.

Mathews, Mitford McLeod, ed. *Beginnings of American English*. Chicago: University of Chicago Press, 1931. Excerpts from eighteenth- and early nineteenth-century writings on American English are presented in chronological order. Authors include Noah Webster and James Fenimore Cooper. An index lists words and expressions mentioned in the essays.

Mencken, H. L. *The American Language*. 4th ed. 1936. New York: Alfred A. Knopf, 2000. Mencken's book is the first to undertake a thorough, organized exploration of the origins and characteristics of American English. The fourth edition discusses colloquial expressions, regionalisms, and slang from the colonial era to the 1930s. Etymological theories are usually documented with footnotes.

Periodicals

American Speech. Tuscaloosa, AL: American Dialect Society. 1925–1999; Durham, NC: Duke University Press, 2000–. This quarterly journal presents articles on all aspects of the American language, both historical and current. It often features discussions of slang and colloquial speech.

Dialect Notes. New Haven, CT: American Dialect Society, 1890–1896. This quarterly publication focuses on word lists from different regions of the United States, as well as slang and jargon of various special groups.

Web Sites

http://www.americandialect.org. The American Dialect Society's Web site includes the archives for the society's e-mail discussion list. North American English is the main discussion topic, especially in the areas of slang, dialects, new words, and word histories. The archives cover 1992 to the present. They are searchable by keyword, author, and date.

http://www.barrypopik.com. Barry Popik's "Big Apple" site explores in detail the origins of a number of New York–related nicknames, words, and expressions. The site also includes nicknames of several other cities and a comprehensive discussion of *the whole nine yards*.

http://www.phrases.org.uk. Gary Martin founded the Phrase Finder site, which offers a discussion forum on the origins of phrases and sayings. Discussions of more than twelve hundred phrases can be accessed alphabetically or by keyword search.

http://www.worldwidewords.org. Michael Quinion, author of this site, writes about "international English from a British point of view." The site offers brief essays on the origins of hundreds of words and expressions, indexed alphabetically. It also features longer pieces on various aspects of English usage and history.

http://www.word-detective.com. The Word Detective site is the online version of Evan Morris's column, in which he answers readers' questions about the origins of English words and expressions. The site includes an archive of old columns, indexed alphabetically.

http://www.wordorgins.org. Wordorigins.org, written by Dave Wilton, is "devoted to the origins of words and phrases." Wilton concentrates on puncturing etymological myths. Brief essays on about four hundred words and expressions are listed alphabetically.

INDEX OF PHRASES